Schizophrenia in Focus

IN FOCUS series

The *In Focus* series is a group of introductory texts to the pharmaceutical care of patients with chronic conditions.

Pharmacy can play a large part in the management of chronic conditions and titles in the *In Focus* series provide practical information on the pharmaceutical care, medication and management of patients.

Each title includes an introduction to the condition; signs, symptoms and diagnosis; prevention and management; monitoring and treatment (including alternative treatments); care of the patient and the future.

Aimed at practising pharmacists in hospital and community, these introductory books will also be helpful to pre-registration and undergraduate pharmacy students, and healthcare professionals with an interest/working in the field of the specific chronic disease.

Available titles in the series:
Diabetes in Focus, 2nd edition, *Anjana Patel*
Osteoporosis in Focus, *Niall Ferguson*
Schizophrenia in Focus, *David Taylor*

Forthcoming
Asthma in Focus, *Anna Murphy*
Parkinson's Disease in Focus, *Charles Tugwell*
Stroke in Focus, *Derek Taylor*

Schizophrenia in Focus

David M Taylor

BSc, MSc, PhD, MRPharmS

Chief Pharmacist, South London and Maudsley NHS Trust, London, UK
Honorary Senior Lecturer, Institute of Psychiatry, London, UK

London • Chicago   **Pharmaceutical Press**

Published by the Pharmaceutical Press
An imprint of RPS Publishing

1 Lambeth High Street, London SE1 7JN, UK
100 South Atkinson Road, Suite 206, Grayslake, IL 60030-7820, USA

© Pharmaceutical Press 2006

 is a trademark of RPS Publishing

RPS Publishing is the wholly owned publishing organisation of the
Royal Pharmaceutical Society of Great Britain

Typeset by Type Study, Scarborough, North Yorkshire
Printed in Great Britain by TJ International, Padstow, Cornwall

ISBN 0 85369 607 1
ISBN-13 978-0-85 369-607-0

A catalogue record for this book is available from the British Library

Contents

Preface

Schizophrenia is one of the most commonly encountered conditions in modern-day pharmacy. Its prevalence and chronicity ensure that pharmacists in both primary and secondary care will frequently be presented with opportunities to improve the lives of people with this often devastating condition. Already, the contributions of pharmacists are widely recognised and appreciated by mental health charities and patients, who often describe pharmacists as the most trustworthy and reliable sources of information. Disturbingly, however, some pharmacists do little more than dispense medicines for people with schizophrenia and, partly as a consequence, a great many people with schizophrenia know very little about the medicines that they are asked to take. In the absence of good information, many people make decisions about their medications based on hearsay or anecdote, which can often result in adverse or disastrous consequences.

What are the reasons behind the reluctance of some pharmacists to make a positive difference to quality of life in schizophrenia? Presumably some pharmacists have insufficient knowledge of the condition and its treatment. Some may have fears about people with schizophrenia – that they think differently and are unpredictable or violent.

This book is aimed not only at pharmacists working in primary care, but also at pharmacists and other healthcare professionals new to secondary care and those intending to specialise in mental health. More experienced specialist pharmacists will also find this book interesting and valuable – efforts have been made to examine carefully and question long-accepted theories of psychotic illness and treatment. In addition, information provided on individual drugs is comprehensive enough to be a valuable resource to specialists in psychiatry. Members of other professions will undoubtedly find much of this book useful as a medicines-centred information resource.

David Taylor
April 2006

About the author

David Taylor is the Chief Pharmacist at London's Maudsley Hospital and honorary senior lecturer at the Institute of Psychiatry. He has worked at the Maudsley Hospital for more than 10 years, having previously held academic and hospital practice posts in London. His qualifications include a BSc in pharmacy, an MSc in clinical pharmacy and a PhD in clinical pharmacology from the Institute of Psychiatry.

Dr Taylor is the lead author of the *Maudsley Prescribing Guidelines* and has contributed as author or editor to several other textbooks of psychopharmacology, including *The Use of Drugs in Psychiatry* [1] and *Case Studies in Psychopharmacology* [2]. His research interests include prescribing practice, pharmacoeconomics, pharmacokinetics and adverse effects of psychotropic drugs. On these subjects he has published more than 100 papers in pharmacy and psychiatric journals, often collaborating with medical colleagues at the Institute of Psychiatry. Dr Taylor is a member of editorial boards for six major journals (including *CNS Drugs*, *Acta Psychiatrica Scandinavica* and *Journal of Psychopharmacology*) and serves as a referee for more than 30 others. He has led several professional and practice initiatives in the UK and was the foundation president of the College of Mental Health Pharmacists. Dr Taylor has frequently acted as an expert advisor on UK National Institute for Clinical Excellence guidance and his awards include the UK Psychiatric Pharmacy Group award for exceptional contributions to psychiatric pharmacy.

References

1. Cookson J, Taylor D, Katona C. *The Use of Drugs in Psychiatry*. London: Gaskell, 2004.
2. Taylor D, Paton C (eds). *Case Studies in Psychopharmacology*, 2nd edn. London: Taylor and Francis, 2002.

1

Schizophrenia – in two minds

What is schizophrenia?

The lay person's idea of a 'schizophrenic' is that of somebody with a 'split personality' and a predilection for random acts of violence. What is understood by the phrase 'split personality' presumably varies from one person to another but one supposes it broadly reflects the view that people with schizophrenia have two or more different psychological identities (in the manner one assumes of Dr Jekyll and Mr Hyde).

That such ideas persist today is partly a consequence of the media's continual prejudice against people with mental illness, which perhaps in turn reflects on our own fear-driven, unconscious desire to distance ourselves from people who appear different and are difficult to understand. This overt and unchallenged prejudice coexists, ironically, with a widely held belief that mental health services cruelly treat people who are mildly and pleasantly eccentric and clearly not at all mentally ill (as in the film *One Flew Over the Cuckoo's Nest*). Perhaps implicit in this latter belief is that shock treatments and psychosurgery are cruel when administered to eccentrics but necessary and desirable for the truly insane.

As is often observed, public confusion results at least partly from professional vacillation. This may be the case with schizophrenia, where experts have argued for many years over the causes of schizophrenia. Even today, there is considerable doubt even over the *existence* of schizophrenia itself. In 2003, a debate was held at the Institute of Psychiatry in London, in which it was proposed that schizophrenia did not exist. The final vote on this motion was a tie: half the audience (consisting of world experts, practising clinicians, patients and carers) felt that schizophrenia was indeed a discrete illness, half felt that it was not.

Both sides have some weighty support. Those who recognise schizophrenia as a single disease entity point to evidence suggesting similar anatomical and functional abnormalities in those diagnosed with schizophrenia, its characteristic response to antipsychotic drugs and the categorical differences between beliefs and experiences of those with schizophrenia and those of the 'normal' population. In contrast, the main argument used by those who deny the existence of schizophrenia is that a diagnosis of schizophrenia is hopelessly uninformative: it predicts very little. That is to say, a diagnosis of schizophrenia on its own will not inform exactly what symptoms might be expected, the likely outcome (recovery, chronicity, severity) or likely response to treatment. Opponents of the schizophrenia classification also note that many of the 'symptoms' of schizophrenia are commonly seen in normal populations. For example, as many as one in 20 people regularly hears voices, and delusional behaviour is virtually endemic – think of smokers and alcohol misusers who deny their addiction and the huge numbers of people who believe in, say, astrology, homeopathy or telepathy. Paranoid beliefs, too, are also common. A French study of patients attending a general practice clinic found that more than a quarter reported that they felt that they were being persecuted in some way (none of these people was diagnosed with a mental illness) [1].

These observations, from both camps, do not really allow any definitive conclusion to be drawn. They do however point the way to an approach to schizophrenia which acknowledges uncertainty. When dealing with people with schizophrenia and with their carers it is important to be open-minded (this illness may or may not exist), non-judgemental ('symptoms' of schizophrenia are common to all of us) and non-prejudicial (people with a diagnosis of schizophrenia are people, not 'schizophrenics'). As we will see, alienation from society is a precipitant of schizophrenia, so professional honesty, candour and respect are important remedial factors.

At this early stage it is also worth examining the association between schizophrenia and violent behaviour. Newspapers frequently report murders or assaults committed by (as they are always described) 'paranoid schizophrenics'. Accompanying editorials lament the failure of community care and call for more secure and more widespread incarceration of people with severe mental illness.

The truth is rather different. Of 500 murders committed in the UK each year, only 50 are said to have been committed by someone with 'diminished responsibility'; only half of these have psychotic illness – that is, 25 a year, at most [2]. Since the introduction of community care the number of murders committed by people with a mental illness has fallen slightly [3]. Over the same period, murders by strangers have grown in number, with many associated with alcohol or substance misuse [4]. In fact, substance misuse is much more clearly associated with violent behaviour than is schizophrenia [5]. The proportion of violent crime in society attributable to schizophrenia is very small indeed [6].

History and diagnosis

Madness or psychosis (a loss of reality) has been observed and reported for millennia. However, only in the early nineteenth century did the discipline of psychiatry arise as a specialty within the field of medicine. Later in that century Emil Kraepelin, a German psychiatrist, developed in earnest a system of classifying mental illness, particularly psychosis. Kraepelin had observed that, in medicine, a particular disease process produced identical symptoms, pathology and aetiology. He assumed that the same would be true of mental illness and set about classifying psychosis by symptoms (contemporary science being unable to shed much light on disease process, pathology or aetiology). Two groupings were suggested. The first, *dementia praecox* (senility of the young), included hebephrenia (a kind of childish insanity), catatonia and dementia paranoides (paranoia) and was said to follow a chronic course. Dementia praecox was also said to be characterised by irreversible decline in cognitive function. The second, *manic-depressive insanity*, followed a fluctuating course with periods of illness interspersed with normality.

In 1911 the Swiss psychiatrist Eugen Bleuler coined the term *schizophrenia* to replace dementia praecox, having observed that the latter did not always occur in the young, and did not always have a deteriorating course. Bleuler intended to encapsulate the fundamental nature of the condition by alluding to the splitting (*schizo-*) of mental faculties (*-phrenia*) (personality, memory and perception) from each other. Interestingly, both he and Kraepelin were convinced of a biological cause for the condition (e.g. some metabolic blood disorder or other). Bleuler used Freud's theories to explain the widely different symptoms of schizophrenia as having a shared psychological mechanism. He described the main symptoms: thought disorder, blunting of affect (i.e. near-absent expressions of glee or sadness) and autism (essentially social withdrawal). Hallucinations and delusions were considered not as core symptoms but as reactions to the disease itself.

Another psychiatrist, Karl Jaspers, later developed Bleuler's ideas by suggesting that schizophrenic delusions were incapable of being understood. This observation ultimately led to psychosis being distinguished from neurosis (in which some sense could be made of the patient's beliefs). Jaspers later facilitated the appointment of another German psychiatrist, Kurt Schneider, who developed the use of 'first-rank' symptoms of schizophrenia (Diagnostic focus 1.1).

By the 1970s it became clear that diagnostic criteria for schizophrenia varied considerably from one country to another. European psychiatrists, for example, tended to use Schneider's criteria whereas

DIAGNOSTIC FOCUS 1.1

Schneider's first-rank symptoms

Auditory hallucinations
Hearing voices talking to or about the patient

Thought insertion or withdrawal
Sensation of thoughts being put into or taken from the patient's mind

Thought broadcasting
Sensation of one's thoughts being heard by others

Passivity feelings
Sensation of being under external control or receiving bodily sensations from another source

Primary delusions
Delusions arising complete based upon experience considered by others to be normal

---

American clinicians employed a wider, psychoanalytical approach. Moreover, there were clear difficulties in distinguishing normality from schizophrenia, as evidenced by the famous Rosenhan experiment of the early 1970s (Box 1.1).

Attempts have since been made to define schizophrenia more precisely and uniformly so as to allow cross-cultural studies of prevalence,

---

Box 1.1 The Rosenhan experiment [7]

Rosenhan, a professor of psychology at Stanford University in California, employed eight pseudo-patients ('normal' individuals coached to feign psychosis) to pretend to be mentally ill to gain admission to hospital. Each pseudo-patient complained of hearing voices saying 'empty', 'hollow' or 'thud'. In other respects they behaved normally. All eight were admitted to hospital. All eight were diagnosed with schizophrenia. Despite reverting to entirely normal behaviour after admission, the pseudo-patients remained in hospital for an average of 19 days.

The pseudo-patients took notes on their experiences, first in secret, then openly since no one observed them. On average, daily contact with medical or nursing staff was 6.8 minutes. No healthcare worker suspected the pseudo-patients were 'normal' but around a third of patients they met made comments suggesting that they, the patients, had spotted them as impostors.

DIAGNOSTIC FOCUS 1.2

Criteria for schizophrenia in *Diagnostic and Statistical Manual* (DSM-IV) [8]

(A) Characteristic symptoms of the active phase
Two (or more) of the following, each present for a significant portion of time during a 1-month period (or less if successfully treated):

1. Delusions
2. Hallucinations
3. Disorganised speech (e.g. frequent derailment or incoherence)
4. Grossly disorganised or catatonic behaviour
5. Negative symptoms, i.e. affective flattening, alogia or avolition

(B) Social/Occupational dysfunction
For a small portion of the time since the onset of the disturbance, one or more major areas of functioning such as work, interpersonal relations or self-care, are markedly below the level achieved prior to the onset (or when the onset is in childhood or adolescence, failure to achieve expected level of interpersonal, academic or occupational achievement)

(C) Duration
Continuous signs of the disturbance persist for at least 6 months. This 6-month period must include at least 1 month of symptoms (or less if successfully treated) that meet criterion A (i.e. active-phase symptoms) and may include periods of prodromal or residual symptoms, the signs of the disturbance may be manifested by only negative symptoms or two or more symptoms listed in criterion A present in an attenuated form (e.g. odd beliefs, unusual perceptual experiences)

(D) Schizoaffective and mood disorder exclusion
Schizoaffective disorder and mood disorder with psychotic features have been ruled out because either (1) no major depressive, manic or mixed episodes have occurred concurrently with the active-phase symptoms, or (2) if mood episodes have occurred during active-phase symptoms, their total duration has been brief relative to the duration of the active and residual periods.

(E) Substance/General medical condition exclusion
The disturbance is not due to the direct physiological effects of a substance (e.g. a drug of abuse, a medication) or a general medical condition

(F) Relationship to a pervasive developmental disorder
If there is a history of autistic disorder or another pervasive development disorder, the additional diagnosis of schizophrenia is made only if prominent delusions are also present for at least 1 month (or less so if successfully treated)

incidence and genetic linkage, amongst other factors. The two most widely used criteria appear in the *Diagnostic and Statistical Manual* (DSM) [8] and the *International Classification of Diseases* (ICD) [9]. In 2006, these publications are in their fourth (DSM-IV) and 10th (ICD-10) editions, respectively. Diagnostic focus boxes 1.2 and 1.3 outline diagnostic criteria for schizophrenia stipulated in these editions.

DIAGNOSTIC FOCUS 1.3

Symptomatic criteria for schizophrenia in *International Classification of Diseases* (ICD-10) [9]

The normal requirement for a diagnosis of schizophrenia is that a minimum of one very clear symptom (and usually two or more if less clear-cut) belonging to any one of the groups listed as (a)–(d) below, or symptoms from at least two of the groups referred to as (e)–(h), should have been clearly present for most of the time during a period of 1 month or more.

(a) Thought echo, thought insertion or withdrawal and thought broadcasting

(b) Delusions of control, influence or passivity, clearly referred to body or limb movements or specific thoughts, actions or sensations: delusional perceptions

(c) Hallucinatory voices giving a running commentary on the patient's behaviour, or discussing the patient among themselves, or other types of hallucinatory voices coming from some part of the body

(d) Persistent delusions of other kinds that are culturally inappropriate and completely impossible

(e) Persistent hallucinations in any modality, when accompanied by fleeting or half-formed delusions without clear affective content, or by persistent overvalued ideas, or when occurring every day for weeks or months on end

(f) Breaks or interpolations in the train of thought, resulting in incoherence or irrelevant speech, or neologisms

(g) Catatonic behaviour, such as excitement, posturing, waxy flexibility, negativism and stupor

(h) 'Negative' symptoms such as marked apathy, paucity of speech, and blunting or incongruity of emotional responses, usually resulting in social withdrawal and lowering of social performance; it must be clear that these are not due to depression or to neuroleptic medication

(i) A significant and constant change in the overall quality of some aspects of personal behaviour, manifest as a loss of interest, aimlessness, idleness, a self-absorbed attitude and social withdrawal

These diagnostic schedules reveal two major problems. First, ICD-10 and DSM-IV are not identical. This suggests lack of agreement over the exact symptomatic nature of schizophrenia and presents difficulties in interpreting data derived from analyses using one or other of the schedules. Second, the facility to diagnose schizophrenia on the basis of a selection of signs and symptoms being present (e.g. only two of five) means that two people can be diagnosed with schizophrenia without sharing a single symptom. Thus a typical person with schizophrenia cannot be defined. One can however describe the most commonly encountered symptoms and these are listed in Diagnostic focus 1.4.

 DIAGNOSTIC FOCUS 1.4

The most frequent symptoms of acute schizophrenia [10]	
Symptoms	**Frequency (%)**
Lack of insight	97
Auditory hallucination	74
Ideas of reference	70
Suspiciousness	66
Flatness of affect	66
Voices speaking to the patient	65
Delusional mood	64
Delusions of persecution	64
Thoughts spoken aloud	50

Both ICD and DSM recognise subtypes of schizophrenia, such as *paranoid*, *hebephrenic* or *disorganised*, *catatonic* and *residual*. The validity of these subtypes is even less certain than that of schizophrenia.

The symptoms of schizophrenia are now usually ascribed to one of three major categories [11]. Positive symptoms (exaggerations of normal function) occur in acute episodes or relapses and include delusions and hallucinations. They may be subdivided into symptoms of psychosis (e.g. hallucinations) and disorganisation (e.g. thought disorder, confusion). Negative symptoms (a loss of normal functions) tend to be more persistent and include social withdrawal, apathy, alogia and lack of volition. Cognitive symptoms also persist and may pre-date the onset of other symptoms [12, 13]. They include deficiencies in memory and in abstract reasoning.

The course of schizophrenia

A typical case of schizophrenia might begin in a person's early adult life with a psychotic episode and continue throughout life with persistent negative and cognitive symptoms interrupted by occasional psychotic breakdowns. Some people (a minority) may suffer only one psychotic episode, have few residual symptoms and live essentially normal lives. Others never recover from their first psychotic breakdown and remain in a continuous state of psychosis. In fact, most cases of schizophrenia are said to follow one of seven patterns [14], which can be condensed into three broad outcomes: (1) continuous course (no relapses or remissions); (2) undulating course (relapses with or without residual symptoms in remissions); and (3) atypical course (various types but including long-term improvement after continuous course). Whatever the clinical course of schizophrenia, functional disability is common: very few people with schizophrenia are in full-time employment.

CASE STUDY 1.1

Jayne

Jayne is a 25-year-old Asian woman admitted to an acute medical ward having been found unconscious in her flat. Her flatmate and her mother provide the patient's history. Jayne's childhood was apparently unremarkable; she did well at school and entered university. Towards the end of her third year, Jayne's behaviour became unusual: she seemed to prefer being on her own and stayed up most nights, sleeping during the day. She attended for her finals, but in one examination wrote nothing, left after 20 minutes and was not seen again for 2 weeks. On returning to her flat, she accused her flatmate of plotting to ruin her financially and of 'shopping' her 'to the CIA'. Jayne was then frequently seen to be responding to unheard questions or statements. Several weeks later she began wearing only black clothes and eating only liquid foods such as soup. Later still, she was heard talking to herself and refused to leave her room.

Tests reveal that Jayne is suffering from malnutrition and scurvy. A psychiatrist's opinion is sought.

Prevalence

The prevalence of schizophrenia has been estimated to be between 1.4 and 4.6 per thousand population and the incidence from 0.09 to 0.57 per thousand per year [15]. In the UK this means around 250 000 people will have been diagnosed with schizophrenia, with perhaps

CASE STUDY 1.2

Katherine

Katherine is a 34-year-old optician. She has experienced two psychotic episodes in the last 10 years and is currently maintained on quetiapine 300 mg daily. This is her description of her first experience of psychosis:

'I had been working for 4 or 5 years and was living at my parents' home. One morning I was taking a shower and the water suddenly became very hot. Almost immediately I became convinced that my mother was trying to kill me – her switching on the washing machine and altering the shower temperature was irrefutable proof of this. We later went to the shops but I insisted on sitting in the back seat of the car. My mother's driving seemed very dangerous and this further convinced me of her malevolent intentions. When we returned, I ran to the next-door neighbours (whom I barely knew) because I was so frightened. Around this time I began to hear voices – I could hear members of my family talking about me. This only added to my terror.

'I felt that I had to run away to think clearly so I "borrowed" my mother's car and drove for 6 hours. All the time my mind was racing at tremendous speed: ideas and possibilities flooded through my brain. I also felt (with 100% certainty) that I could directly sense my friends' problems in some way, and I began praying for them.

'Later I checked into a hotel but I couldn't sleep because of the voices and because I could hear stones hitting the window (I assumed people were throwing them at me). I checked out at 5.00 a.m. and drove off again, stopping at a service station some hours later. At the service station I became convinced that the Tannoy speakers were really cameras spying on me. I also became convinced that my husband had AIDS and was being kept in a hospice.

'By this time I was more or less paralysed by numerous terrors. I sat in the car and refused to move. The police were called and I was arrested. A few days later I was admitted to hospital. By then I was hearing my own thoughts spoken aloud.

'After 2 or 3 weeks of treatment I began to gain some insight and after 4 weeks was discharged well. By then I could see that my beliefs and experiences were not "real" but they had certainly felt real and nobody could have convinced me otherwise.'

---

10 000–20 000 new cases diagnosed each year. Prevalence and incidence do not seem to vary substantially around the world, but the wide variations in the magnitude of estimates do suggest variation over time and perhaps with place [16] (Box 1.2).

Box 1.2 Summary

- Schizophrenia is probably a heterogeneous disorder – that is, an umbrella term for a variety of syndromes
- Schizophrenia is not clearly associated with violence or homicide – fewer than 5% of murders are committed by psychotic individuals
- The symptoms of schizophrenia are classified in *Diagnostic and Statistical Manual* (DSM) and *International Classification of Diseases* (ICD)
- Most common symptoms are auditory hallucinations, ideas of reference and suspiciousness
- Schizophrenia follows a varied, unpredictable course but nearly all people with a diagnosis of schizophrenia are sufficiently impaired that they are unable to work
- Prevalence of schizophrenia is up to around 0.5% with little variation from one country to another

---

References

1.   Verdoux H, Maurice-Tison S, Gay B *et al.* A survey of delusional ideation in primary care patients. *Psychol Med* 1998; 28: 127–134.
2.   Szmukler G. Homicide inquiries: what sense do they make? *Psychiatr Bull* 2000; 24: 6–10.
3.   Taylor P J, Gunn J. Homicides by people with mental illness: myth and reality. *Br J Psychiatry* 1999; 174: 9–14.
4.   Shaw J, Amos T, Hunt I M *et al.* Mental illness in people who kill strangers: longitudinal study and national clinical survey. *BMJ* 2004; 328: 734–737.
5.   Soyka M. Substance misuse, psychiatric disorder and violent and disturbed behaviour. *Br J Psychiatry* 2000; 176: 345–350.
6.   Walsh E, Buchanan A, Fahy T. Violence and schizophrenia: examining the evidence. *Br J Psychiatry* 2002; 180: 490–495.
7.   Rosenhan D L. On being sane in insane places. *Science* 1973; 179: 250–258.
8.   American Psychiatric Association. *Diagnostic and Statistical Manual of Mental Disorders*, 4th edn. Washington, DC: American Psychiatric Association, 1994.
9.   World Health Organization. *The ICD-10 Classification of Mental and Behavioural Disorders*. Geneva: World Health Organization, 1992.
10. Carpenter W T Jr, Strauss J S, Bartko J J. Flexible system for the diagnosis of schizophrenia: report from the WHO international pilot study of schizophrenia. *Science* 1973; 21: 1275–1278.
11. Andreasen N C. Symptoms, signs, and diagnosis of schizophrenia. *Lancet* 1995; 346: 477–481.
12. Kremen W S, Buka S L, Seidman L J *et al.* IQ decline during childhood and adult psychotic symptoms in a community sample: a 19 year longitudinal study. *Am J Psychiatry* 1998; 155: 672–677.
13. Russell A J, Munro J C, Jones P B *et al.* Schizophrenia and the myth of intellectual decline. *Am J Psychiatry* 1997; 154: 635–639.

14. Bleuler M. *The Schizophrenic Disorders: Long Term Patient and Family Studies*. New Haven, CT: Yale University Press, 1978.
15. Gelder M G, Lopez-Ibor J J, Andreasen N (eds). *New Oxford Textbook of Psychiatry*. Oxford: Oxford University Press, 2000.
16. Godner E M, Hsu L, Waraich P, Somer J M. Prevalence and incidence studies of schizophrenic disorders: a systematic review of the literature. *Can J Psychiatry* 2002; 47: 833–843.

2

The causes of schizophrenia

Despite nearly a century of investigation, the causes of schizophrenia remain unclear. There are three possible reasons for this failure to discover the aetiology of the illness: (1) there may be many causes of schizophrenia; (2) schizophrenia may not exist as a single disease entity; or (3) schizophrenia may be caused by something not so far investigated. The second of these possibilities can be best illuminated by fictitious example. Imagine that medical science cannot distinguish between asthma, chronic obstructive pulmonary disease and pneumonia, and inadvertently groups them together under a collective term, say, phlegmosis. Epidemiological studies would reveal that phlegmosis can be related to congenital atopy, smoking and influenza, suggesting multiple causes and elucidating no single cause. Thus, in the case of schizophrenia, the failure to find a cause may indicate erroneous grouping of illnesses or conditions under a single term.

Notwithstanding this possibility, all studies of the aetiology of schizophrenia assume its existence and most use modern diagnostic criteria such as the *Diagnostic and Statistical Manual* (DSM) and *International Classification of Diseases* (ICD) to identify the condition. Conclusions drawn from these studies are summarised below.

Season of birth

Several studies have indicated that those later diagnosed with schizophrenia are relatively more likely to have been born in late winter or early spring [1, 2]. This suggests a link to maternal respiratory viral infection, an association supported by some but not all analyses of maternal influenza and schizophrenia [3]. Even those studies supporting a link suggest only a small excess of births in February, March or April, so the effect is weak.

Obstetric complications

Problems shortly before or at the time of birth have long been associated with an increased risk of schizophrenia [4]. It has been postulated that hypoxic events at birth set in train neurochemical and structural changes that later lead to schizophrenia. It is also possible that a genetic predisposition to schizophrenia in the fetus affects *in utero* development and somehow provokes a higher than expected rate of complications [5]. Complications of pregnancy, abnormal fetal growth and complications of delivery all seem to be associated with a later diagnosis of schizophrenia [6], although there remains some debate over this [7]. Again, the overall effect is small.

Genetics

There is little doubt that genes play a major part in schizophrenia. The lifetime risk of schizophrenia is around 1%; in people born to parents who both have a diagnosis of schizophrenia the lifetime risk approaches 50% [8]. Higher risks are also seen in identical and non-identical twins of those diagnosed with schizophrenia (using either DSM or ICD) [9]. In fact, the likelihood of diagnosis with schizophrenia is directly proportional to the closeness and number of relatives with the same diagnosis. This increased risk of schizophrenia persists even when offspring are 'adopted away' from affected family members [3, 8].

The mechanism by which schizophrenia is genetically transmitted has yet to be elucidated and is the subject of intensive research.

Environment

Given that concordance for diagnosis of schizophrenia in identical twins is substantially less than 100%, environmental factors are very likely to have significant influence on the emergence of schizophrenia. Indeed, as many as 60% of all those diagnosed with schizophrenia have no first- or second-degree relatives with the condition [10].

An urban environment seems to be particularly likely to give rise to schizophrenia and other psychoses [11], with risk of emergence of psychotic symptoms increasing with size of population [12].

Migration also appears to be a risk factor for schizophrenia [13]. Interestingly, risk increases as the size of a migrant ethnic population decreases, that is, the incidence of schizophrenia in ethnic minorities is greater when they comprise a smaller proportion of the population [14].

Both urbanicity and ethnic minority status can be seen as being strongly related to alienation of individuals in society. This suggests that the extent to which people feel distanced from local society governs to some extent their risk of schizophrenia. A link between this and paranoid symptoms so frequently seen in schizophrenia is an intriguing possibility not so far established.

Linked to urbanicity influences is the use of cannabis – a largely urban pursuit. Cannabis, particularly delta-9-tetrahydrocannabinol, produces psychotic symptoms in some people [15] and the use of cannabis is associated with later diagnosis of schizophrenia in those showing a particular genetic form of catechol-*o*-methyltransferase [16].

In the past, it has been suggested that the family environment or, more specifically, poor parenting was responsible for many cases of schizophrenia. It is now thought that the family environment has no effect on the emergence or development of schizophrenia. Nonetheless, a family environment with high expressed emotion (criticism, hostility, emotional overinvolvement) does affect time to relapse [17] and studies show that family therapy aimed at reducing expressed emotion substantially prolongs time to relapse [18].

Clearly, it is possible, if not probable, given the example of cannabis, that genetic and environmental influences interact – that there is a genetic predisposition to schizophrenia which is only expressed under certain environmental conditions. There is also a possibility that two forms of schizophrenia exist – a genetic and an environmental form [19] (Epidemiology focus 2.1).

EPIDEMIOLOGY FOCUS 2.1

Causes of schizophrenia		
Cause	**Extent of influence**	**Strength of supporting evidence**
Season of birth	+	+
Birth complications	+	+
Genetics	+++	+++
Environment		
Urbanicity	++	+++
Migration	++	+++
Cannabis	+ or ++	++
Family	–	–

References

1. Hare E H. Seasonal variations in psychiatric illness. *Trends Neurosci* 1980; 3: 295–298.

2. Mortensen P B, Pedersen C B, Westergaard T *et al*. Effects of family history and place and season of birth on the risk of schizophrenia. *N Engl J Med* 1999; 340: 603–608.

3. Wright I, Woodruff P. Aetiology of schizophrenia. *CNS Drugs* 1995; 3: 126–144.

4. Kendell R E, Juszczak E, Cole S K. Obstetric complications and schizophrenia: a case control study based on standardised obstetric records. *Br J Psychiatry* 1996; 168: 556–561.

5. Cannon M, Murray R M. Neonatal origins of schizophrenia. *Arch Dis Child* 1998; 78: 1–3.

6. Cannon M, Jones P B, Murray R M. Obstetric complications and schizophrenia; historical and meta-analytic review. *Am J Psychiatry* 2002; 159: 1080–1092.

7. Crow T J. Obstetric complications and schizophrenia. *Am J Psychiatry* 2003; 160: 1011–1012.

8. McGuffin P, Owen M J, Farmer A E. Genetic basis of schizophrenia. *Lancet* 1995; 346: 678–682.

9. Cardno A G, Marshall E J, Coid B *et al*. Heritability estimates for psychotic disorders. *Arch Gen Psychiatry* 1999; 56: 162–168.

10. Bleuler M. *The Schizophrenic Disorders*. New Haven, CT: Yale University Press, 1978.

11. Van Os J, Hanssen M, Bijl R V, Vollebergh W. Prevalence of psychotic disorder and community level of psychotic symptoms. *Arch Gen Psychiatry* 2001; 58: 663–668.

12. Van Os J, Hanseen M, Bak M *et al*. Do urbanicity and familial liability co-participate in causing psychosis? *Am J Psychiatry* 2003; 160: 477–482.

13. Cantor-Graae E, Pedersen C B, McNeil T F, Mortensen P B. Migration as a risk factor for schizophrenia: a Danish population-based cohort study. *Br J Psychiatry* 2003; 182: 117–122.

14. Boydell J, van Os J, McKenzie K *et al*. Incidence of schizophrenia in ethnic minorities in London: ecological study interactions with environment. *BMJ* 2001; 323: 1336.

15. D'Souza D C, Perry E, MacDougall L *et al*. The psychotomimetic effects of intravenous delta-9-tetrahydrocannabinol in healthy individuals: implications for psychosis. *Neuropsychopharmacology* 2004; 29: 1558–1572.

16. Caspi A, Moffitt T E, Cannon M *et al*. Moderation of the effect of adolescent-onset cannabis use on adult psychosis by a functional polymorphism in the catechol-o-methyltransferase gene: longitudinal evidence of a gene × environment interaction. *Biol Psychiatry* 2005; 57: 1117–1127.

17. Anderson J, Adams C. Family interventions in schizophrenia. *BMJ* 1996; 313: 505–506.

18. Leff J. Working with the families of schizophrenic patients. *Br J Psychiatry* 1994; 23: 71–76.

19. Van Os J, McGuffin P. Can the social environment cause schizophrenia? *Br J Psychiatry* 2003; 182: 291–292.

3

Pathology of schizophrenia

Anatomical changes

Research has uncovered subtle anatomical differences between brains of those with a diagnosis of schizophrenia and normal controls but there appear to be no gross anatomical lesions in schizophrenia. Establishing that subtle differences do exist has been hampered by the wide variation seen in normal controls and by the possibility that schizophrenia is clinically and aetiologically a heterogeneous disorder (as already discussed). Single studies of anatomical differences are often not uniformly replicated and so our understanding is perhaps best informed by systematic review or meta-analysis. These methods are of course better able, statistically, to identify subtle or small differences revealed by modern scanning techniques.

Most of the identified anatomical abnormalities in schizophrenia relate to differences in the volume of various brain structures. A comprehensive analysis of studies in this area [1] suggested that some structures are increased in size, such as cerebral ventricles [2], but most show small decreases in schizophrenia (Table 3.1). Overall brain size is also slightly reduced in schizophrenia. It is not clear whether or not these differences represent causative factors, risk factors or coincidental anomalies [3].

Some other anatomical associations with schizophrenia include alterations in the normal pattern of brain asymmetry and reduced blood flow in the frontal lobe ('hypofrontality') [4], although the latter remains somewhat controversial [5]. None of the abnormalities so far observed

Table 3.1 Size of brain structures in schizophrenia [1]

Structure	Mean size*
Brain (cerebral volume)	98%
Ventricles (all combined)	126%
Hippocampus	98% (L); 97% (R)
Amygdala	94% (L); 94% (R)
Basal ganglia structures	104–121% (L); 102–124% (R)

*Normal = 100% in each case.

are sufficiently marked either alone or when combined with other abnormalities to allow diagnosis of schizophrenia.

Histological studies [6] support the concept that schizophrenia is a neurodevelopmental disorder. That is, schizophrenia is said to arise because of pathological abnormalities in the brain's early development which only later give rise to the full syndrome of symptoms of the disorder. This now well-established theory is supported by much of the foregoing and more besides. Histological studies show abnormal cell migration patterns; anatomical studies show abnormalities probably resulting from defective neurodevelopment; premorbid cognitive and motor abnormalities are common; and birth or *in utero* complications provide a plausible starting point for abnormal development [7].

Further elucidation of the processes involved in the development of schizophrenia has the potential to allow effective intervention in individuals at risk, in the eventual hope of preventing symptoms arising (Anatomy focus 3.1).

ANATOMY FOCUS 3.1

Anatomical changes in schizophrenia	
Brain size	Reduced
Ventricles	Enlarged
Basal ganglia	Enlarged

References

1. Wright I C, Rabe-Hesketh S, Woodruff P W R *et al*. Meta-analysis of regional brain volumes in schizophrenia. *Am J Psychiatry* 2000; 157: 16–25.
2. Van Horn J D, McManus I C. Ventricular enlargement in schizophrenia. A meta-analysis of studies of the ventricle:brain ratio (VBR). *Br J Psychiatry* 1992; 160: 687–697.
3. Chua S E, McKenna P J. Schizophrenia – a brain disease? A critical review of structural and functional cerebral abnormality in the disorder. *Br J Psychiatry* 1995; 166: 563–582.
4. Wright I, Woodruff P. Aetiology of schizophrenia: a review of theories and their clinical and therapeutic implications. *CNS Drugs* 1995; 3: 126–144.
5. Gur R C, Gur R E. Hypofrontality in schizophrenia: RIP. *Lancet* 1995; 345: 1383–1384.
6. Akbarian S, Bunney W E, Potkin S G *et al*. Altered distribution of nicotinamide–adenine dinucleotide phosphate–diaphorase cells in frontal lobe of schizophrenics implies disturbances of cortical development. *Arch Gen Psychiatry* 1993; 50: 169.
7. Weinberger D R. From neuropathology to neurodevelopment. *Lancet* 1995; 346: 552–557.

4

The neurochemistry of schizophrenia

Our knowledge of the neurochemical abnormalities associated with schizophrenia has grown substantially over the past decade or so. Five decades ago, the accidental discovery of chlorpromazine's antipsychotic action led, eventually, to a better understanding of the neuronal nature of schizophrenia. More recently, modern techniques for *in vivo* imaging of neurotransmitter receptors have advanced our understanding still further. Nonetheless, the true and complete neurochemical nature of schizophrenia is still to be elucidated and drug efficacy remains somewhat limited, with no major advance since the introduction of clozapine, a drug first synthesised in the 1950s. In fact, our knowledge of the neurochemistry of schizophrenia is such that we cannot say with certainty whether we know almost nothing or almost everything – it is not clear whether or not we are 1 year or a 100 years away from a major therapeutic breakthrough.

In this chapter, we examine neurochemical candidates in schizophrenia and summarise knowledge of their suspected or established involvement in the disorder.

Dopamine

Dopamine is synthesised in neurones from extracellular tyrosine via dihydrophenylalanine. Intracellular dopamine levels are controlled by the enzyme monoamine oxidase. After release, dopamine may be taken back up into the presynaptic neurone or metabolised by catechol-o-methyl transferase. In the brain, dopamine interacts with a range of postsynaptic dopamine receptors (D_1–D_5; Figure 4.1). There are four major dopaminergic pathways:

1. the nigrostriatal pathway, controlling motor activities
2. the mesolimbic pathways, controlling reward, pleasure and many behaviours
3. the mesocortical pathway, which has uncertain function but contributes to cognition and volition
4. the tuberoinfundibular pathway, controlling production of prolactin

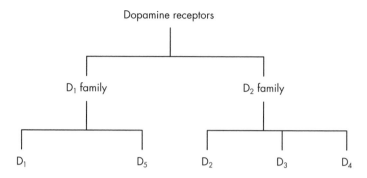

Figure 4.1   Dopamine receptor classification.

As is well known, the dopamine theory of schizophrenia has its origin in early observation of the pharmacological actions of antipsychotics such as reserpine [1] and chlorpromazine [2]. The theory is further supported by the neurochemically unique correlation between *in vitro* activity at dopamine receptors and clinical dose [3] and the observed pro-psychotic effects of dopamine agonists such as amfetamine [4]. It became accepted that schizophrenia was a condition associated with, or caused by, dopamine overactivity.

Over the last decade or so, the dopamine theory of schizophrenia has suffered numerous blows to its status as accepted fact. Some rather confusing and contradictory evidence comes from neuroimaging studies (Box 4.1). In the 1980s an *in vivo* positron emission tomography (PET) study of antipsychotic-naive patients using the ligand [^{11}C] N-methyl-spiperone [5] suggested an increase in dopamine (D_2, D_3, D_4) receptor numbers in schizophrenia, so supporting the dopamine theory of schizophrenia. However, later, studies using a more specific ligand, [^{11}C] raclopride, found no increase in D_2 or D_3 receptors [6]. In addition to this, neuroimaging studies in patients receiving antipsychotics were able to show, first, that antipsychotics sometimes failed to be effective despite high dopamine receptor binding and, second, that the supremely effective antipsychotic clozapine was able to induce response despite low D_2 receptor occupancy [7, 8].

Recent research has also attempted to determine which type or types of dopamine receptor might be involved in the neurochemistry of schizophrenia.

D_1 *receptors* are concentrated in the caudate putamen, the nucleus accumbens and the olfactory tubercle but are highly abundant, being found in cortical and limbic regions. There is limited evidence that D_1

Box 4.1 Neuroimaging

Neuroimaging involves the use of radiolabelled receptor-binding compounds (ligands) to identify the location and number of specific neurochemical receptors. The technique is suitable for *in vitro* and *in vivo* studies but the latter are generally more illuminating. The radiolabelled compound is usually a specific antagonist of a certain receptor or receptor type. Examples include [^{11}C] *N*-methylspiperone (D_2, D_3, D_4 receptors); [^{11}C] raclopride (D_2, D_3); [^{11}C] SCH 23390 (D_1); [^{123}I] epidepride (D_2, D_3); [^{123}I]-iodobenzamide and R 91150 ($5HT_{2a}$).

There are two major experimental methods: PET and single photon emission tomography (SPET). Both are able to image receptor location, receptor density and numbers of free (unbound) receptors. Both have two potential sources of error: (1) specificity of ligands for receptor types and (2) the competition for receptor sites between the ligand, endogenous neurotransmitter and any drug present. Ligands are therefore specially selected for their specificity and their receptor affinity so that specific, free receptors can be imaged (the ligand should not, for example, displace the drug under investigation from receptor sites).

---

receptor numbers are reduced in schizophrenia but this is not conclusive [8]. Some PET studies have detected reduced D_1 density [9]; others have not [10]. Newly developed ligands such as [^{11}C] NNC 112 may help clarify the situation [11].

A reduction in D_1 receptor density is an intriguing possibility, which, counterintuitively, supports the dopamine hypothesis. It is possible that antipsychotics (which in general block D_2 receptors but not D_1) may induce increased dopamine turnover which may compensate for the pathological reduction in D_1 numbers and perhaps restore the balance in D_1/D_2 stimulation [8]. This explanation stands whether D_1 receptors are primarily postsynaptic or presynaptic autoreceptors. It is noteworthy that a specific D_1 antagonist SCH39166 seems to cause deterioration of psychotic symptoms [12], while clozapine appears to be a D_1 receptor agonist [13].

D_2 receptors are the most abundant dopamine receptors in the brain with widespread distribution but particular concentration in the basal ganglia (striatum, putamen). Measurements of D_2 receptor numbers in schizophrenia have provided conflicting results, largely as a consequence of the use of antipsychotics which share a propensity for D_2 antagonism and inevitably affect D_2 receptor density. *In vivo* neuroimaging studies in drug-naive subjects generally suggest increased D_2

receptor density in the striatum with perhaps decreased receptor numbers in the anterior cingulate cortex [14]. Those with schizophrenia also seem to show an exaggerated response to amfetamine – striatal dopamine release is significantly greater than in normal controls [15].

D_2 receptor antagonism remains the most plausible and well-supported method by which antipsychotics exert their effects [7, 8]. Neuroimaging studies confirm the D_2 receptor-blocking action of all antipsychotics but these studies are limited by their lack of specificity for different dopamine receptor subtypes and their restricted capacity for imaging receptor density in areas of the brain with few receptors (e.g. extrastriatal structures). Improved techniques may eventually be illuminating, as may genetic studies, which have already proposed an association between a polymorphism of a D_2 receptor gene and a diagnosis of schizophrenia [16].

Investigation into the role of D_3 *receptors* in schizophrenia has been severely hampered by the absence of a specific D_3 ligand [8]. D_3 receptors appear to be predominantly found in limbic areas of the brain – the sites of emotional processing. As such, they are potential candidates for involvement in the symptoms of schizophrenia and for targets for antipsychotic action. D_3 receptor densities may be increased in the brains of those with schizophrenia [17], although the evidence for this is slim. Knowledge of the role of D_3 receptors is likely to develop more quickly now that specific ligands such as $[^{125}I]$7-hydroxy-PIPAT have begun to be used [17–19]. Genetic studies may also be productive: it has been suggested that D_3 receptor messenger RNA is increased in white blood cells of those with schizophrenia [20].

In the 1990s there was considerable excitement over the role of D_4 *receptors*. This excitement and resultant flurry of activity followed the apparent discovery of a sixfold increase in D_4 receptor numbers in schizophrenia [21]. Clozapine was also noted to be a potent D_4 receptor antagonist [22]. However, the D_4 receptor theory of schizophrenia was short-lived: other workers failed to replicate original findings [8] and the D_4 antagonist fananserin was found to have no antipsychotic effects [23].

The role of dopamine D_5 *receptors* in schizophrenia is unclear and their function is unknown. Studies examining associations between genetic mutations of the D_5 gene and schizophrenia have produced contradictory results [24, 25] (Dopamine focus 4.1).

DOPAMINE FOCUS 4.1

Dopamine activity in schizophrenia		
Brain region	**Dopamine activity**	**Associated symptoms**
Broca's area	↑	Auditory hallucinations
Superior temporal gyrus	↑	Auditory hallucinations
Cingulate gyrus	↑	Passivity experiences
Hippocampus	↑	Positive symptoms
Prefrontal cortex	↓	Negative symptoms
Anterior cingulate	↓	Thought disorder
		Attention deficit

Serotonin

Serotonin or 5-hydroxytryptamine (5HT) has been suspected to be involved in psychiatric symptoms since it was noted that the hallucinogen lysergic acid diethylamide (LSD) possessed serotonergic properties [26]. The serotonergic system is known to interact closely with dopaminergic systems. Genetic profiling and molecular cloning have identified many receptor subtypes very few of which have been carefully scrutinised for a role in the symptoms of schizophrenia. Most research has centred on the $5HT_{2A}$ receptor [8]: the newer atypical antipsychotics generally possess potent $5HT_{2A}$ antagonist activity (Figure 4.2).

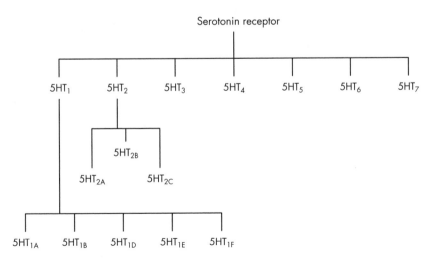

Figure 4.2   Serotonin receptor classification.

A series of imaging studies using the SPET ligand ^{123}I-5-I-R91150 has shown that a variety of atypicals produce very high occupancies of cortical 5HT$_{2A}$ receptors, often at very low doses [27]. In addition, both *in vivo* and postmortem binding studies (using a variety of ligands: [125I] LSD, [3H] ketanserin, [3H] spiperone) tend to suggest a decreased density of 5HT$_{2A}$ receptors in the brains of those with a diagnosis of schizophrenia [28]. Moreover, 5HT$_{2A}$ gene polymorphisms seem to predict response to the atypical antipsychotic clozapine [29, 30].

These observations provided compelling evidence for the involvement of 5HT$_{2A}$ function in schizophrenia and provoked the development of a highly selective 5HT$_{2A}$ antagonist (M-100907) as a putative antipsychotic [31]. M-100907 produced very high (> 90%) cortical occupancy at the clinical doses evaluated [32] but was found to be ineffective in psychosis [31]. At around the same time, it was noted that 5HT$_{2A}$ receptor antagonism was not necessary for atypical action (amisulpride is atypical) and that it did not protect against extrapyramidal adverse effects or hyperprolactinaemia produced by typical drugs [33]. These later observations have provoked a reconsideration of the role of 5HT$_{2A}$ receptors in schizophrenia and in antipsychotic action [28].

Of the other serotonin receptors investigated, none has been clearly implicated in the pathophysiology of schizophrenia. 5HT$_{1A}$ agonism seems to promote increased dopamine activity in the prefrontal cortex and so 5HT$_{1A}$ agonists may be effective in treating negative symptoms [34]. This activity is shown by drugs such as clozapine, ziprasidone and aripiprazole. Antagonism of 5HT$_{2C}$ receptors is probably responsible for antipsychotic-induced weight gain (see later) but does not seem to be involved in the pathophysiology of schizophrenia. 5HT$_3$ receptors also appear not to be involved [35]. The possible contribution of 5HT$_4$, 5HT$_5$, 5HT$_6$ and 5HT$_7$ receptors remains under investigation. Several newer antipsychotics are 5HT$_6$ and 5HT$_7$ antagonists [36] and a selective 5HT$_6$ antagonist, SB271046, is being evaluated as a possible antipsychotic. Polymorphisms in the gene coding for 5HT$_6$ receptors do not, however, predict response to clozapine [37].

Glutamate

Glutamate is an amino acid transmitter and the main excitatory transmitter in the brain. Glutamate is synthesised in neurones or in adjacent glial cells from glutamine. The action of the transmitter may be terminated either by reuptake into the neurone or uptake into glial cells. The glutamate system influences many other neuronal networks, including dopaminergic systems [38], and appears both to stimulate and inhibit dopamine release, depending on the conditions and location. Cerebro-spinal fluid glutamate levels may be altered in people with schizophrenia [8, 39].

The structure and function of glutamate receptors are decidedly complex. There are two major types of receptor (Figure 4.3): (1) ionotropic receptors, which incorporate a gated cation channel (i.e. neuronal trans-mission relies on cation influx but in the resting state the ion channel is blocked or 'gated' by a magnesium ion); and (2) metabotropic receptors, which enable transmission via G proteins or second messenger systems.

The ionotropic N-methyl-D-aspartic acid (NMDA) receptor has been most intensively investigated in regard to its potential involvement in schizophrenia. This receptor complex incorporates several receptor sites both outside and within the ion channel. Glutamate and glycine sites outside the channel must be occupied for the channel to open. The channel may be blocked by compounds such as ketamine and phencycli-dine (PCP; angel dust) which bind inside the channel and prevent cation influx. Both drugs produce sensory disturbances and other symptoms similar to those seen in schizophrenia [40].

Influx of Na+ or Ca2+ ions is essential for neuronal depolarisation and excitatory function. Influx of calcium ions for example sets in chain a number of cellular responses which form the basis for learning and memory. Overactivation of NMDA and other glutamate receptors may lead to excessive calcium influx and cell damage or cell death. This may be the basis for neurone loss in ischaemia and epilepsy [41].

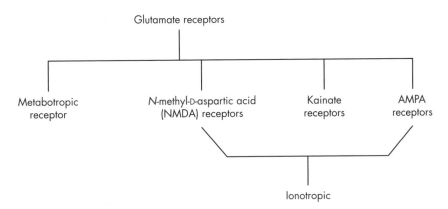

Figure 4.3   Glutamate receptor classification. (AMPA, alpha-amino-3-hydroxy-5-methyl-4-isoxazoleproprionic acid.)

Over the past 10 years or so an NMDA receptor hypofunction model of schizophrenia has emerged [42]. A reduction in NMDA function is said, acutely, to allow increased release of mesolimbic dopamine and, chronically, to afford decreased release in the prefrontal cortex. This 'picture' of dopamine dysfunction fits exactly with our current understanding of the basis of schizophrenia. It has further been postulated that NMDA hypofunction might in some way lead to compensatory overstimulation of non-NMDA glutamate receptors and so account for cognitive decline seen in schizophrenia (via excitatory neurotoxicity). Certainly acute antagonism of NMDA receptors with ketamine leads to cognitive defects (particularly of memory) very similar to those seen in schizophrenia [39].

The developing acceptance of glutamate's involvement in the pathology of schizophrenia has led to therapeutic trials of glutamate agonists and antagonists. The glutamate co-agonist glycine seems to augment negative-symptom response to antipsychotics [43] but, intriguingly, not clozapine [44]. The glutamate antagonist lamotrigine also seems to have antipsychotic properties, particularly in relation to positive symptoms [45]. It is suggested that glycine partial agonists such as clozapine increase neuronal depolarisation at low concentrations and inhibit depolarisation at higher levels [39]. The glycine partial agonist D-cycloserine improves negative symptoms when added to typical antipsychotics [46] and to risperidone [47]. There are several glutamate agonists (CX-516; LY 379269) under investigation as potential antipsychotics [48].

Gamma-aminobutyric acid

Gamma-aminobutyric acid (GABA) is synthesised from glutamate by the enzyme glutamate decarboxylase and is the main inhibitory transmitter in the brain. It interacts with a variety of postsynaptic receptors – $GABA_A$, $GABA_B$ and $GABA_C$ – before being actively transported into glial cells or presynaptic neurones. Like glutamate, GABA is very widely distributed in the brain.

GABA receptor function is complex. $GABA_A$ and $GABA_C$ receptors are ionotropic, being made up of subunits enclosing an ion channel. Stimulation of these receptors opens the ion channel and allows influx of chloride ions which hyperpolarise the postsynaptic neurone and hence provide inhibitory action. $GABA_B$ receptors are metabotropic and linked to G proteins.

Data from animal models and postmortem studies strongly suggest that schizophrenia is associated with a reduction in GABA activity in a number of brain areas, including the cortex and mesolimbic system [49].

In vivo neuroimaging studies using the GABA$_A$ ligand [^{123}I] iomazenil also suggest a cortical GABA deficit in schizophrenia [50]. These observations have led to a 'GABA deficit' theory of schizophrenia which posits that excessive dopaminergic activity is at least in part a result of a reduction in the inhibitory influence of GABA in the brain.

This theory would suggest that GABA agonists might be effective in the treatment of schizophrenia. Evidence for this, however, is not strong. Antipsychotics, both typical and atypical, seem to affect GABA function, and some GABA$_A$ agonists (benzodiazepines, valproate) have a small but positive effect on symptoms when added to antipsychotics [49]. The lack of any major effect has provoked some workers to suggest that inhibitory deficit in schizophrenia is unrelated to GABA [51]. In addition there appear to be no GABA agonists currently being developed for the treatment of schizophrenia.

Essential fatty acids

Polyunsaturated fatty acids make up about 20% of the dry weight of the brain; they are essential constituents of cell membranes and act as precursors to a multitude of physiologically active substances [52]. The polyunsaturated fatty acids linoleic acid and gamma linoleic acid are termed 'essential' because they cannot be synthesised in the body and so need to be ingested. Each compound is modified in the body to produce a variety of structurally distinct fatty acids with various physiological functions.

The potential involvement of fatty acids in schizophrenia was first considered in the 1970s when it was suggested that schizophrenia might be related to prostaglandin excess or deficiency [53]. Polyunsaturated fatty acids are essential precursors of prostaglandins and it was observed that inflammatory conditions such as rheumatoid arthritis were uncommon in schizophrenia. Prostaglandin-related skin flushing is also reduced or absent in people with schizophrenia administered niacin [54]. A theory of abnormal phospholipid metabolism in schizophrenia has arisen, promulgated largely, but not solely, by the late Dr David Horrobin. Support for this theory is provided by the above observations and by other studies reporting changes in prostaglandin function and functional magnetic resonance studies in schizophrenia suggesting lowered phospholipid synthesis in schizophrenia [52, 53].

Clinical trials of essential fatty acids have produced mixed results [55]. Omega-6 fatty acids derived from linoleic acids seem to be ineffective when added to existing antipsychotic treatment but the omega-3 compounds docosahexanoic acid and particularly eicosapentanoic acid produce fairly reliable, if minimal, clinical improvement.

Opiate receptors

The opioid agonist and analgesic pentazocine has psychosis-inducing properties and it has been suggested that sigma antagonists might have active antipsychotic actions. Sigma receptors are found in the same brain regions as dopamine receptors and some conventional antipsychotics are sigma antagonists [40]. Trials of more selective sigma antagonists have proved disappointing: some are ineffective [40, 56], whereas others, such as panamesine (EMB 57445), are effective [57] but may work as dopamine receptor antagonists [58]. Despite these findings, a relatively large number of sigma ligands have been patented as putative anti-psychotics [59]. Antagonists of opiate kappa receptors may also have antipsychotic properties [8].

Neuropeptides

The brain contains a great many peptide molecules which are thought to be involved in neurone function. Two particular neuropeptides appear to be co-located with dopaminergic pathways: cholecystokinin and neurotensin. Antipsychotics seem to affect neurotensin gene expression and neurotensin function [60]. Research continues and there are a handful of neurotensin agonists in development (e.g. PD-149163; NT69-L) [48]. Early research has also investigated an association between the neurotensin receptor gene with schizophrenia and clozapine response [61].

Adenosine

Adenosine is also widely co-localised with dopamine in the brain. Agonists at the adenosine A_{2A} receptors appear to reduce dopamine release and may have antipsychotic properties in animal models [48]. The adenosine reuptake inhibitor dipyridamole seems to be effective in conjunction with haloperidol [62].

Reproductive hormones

The symptoms of schizophrenia have a close temporal relationship with puberty and ageing: symptoms are extremely rare before the onset of puberty and less severe in chronic patients in middle and late age. It has been postulated that schizophrenia may arise as a result of excessive inhibitory response to the excitatory hormonal flood in puberty [63]. There is also a modicum of evidence that oestrogen is antipsychotic when added to standard treatment [64, 65].

Acetylcholine

In many brain areas the dopaminergic system is antagonised by the cholinergic system. Muscarinic receptor numbers may be reduced in schizophrenia [66] and the M1/M4 receptor agonist xanomeline appears to have antipsychotic actions [67].

Conclusion

The neurochemical basis of schizophrenia and psychosis in general remains unclear and poorly understood. There is some confidence over the extensive contribution of dopamine excess to psychotic symptoms but beyond this there is little certainty. Viewing schizophrenia, or at least positive psychotic symptoms, simply as a product of dopamine excess is clearly illogical since dopamine antagonists are only effective against some symptoms in some people.

Our limited understanding of the neurochemical basis of schizophrenia is undoubtedly associated with our inability to comprehend the complexity of the network of neuronal systems that make up the brain. Many neuronal systems influence many others in many parts of the brain. Confusingly, some systems exert different effects on other systems at different times. In addition, the function of many neurochemicals remains to be established.

It follows that we cannot know the precise neurochemical basis of schizophrenia or psychosis (Neurochemistry focus 4.2). There may be defects in all of the neuronal systems above, in just some of them, or in none of them (but some other, so far undiscovered, neurochemical). Antipsychotic action may be shown by dopamine antagonists, serotonin antagonists, glutamate agonists and antagonists (!), GABA agonists, sigma antagonists, adenosine agonists and cholinomimetics (to give an incomplete list). It remains to be demonstrated that combinations of effects clearly afford relatively improved efficacy. Much, very much, is still to be uncovered.

NEUROCHEMISTRY FOCUS 4.2

Neurochemistry of schizophrenia	
Neurotransmitter	**Evidence for involvement in schizophrenia**
Dopamine	All active antipsychotics are dopamine antagonists.
	Dopamine agonists are propsychotic
5HT	Many antipsychotics are $5HT_2$ antagonists. Genetic form of $5HT_{2A}$ receptor may predict response to clozapine
Glutamate	Ketamine and PCP NMDA antagonists) cause schizophrenia-like symptoms. Glutamate co-agonists mildly antipsychotic
GABA	Weak evidence of reduced GABA activity in schizophrenia
Opiates	Sigma receptor antagonists may be antipsychotic
Neurotensin	Neurotensin agonists may be antipsychotic
Acetylcholine	Some cholinergic agonists are antipsychotic

References

1. Carlsson A, Rosengren E, Bertler A, Nilsson J. Effect of reserpine on the metabolism of catecholamines. In: Garattini S, Getti V, eds. *Psychotropic Drugs.* Amsterdam: Elsevier, 1957: 363–372.
2. Carlsson A, Lindqvist M. Effect of chlorpromazine or haloperidol in formation of 3-methoxytyramine or normetanephrine in mouse brain. *Acta Pharmacol Toxicol* 1963; 20: 140–144.
3. Creese I, Burt D R, Snyder S H. Dopamine receptor binding predicts clinical and pharmacological potencies of antischizophrenic drugs. *Science* 1976; 192: 481–483.
4. Randrup A, Munkvad I. Stereotyped activities produced by amfetamine in several animal species and man. *Psychopharmacology* 1967; 11: 300–310.
5. Wong D F, Wagner H N, Tune L E *et al.* Positron emission tomography reveals elevated D_2 dopamine receptors in drug-naive schizophrenics. *Science* 1986; 234: 1558–1563.
6. Farde L, Wiesel F-A, Stone-Elander S *et al.* D_2 dopamine receptors in neuroleptic-naive schizophrenic patients. *Arch Gen Psychiatry* 1990; 47: 213–219.
7. Jones H M, Pilowsky L S. Dopamine and anti-psychotic drug action revisited. *Br J Psychiatry* 2002; 181: 271–275.
8. Sedvall G, Farde L. Chemical brain anatomy in schizophrenia. *Lancet* 1995; 346: 743–749.
9. Okubo Y, Suhara T, Suzuki K *et al.* Decreased prefrontal D_1 receptors in schizophrenia revealed by PET. *Nature* 1997; 385: 634–636.

10. Karlsson P, Farde L, Halldin C, Sedvall G. PET study of D_1 dopamine receptor binding in neuroleptic-naive patients with schizophrenia. *Am J Psychiatry* 2002; 159: 761–767.

11. Halldin C, Foged C, Chou Y H *et al.* Carbon-11-NNC 112: a radioligand for PET examination of striatal and neocortical D_1-dopamine receptors. *J Nuclear Med* 1998; 39: 2061–2068.

12. Karlson P, Smith L, Farde L *et al.* Lack of apparent antipsychotic effect of the D_1-dopamine receptor antagonist SCH39166 in acutely ill schizophrenic patients. *Psychopharmacology* 1995; 121: 309–316.

13. Oerther S, Ahlenius S. Atypical antipsychotics and dopamine D_1 receptor agonism: an *in vivo* experimental study using core temperature measurements in the rat. *J Pharmacol Exp Ther* 2000; 292: 731–736.

14. Wong D F. *In vivo* imaging of D_2 dopamine receptors in schizophrenia. *Arch Gen Psychiatry* 2002; 59: 31–34.

15. Abi-Dargham A, Gil R, Krystal J *et al.* Increased striatal dopamine transmission in schizophrenia: confirmation in a second cohort. *Am J Psychiatry* 1998; 155: 761–767.

16. Glatt S J, Faraone S V, Tsuang M T. Meta-analysis identifies an association between the dopamine D_2 receptor gene and schizophrenia. *Mol Psychiatry* 2003; 8: 911–915.

17. Gurevich E V, Bordelon Y, Shapiro R M *et al.* Mesolimbic dopamine D_3 receptors and use of antipsychotics in patients with schizophrenia. *Arch Gen Psychiatry* 1997; 54: 225–232.

18. Stanwood G D, Artymyshyn R P, Kung M P *et al.* Quantitative autoradiographic mapping of rat brain dopamine D_3 binding with [^{125}I]7-OH-PIPAT: evidence for the presence of D_3 receptors on dopaminergic and non-dopaminergic cell bodies and terminals. *Pharmacol Exp Ther* 2000; 295: 1223–1231.

19. Stanwood G D, Lucki I, McGonigle P. Differential regulation of dopamine D_2 and D_3 receptors by chronic drug treatments. *Pharmacol Exp Ther* 2000; 295: 1232–1240.

20. Ilani T, Ben-Shachar D, Strous R D *et al.* A peripheral marker for schizophrenia: increased levels of D_3 dopamine receptor mRNA in blood lymphocytes. *Proc Natl Acad Sci USA* 2001; 98: 625–628.

21. Seeman P, Guan H C, Van Tol H H M. Dopamine D_4 receptors elevated in schizophrenia. *Nature* 1993; 365: 441–445.

22. Seeman P. Dopamine receptor sequences: therapeutic levels of neuroleptics occupy D_2 receptors, clozapine occupies D_4. *Neuropsychopharmacology* 1992; 7: 261–284.

23. Truffinet P, Tamminga C A, Fabre L F *et al.* Placebo controlled study of D_4/5-HT_{2a} antagonist fananserin in the treatment of schizophrenia. *Am J Psychiatry* 1999; 156: 419–425.

24. Sobell J L, Lind T J, Sigurdson D C *et al.* The D_5 dopamine receptor gene in schizophrenia: identification of a nonsense change and multiple missense changes but lack of association with disease. *Hum Mol Genet* 1995; 4: 507–514.

25. Muir W J, Thomson M L, McKeon P *et al.* Markers close to the dopamine D_5 receptor gene (*DRD5*) show significant association with schizophrenia but not bipolar disorder. *Am J Med Genet* 2001; 105: 152–158.

26. Woolley D, Shaw E. A biochemical and pharmacological suggestion about certain mental disorders. *Proc Natl Acad Sci USA* 1954; 40: 228–231.

27. Travis M J. Receptor imaging with SPET. *J Adv Schizophr Brain Res* 2001; 3: 79–86.

28. Dean B. The cortical serotonin$_{2A}$ receptor and the pathology of schizophrenia: a likely accomplice. *J Neurochem* 2003; 85: 1–15.

29. Arranz M J, Collier D A, Munro J et al. Analysis of a structural polymorphism in the 5HT$_{2A}$ receptor and clinical response to clozapine. *Neurosci Lett* 1996; 217: 177–178.

30. Arranz M J, Munro J, Owen M J et al. Evidence for association between polymorphisms in the promoter and coding regions of the 5HT$_{2A}$ receptor gene and response to clozapine. *Mol Psychiatry* 1998; 3: 61–66.

31. De Paulis T. M-100907 (Aventis). *Curr Opin Invest Drugs* 2001; 2: 123–132.

32. Talvik-Lotfi M, Nyberg S, Nordstrom A L et al. High 5HT$_{2A}$ receptor occupancy in M100907 treated schizophrenic patients. *Psychopharmacology* 2000; 148: 400–403.

33. Kapur S, Roy P, Daskalakis J et al. Increased dopamine D$_2$ receptor occupancy and elevated prolactin level associated with addition of haloperidol to clozapine. *Am J Psychiatry* 2001; 158: 311–314.

34. Bantick R A, Deakin J F W, Grasby P M. The 5HT$_{1A}$ receptor in schizophrenia: a promising target for novel atypical neuroleptics? *J Psychopharmacol* 2001; 15: 37–46.

35. Gutierrez B, Arranz M J, Huezo-Diaz P et al. Novel mutations in 5HT$_{3A}$ and 5HT$_{3B}$ receptor genes not associated with clozapine response. *Schizophr Res* 2002; 58: 93–97.

36. Lawler C P, Prioleau C, Lewis M M et al. Interactions of the novel antipsychotic aripiprazole (OPC-14597) with dopamine and serotonin receptor subtypes. *Neuropsychopharmacology* 1999; 20: 612–627.

37. Masellis M, Basile V S, Meltzer H Y et al. Lack of association between the T→C 267 serotonin 5HT$_6$ receptor gene (*HTR6*) polymorphism and prediction of response to clozapine in schizophrenia. *Schizophr Res* 2001; 47: 49–58.

38. Halpain S, Girault J A, Greengard P. Activation of NMDA receptors induces phosphorylation of DARPP-32 in rat striatal slices. *Nature* 1990; 343: 369–372.

39. Goff D C, Coyl J T. The emerging role of glutamate in the pathophysiology and treatment of schizophrenia. *Am J Psychiatry* 2001; 158: 1367–1377.

40. Wright I, Woodruff P. Aetiology of schizophrenia. A review of theories and their clinical and therapeutic implications. *CNS Drugs* 1995; 3: 126–144.

41. Olney J W. Excitatory amino acids and neuropsychiatric disorders. *Biol Psychiatry* 1989; 26: 505–525.

42. Lewis A D, Lieberman J A. Catching up on schizophrenia: natural history and neurobiology. *Neuron* 2000; 28: 325–334.

43. Javitt D C, Silipo G, Cienfuegos A et al. Adjunctive high dose glycine in the treatment of schizophrenia. *Neuropsychopharmacology* 2001; 4: 385–391.

44. Evins A E, Fitzgerald S M, Wine L et al. Placebo-controlled trial of glycine added to clozapine in schizophrenia. *Am J Psychiatry* 2000; 157: 826–828.

45. Tiihonen J, Hallikainen T, Ryynanen O P et al. Lamotrigine in treatment-resistant schizophrenia: a randomised placebo-controlled crossover trial. *Biol Psychiatry* 2003; 54: 1241–1248.

46. Goff D C, Tsai G, Levitt J *et al.* A placebo-controlled trial of D-cycloserine added to conventional neuroleptics in patients with schizophrenia. *Arch Gen Psychiatry* 1999; 56: 21–27.

47. Evins A E, Amico E, Posever T A *et al.* D-Cycloserine added to risperidone in patients with primary negative symptoms of schizophrenia. *Schizophr Res* 2002; 56: 19–23.

48. Mortimer A M. Novel antipsychotics in schizophrenia. *Expert Opin Invest Drugs* 2004; 13: 315–329.

49. Wassef A, Baker J, Kochan L D. GABA and schizophrenia: a review of basic science and clinical studies. *J Clin Psychopharmacol* 2003; 23: 601–640.

50. Busatto F G, Pilowsky L S, Costa D C *et al.* Correlation between reduced *in vivo* benzodiazepine receptor binding and severity of psychotic symptoms in schizophrenia. *Am J Psychiatry* 1997; 154: 56–63.

51. Lara D R. Inhibitory deficit in schizophrenia is not necessarily a GABAergic deficit. *Cell Mol Neurobiol* 2002; 22: 239–247.

52. Walker N P, Fox H C, Whalley L J. Lipids and schizophrenia. *Br J Psychiatry* 1999; 174: 101–104.

53. Fenton W S, Hibbeln J, Knable M. Essential fatty acids, lipid membrane abnormalities, and the diagnosis and treatment of schizophrenia. *Biol Psychiatry* 2000; 47: 8–21.

54. Ward P E, Sutherland J, Glen E M T, Glen A I M. Niacin skin flush in schizophrenia: a preliminary report. *Schizophr Res* 1998; 29: 269–274.

55. Emsley R, Oosthuizen P, Van Resburg S J. Clinical potential of omega-3 fatty acids in the treatment of schizophrenia. *CNS Drugs* 2003; 17: 1081–1091.

56. Borison R L, Diamond B I, Dren A T. Does sigma receptor antagonism predict clinical antipsychotic efficacy? *Psychopharmacol Bull* 1991; 27: 103–106.

57. Hubert M T, Gotthart U, Schreiber W, Krieg J C. Efficacy and safety of the sigma receptor ligand EMD 57445 (panamesine) in patients with schizophrenia: an open clinical trial. *Pharmacopsychiatry* 1999; 32: 68–72.

58. Grunder G, Muller M J, Andreas J *et al.* Occupancy of striatal D(2)-like dopamine receptors after treatment with the sigma ligand EMD 57445, a putative atypical antipsychotic. *Psychopharmacology (Berl)* 1999; 146: 81–86.

59. Sodhi M S, Murray R M. Future therapies for schizophrenia. *Expert Opin Ther Patents* 1997; 7: 151–165.

60. Binder E B, Kinkead B, Owens M J, Nemeroff C B. Neurotensin and dopamine interactions. *Pharmacol Rev* 2001; 53: 453–486.

61. Huezo-Diaz P, Arranz M J, Munro J *et al.* An association study of the neurotensin receptor with schizophrenia and clozapine response. *Schizophr Res* 2004; 66: 193–195.

62. Akhondzadeh S, Shasavand E, Jamilian H *et al.* Dipyridamole in the treatment of schizophrenia: adenosine–dopamine receptor interactions. *J Clin Pharm Ther* 2000; 25: 131–137.

63. Stevens J R. Schizophrenia: reproductive hormones and the brain. *Am J Psychiatry* 2002; 159: 713–719.

64. Akhondzadeh S, Nejastifa A A, Amini H *et al.* Adjunctive estrogen treatment in women with chronic schizophrenia: a double-blind, randomized, and placebo-controlled trial. *Prog Neuropsychopharmacol Biol Psychiatry* 2003; 27: 1007–1012.

65. Kulkarni J, Riedel A, de Castella A R *et al.* A clinical trial of adjunctive oestrogen treatment in women with schizophrenia. *Arch Women's Mental Health* 2002; 5: 99–104.

66. Raedler T J, Knable M B, Jones D W *et al. In vivo* determination of muscarinic acetylcholine receptor availability in schizophrenia. *Am J Psychiatry* 2003; 160: 118–127.

67. Shannon H E, Rasmussen K, Bymaster F P *et al.* Xanomeline, an M1/M4 preferring muscarinic receptor agonist, produces antipsychotic-like activity in rats and mice. *Schizophr Res* 2000; 42: 249–259.

5

The development and evaluation of antipsychotics

The story of antipsychotic discovery and development essentially began in the 1880s with the synthesis, for use as industrial dyes, of phenothiazine compounds. Many years later, Rhône-Poulenc laboratories developed a number of substituted phenothiazines such as promethazine for use as sedatives and antihistamines. A French surgeon, Henri Laborit, encouraged Rhône-Poulenc to produce compounds which might be useful as premedication agents – drugs which would calm patients pre-operatively and perhaps reduce surgical shock. Laborit was supplied with RP4560, which had been synthesised by Charpentier in 1950 and investigated as an anthelmintic and antihistamine. RP4560 was incorporated into Laborit's 'lytic cocktail', which he used to produce pre-surgical sedation and allow a hypothermic state to be induced and so prolong the time available for cardiac surgery. The effect of RP4560, which later became known as chlorpromazine, was noted by several clinicians: patients became subdued and emotionally unresponsive but were not overtly sedated. These observations led to the experimental use of chlorpromazine in psychosis and agitation. The French psychiatrists Delay and Deniker were the first to report their findings in such patients [1], thus marking the beginning of the antipsychotic era (Development focus 5.1).

Before the discovery and use of chlorpromazine in psychosis no true antipsychotic drug existed. The treatment of psychosis might involve the use of electroconvulsive therapy and insulin coma therapy (the former being effective, the latter very probably not). Drugs available and widely used included chloral, bromides, paraldehyde and barbiturates. None of these had antipsychotic effects *per se*, although all were sedative enough to reduce agitation and anxiety and perhaps to reduce patients' outward expression of psychotic symptoms. Chlorpromazine, it was rather informally observed at the time, seemed to reduce symptoms of psychosis (delusions, hallucinations, thought disorder) even in the absence of overt sedation.

Antipsychotic development

1880s	Synthesis of phenothiazines
1940s	Medicinal use of phenothiazines
1950s	Introduction of chlorpromazine
1960s	Introduction of butyrophenones
	Trials of clozapine
	Antipsychotics shown to be dopamine antagonists
1970s/1980s	Introduction of sulpiride and pimozide
1990s	Reintroduction of clozapine
	Introduction of 'atypicals'
2000s	Introduction of aripiprazole

In the psychoanalysis-dominated world of the 1950s, the idea that a drug might radically improve the symptoms of severe mental illness was revolutionary. Nevertheless, the use of chlorpromazine slowly became more widespread during the early 1950s and the drug was eventually licensed in the USA in 1955 (as an antiemetic: it was still too early to try to convince the regulatory authorities that a drug might truly be an antipsychotic) [2]. Gradually, more compounds were found to be antipsychotic and were marketed. These included the rauwolfia alkaloid reserpine and further substituted phenothiazines such as fluphenazine, prochlorperazine and thioridazine. Later, largely using behavioural screening tests, other chemical groups of antipsychotics were developed, the most notable being the butyrophenones – compounds derived from the opioid analgesic pethidine [3].

For more than 10 years after the discovery of chlorpromazine's antipsychotic effect, there were few clues as to its mode of action. The neurotransmitter dopamine had been identified [4] but few linked it to the effect of antipsychotics. Only later did Carlsson and Lindqvist [5] observe that both chlorpromazine and haloperidol increased the production of dopamine metabolites in mouse brain. From this, the dopamine theory of antipsychotic action (and of schizophrenia) was developed and later strengthened by numerous observations such as those of Seeman and co-workers [6], who correlated clinic dose with molecular affinity for dopamine D_2 receptors (see Chapter 4).

This action might have been predicted somewhat earlier had more been known of the pathology of Parkinson's disease. Early evaluations of chlorpromazine had brought to light its propensity to produce extrapyramidal adverse effects similar in many ways to the symptoms of Parkinson's disease [7]. It is now known that extensive blockade of nigrostriatal dopamine receptors by antipsychotics is the mechanism for inducing extrapyramidal symptoms.

Thus, dopamine receptor antagonism seemed to be necessary for therapeutic effects but also gave rise to adverse effects such as extrapyramidal symptoms. Indeed, in the 1960s it became accepted practice to increase doses of antipsychotics until extrapyramidal effects appeared; this was judged to be a minimum effective dose. The development of antipsychotics, to a large extent, incorporated this accepted wisdom of drug action. Further development produced drugs which tended to affect only dopamine D_2 receptors and to spare other less 'important' receptors. Such drugs included butyrophenones such as droperidol, the diphenylbutylpiperidine pimozide and the substituted benzamide sulpiride.

Research might have continued along the same lines for decades were it not for the synthesis and use of a dibenzodiazepine compound, clozapine. Uniquely, clozapine was an effective antipsychotic but did not give rise to extrapyramidal side-effects. Clozapine was thus the first 'atypical' antipsychotic; other antipsychotics were eventually labelled conventional or 'typical' because they typically engendered such adverse side-effects.

The recognition that extrapyramidal effects need not be inexorably linked to therapeutic effects led eventually to the introduction of a new group of antipsychotics, the atypicals. Amongst these is a compound with close chemical and pharmacological similarity to clozapine, the thienobenzodiazepine olanzapine, and other structurally distinct compounds such as risperidone, sertindole and aripiprazole.

Evaluating antipsychotic effects

Clinical efficacy studies in schizophrenia are usually randomised, double-blind trials that assess symptom changes using recognised, validated rating scales. Broad-based measures include the 18-item Brief Psychiatric Rating Scale (BPRS) [8], the more comprehensive 30-item Positive and Negative Symptom Scale (PANSS) [9] and the rudimentary but meaningful Clinical Global Impression [10].

Positive symptoms are usually evaluated using the positive-symptom subscales (i.e. only those items relating to positive symptoms) of the BPRS or PANSS. Negative symptoms are better assessed using the negative subscale of the PANSS or by specific rating scales such as the Schedule for Assessment of Negative Symptoms [11]. Overall, it is generally held that positive symptoms (essentially categorical departures from 'normality') are more accurately and precisely evaluated than negative symptoms (essentially a *relative* absence of normal behaviours). Other scales for efficacy assessments used in schizophrenia include the Montgomery–Asberg Depression Rating Scale [12], and a variety of quality-of-life scales and global assessment scales.

Adverse effects are also systematically evaluated using validated scales. These scales include the Simpson–Angus Scale (acute extra-pyramidal symptoms) [13], the Barnes Akathisia Scale [14], the Extra-pyramidal Symptoms Rating Scale [15] and the Abnormal Involuntary Movement Scale for tardive dyskinesia [16].

The successful use of all these scales in trials is dependent upon rater training, skill and reliability (including interrater reliability). In practice, many are useful for evaluating progress and tolerability of antipsychotic treatment. A number of practically useful scales are included in the Appendix.

References

1. Delay J, Deniker P. Le traitement des psychoses par une neurolyptique derivée de l'hibernotherapie. *Congrès Med Alienistes Neurologistes France* 1952; 50: 497.
2. Healy D. *The Psychopharmacologists II.* Philadelphia, PA: Lippincott-Raven, 1998.
3. Janssen P A J. The butyrophenone story. In: Ayd F J, Blackwell B, eds. *Discoveries in Biological Psychiatry.* Philadelphia, PA: Lippincott, 1970: 165–179.
4. Bertler Å, Rosengren E. Occurrence of distribution of dopamine in brain and other tissues. *Pharmacol Rev* 1959; 11: 490–493.
5. Carlsson A, Lindqvist M. Effect of chlorpromazine or haloperidol on the formation of 3-methoxytyramine and normetanephrine in mouse brain. *Science* 1963; 127: 471.
6. Seeman P, Lee T, Chou-Wong M *et al.* Antipsychotic drug dose and neuroleptic/dopamine receptors. *Nature* 1976; 261: 717–718.
7. Lehmann H E, Hanrahan A E. CP2: new inhibiting agent for psychomotor excitement and manic states. *Arch Neurol Psychiatry* 1954; 71: 227–237.
8. Overall J E, Gorham D R. The Brief Psychiatric Rating Scale. *Psychol Rep* 1962; 10: 799–812.
9. Kay S R, Fishbein A, Opler L A. Positive and Negative Syndrome Scale (PANSS) for schizophrenia. *Schizophr Bull* 1987; 13: 261–276.
10. National Institute of Mental Health. Clinical global impressions. In: Guy W, ed. *ECDEU Assessment Manual for Psychopharmacology,* revised. Rockville, MD: Department of Health Education and Welfare, 1976: 157–169.
11. Andreasen N. Scale for the Assessment of Negative Symptoms (SANS). *Br J Psychiatry* 1989; 155 (suppl. 7): 53–58.
12. Montgomery S A, Asberg M. A new depression scale designed to be sensitive to change. *Br J Psychiatry* 1979; 134: 382–389.

13. Simpson G M, Angus J W S. A rating scale for extrapyramidal side-effects. *Acta Psychiatr Scand* 1970; 212: 11–19.

14. Barnes T R E. A rating scale for drug-induced akathisia. *Br J Psychiatry* 1989; 154: 672–676.

15. Chouinard G, Ross-Chouinard A, Annable L *et al*. The Extrapyramidal Symptom Rating Scale. *Can J Psychiatry* 1980; 7: 1233.

16. Lane R D, Glazer W M, Hausen T E *et al*. Assessment of tardive dyskinesia using the Abnormal Involuntary Movement Scale. *J Nerv Ment Disord* 1985; 173: 353–357.

6

Conventional antipsychotics

Several terms are used to describe antipsychotic drugs that can be expected to engender acute extrapyramidal effects in normal clinical use. These terms include typical, conventional and first-generation antipsychotics. Before so-called atypical antipsychotics were introduced, typical antipsychotics were, of course, not considered to be a drug subgroup since they represented antipsychotics as a whole. Conventional antipsychotics share very little except their propensity for extrapyramidal side-effects (EPSEs), which is assumed to arise as a consequence of their potent (striatal) dopamine receptor antagonism. Both chemical structure and receptor activity differ markedly within this ersatz grouping of drugs.

Conventional antipsychotics are no longer widely used in the developed world but remain drugs of choice, largely because of relative cost, in developing countries. Many of the pharmacological and clinical data relating to these drugs are now very old and the quality of research poor. Ironically, a better understanding of the effects of these drugs has been provided by their use as standard comparators in trials of newer antipsychotics.

An understanding of the properties of conventional drugs remains important because of their continued use and because of the historical perspective provided by a knowledge of their development and clinical utility. In this chapter we briefly review data relating to this diverse and numerous group of drugs.

Chemistry and pharmacology

The phenothiazines are the most numerous of the conventional antipsychotics. There are three major classes: (1) aliphatic; (2) piperidine; and (3) piperazine.

Phenothiazines

Aliphatic phenothiazines such as chlorpromazine (Figure 6.1) have a carbon chain and amine group substituted at position 10 of the phenothiazine molecule. Other examples include promazine and trifluopromazine, which have different substitutions at position 2 on the phenothiazine structure. Piperidine phenothiazines incorporate a piperidine ring attached by a short carbon chain at position 10. Examples include thioridazine and mesoridazine. Aliphatic and piperidine phenothiazines are sometimes referred to as low-potency neuroleptics because relatively high doses are needed to elicit antipsychotic effects. The third class of phenothiazines are the piperazine phenothiazines, which have a higher potency. Examples include trifluoperazine, fluphenazine and perphenazine. These drugs often have an alcohol moiety substituted on the piperazine structure (R, Figure 6.2) which allows esterification to oil-soluble compounds. These long-chain esters are often dissolved in oils to produce long-acting or depot formulations.

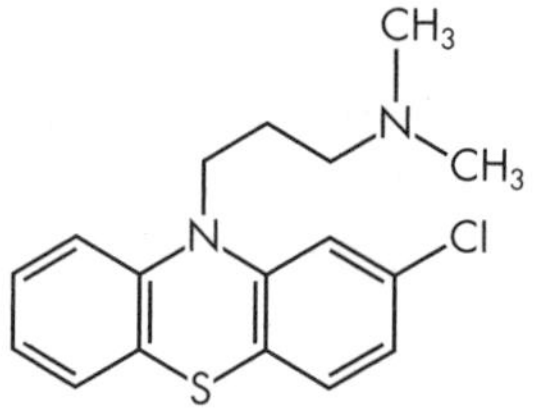

Figure 6.1 Chlorpromazine.

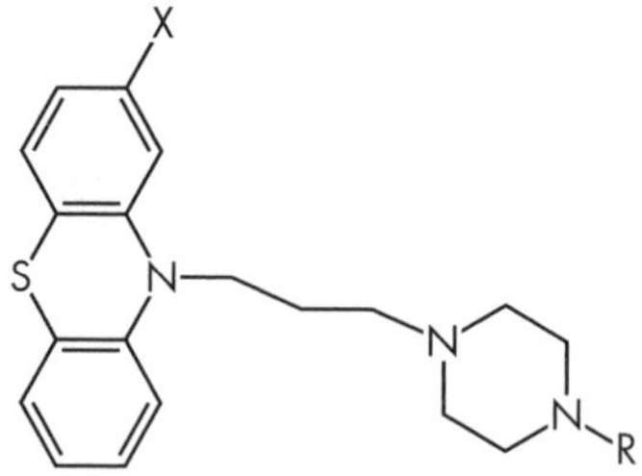

Figure 6.2 Piperazine phenothiazine: basic structure.

Thioxanthines

Piperazine phenothiazines share some characteristics with thioxanthine antipsychotics. Thioxanthines substitute a carbon atom for nitrogen at position 10 of the phenothiazine structure and may also have an alcoholic piperazine moiety attached (Figure 6.3). Examples include flupentixol, zuclopenthixol, thiothixine and chlorprothixine. Certain thioxanthines may be esterified and used in depot formulations. Piperazine phenothiazines and thioxanthines are sometimes referred to as high-potency neuroleptics along with butyrophenones and diphenylbutylpiperidines.

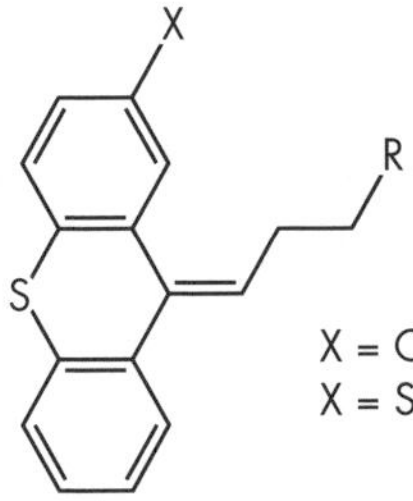

X = Cl   R = N(CH₃)₂   Chlorprothixene
X = SO₂N(CH₃)₂   R = Methylpiperazine   Thiothixene

Figure 6.3 Thioxanthine structure.

Butyrophenones

The structure of butyrophenones differs markedly from phenothiazines. These drugs were developed from pethidine and bear some resemblance to its chemical structure. Haloperidol (Figure 6.4) is the most commonly used of the butyrophenones but droperidol and benperidol are also available in many countries.

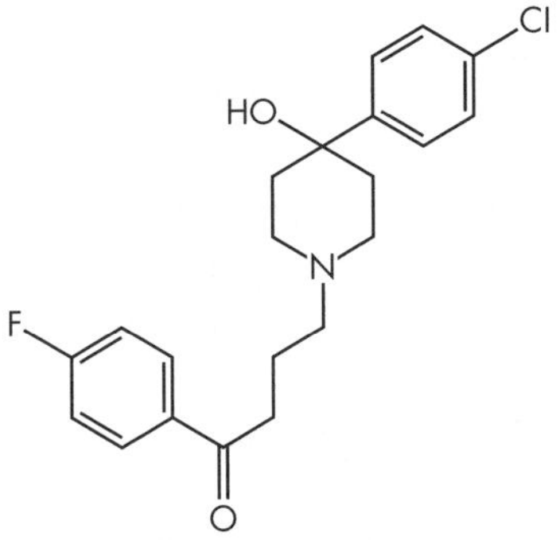

Figure 6.4 Haloperidol.

Others

Other conventional drugs include the diphenylbutylpiperidines pimozide and fluspiriline (Figure 6.5) and the dibenzazepine loxapine.

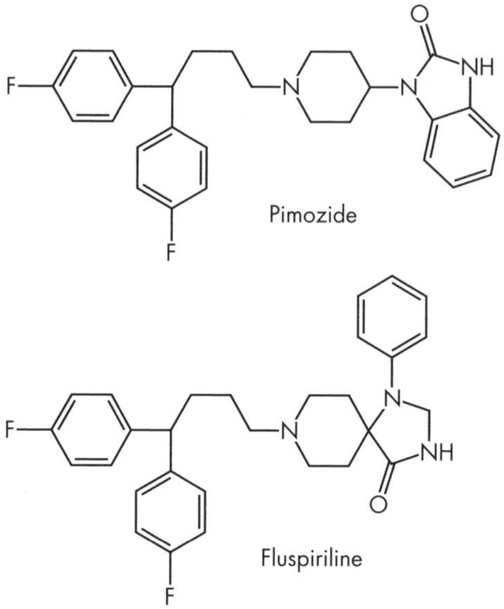

Figure 6.5 The diphenylbutylpiperidines pimozide and fluspiriline.

All conventional antipsychotics are very potent or moderately potent antagonists of dopamine D_2 receptors. Dopamine antagonism is the single important receptor activity of butyrophenones and piperazine phenothiazines – these drugs have insignificant effects at other receptors. Aliphatic and piperidine phenothiazines are characterised by additional antagonistic activity at $5HT_2$, H_1, α_1 and cholinergic receptors. Thioxanthines, diphenylbutylpiperidines and loxapine also show serotonergic antagonism but have minimal activity at other receptors (although loxapine is a fairly potent H_1 antagonist).

Various positron emission tomography studies using ^{11}C-raclopride and ^{11}C-SCH23390 have shown that conventional antipsychotics, used in clinically effective doses, produce striatal D_2 occupancies of between 65% and 89% [1–3]. Conventional drugs appear to have equal affinity for striatal and cortical D_2 receptors (unlike some, or perhaps all, atypical drugs) [4] and this lack of limbic selectivity may mean that conventional antipsychotics are inexorably associated with dopaminergic adverse effects when used at clinically effective doses [5]. Others contend that, even with conventional drugs, dopaminergic adverse effects only occur at D_2 receptor occupancies above that needed for therapeutic efficacy [6]. Even if this is true, doses separating therapeutic and adverse effects may be too similar to be clinically useful [7].

There is some evidence that thioridazine, the most atypical of the conventional drugs, is relatively less likely to cause dopaminergic adverse effects because of lower or looser binding to striatal D_2 receptors [8]. It is also possible that its partial atypicality is a product of its potent anticholinergic properties.

Efficacy

The effectiveness of conventional antipsychotics is visible to the naked eye: phenothiazines such as chlorpromazine were readily observed to be strikingly effective when first used in the 1950s. In first-episode schizophrenia a worthwhile response is seen in the majority of subjects. Over 1 year, response rates are remarkably uniform – rates of 79% [9], 83% [10] and 87% [11] have been reported. It is also noteworthy that atypical drugs such as clozapine are not clearly superior to conventional drugs in first-episode schizophrenia [9].

In relapsed, chronic schizophrenia response is less marked, with around 20–30% showing worthwhile reduction in symptoms and the remainder showing either partial or no response [12]. Some trials show advantages for atypical antipsychotics in this subject group (see later chapters). Chlorpromazine and haloperidol, amongst others, are effective in reducing the risk of relapse in schizophrenia [13, 14]. The same is true of conventional depots, but, somewhat surprisingly, there is no clear evidence that depots are superior to oral treatment in preventing relapse [15, 16]. In fact there is no firm evidence supporting relatively better efficacy for any conventional drug or formulation in any symptom domain. Conventional antipsychotics are not effective in refractory schizophrenia [17].

The optimal dose of conventional antipsychotics has not been clearly established despite more than 50 years of clinical use. Standard reference texts suggest a wide range of allowable doses but these recommendations appear to be based more on historical use than on robust clinical trial data. Take the example of haloperidol. The upper limit of its recommended dose range in the UK was 200 mg/day for many years but is now 30 mg/day, having been 120 mg/day in the time in between. Clinical doses are often in the region of 10–15 mg/day. However, in first-episode subjects, doses of less than 4 mg/day are probably effective [18, 19], and in relapsed schizophrenia doses of between 4 and 7.5 mg/day appear to be optimally effective [20, 21]. In the prevention of relapse, clinical doses of haloperidol decanoate range from 50 to 300 mg/month, but a dose of 50–100 mg/month is probably optimally effective [22] and this dose equates to around 2–3 mg/day intramuscularly or 5–6 mg/day in oral equivalents (allowing for differences in bioavailability). For other conventional drugs, optimal doses are very probably at the lower end of the recommended dose range.

Why higher than necessary doses are prescribed is something of a mystery. Part of the explanation may relate to the limited efficacy of all antipsychotics in relapsed schizophrenia. This is likely to encourage dose increases which are aimed at eliciting or improving response. Another explanation involves the motor adverse effects of conventional drugs. Hostile or overactive patients can be rendered akinetic with high doses of conventional antipsychotics and this may be a bona fide treatment aim. A third reason may be that the sheer range of recommended doses encouraged prescribers to increase doses within this range, assuming either that safety was assured or that efficacy would gradually increase with dose.

Adverse effects

By definition, all conventional antipsychotics are associated with the dopamine-related effects of EPSEs, hyperprolactinaemia, tardive dyskinesia (TD) and neuroleptic malignant syndrome. Acute EPSEs are relatively more common with butyrophenones, piperazine phenothiazines, thioxanthines and pimozide and less common with aliphatic and, particularly, piperidine phenothiazines. (These different frequencies of acute events may confer different rates of longer-term effects such as tardive dyskinesia but there is little research to support this assumption.) Space does not permit a close examination of EPSE severity with each conventional drug but some illustrative examples are now provided. Haloperidol produces EPSEs severe enough to warrant treatment with anticholinergic drugs in at least 50% of patients when used at low doses (8 or 16 mg/day) [21]. Compared with placebo, relative risks of adverse effects have been calculated as follows [14]: dystonia relative risk 4.7, akathisia 6.5 and parkinsonism 8.9. The piperazine phenothiazine trifluoperazine is more than five times more likely to cause extrapyramidal effects than placebo and 66% more likely to cause these effects than chlorpromazine [23]. Pimozide, too, is more likely than other conventional drugs to cause acute EPSEs [24] but thioridazine less likely to be associated with EPSEs [25].

Hyperprolactinaemia is usually seen in nearly all patients receiving conventional antipsychotics at effective doses [5]. TD is also commonly seen. See Chapter 14 for a full discussion of these adverse effects.

Other adverse effects include sedation (aliphatic and piperidine phenothiazines), anticholinergic effects (piperidine phenothiazines), cholestatic jaundice (chlorpromazine), skin hypersensitivity (chlorpromazine), orthostatic hypertension (aliphatic and piperidine phenothiazines), prolongation of the cardiac QT interval (all drugs), weight gain (all drugs) and diabetes (phenothiazines). Many of these adverse effects are discussed in Chapter 15.

Pharmacokinetics

The discovery and development of conventional antipsychotics predate both the use of sophisticated chemical analysis to establish pharmacokinetic profiles and knowledge of hepatic cytochrome function. As a consequence, knowledge of the pharmacokinetic characteristics of many typical drugs is rather poor. Generally, conventional antipsychotics have less than 100% oral bioavailability, are hepatically metabolised and have plasma half-lives of several hours or longer. Again, space does not permit an examination of the kinetic profile of each and every typical drug but some examples are provided below.

Chlorpromazine shows an oral bioavailability of around 32% after a single dose and even lower bioavailability in continuous dosing [26]. It is widely metabolised (by sulphoxidation, hydroxylation and oxidation) to a wide range of compounds (some of which have antipsychotic activity) and has a plasma half-life of around 11 hours [27]. It is not clear which cytochrome enzymes are responsible for chlorpromazine metabolism. Most reported adverse interactions are pharmacodynamic in nature – additive effects with sedatives and anticholinergic agents.

Attempts to define a target range of plasma chlorpromazine concentrations have been unsuccessful, probably because of the large number of active metabolites generated. Therapeutic response may be seen at plasma concentrations of 50–300 µg/L [28].

Haloperidol has been demonstrated to have an oral bioavailability of 60–65% and a plasma half-life of around 20 hours [29]. It is extensively metabolised to a variety of compounds which may possess antipsychotic activity by virtue of sigma receptor antagonism (they are mostly not D_2 antagonists) [30]. The hepatic cytochrome CYP3A4 seems to be the enzyme primarily responsible for haloperidol metabolism, with CYP2D6 also involved to a lesser extent [31]. In fact, patients who are poor CYP2D6 metabolisers are more likely to experience EPSEs with haloperidol [32]. The observation that smoking reduces haloperidol plasma levels suggests that CYP1A2 can also metabolise haloperidol [32, 33]. Haloperidol is an inhibitor of CYP2D6 [31]. Interactions can be expected with other drugs metabolised by CYP2D6 and with inducers of CYP3A4 (carbamazepine) and inhibitors of CYP3A4 (fluoxetine, ketoconazole) or CYP2D6 (fluoxetine, paroxetine, etc.).

Haloperidol plasma levels of 12–30 µg/L have been reported to be associated with clinical effect [34, 35]. However, it is probable that much lower levels are effective: a plasma level of around 2 µg/L (from a dose of 2.5 mg/day) appears to afford *in vivo* D_2 receptor occupancy of more than 80% [36] (10 mg/day would be expected to give a plasma level of around 8 µg/L).

All available conventional *depot antipsychotics* are oil-soluble esters. Depot injections are given intramuscularly as the esterified drug dissolved in a natural oil derived from sesame seeds, coconuts or vegetables. The esterified drug slowly diffuses from the injection site into the blood, where it is very quickly hydrolysed to the parent drug. Because the rate of the drug release is slower than the rate of elimination, the apparent rate of elimination is controlled by release rather than hepatic metabolism. This effectively means that plasma half-life is dependent on rate of drug release. Because of the very slow rate of release, attainment of steady-state plasma levels may be delayed for up to 3 months, during which time plasma levels may quadruple [37]. Most depot preparations are effective when given at intervals of 2–4 weeks. In practice, much shorter intervals are frequently used (typically weekly). There is no evidence to suggest that more frequent administration results in improved efficacy.

The pharmacokinetic characteristics of commonly used depot preparations are given in Pharmacokinetic focus 6.1.

PHARMACOKINETIC FOCUS 6.1

Pharmacokinetic characteristics of depot formulations [37–40]			
Drug	Dose interval (weeks)	Time to peak plasma level (days)	Apparent half-life in clinical use (days)
Flupentixol decanoate	2–4	3–10	17
Fluphenazine decanoate	2–5	1–2	14
Haloperidol decanoate	4	3–9	21
Pipotiazine palmitate	4	10	14–21
Zuclopenthixol decanoate	2–4	4–7	19

Pimozide shows oral bioavailability of 30–60% and a plasma half-life of around 50 hours [41] – long enough for once-weekly administration to be effective [42]. Pimozide is largely metabolised by oxidative N-dealkylation, with some drug excreted unchanged in the urine. None of the metabolites is active [43]. Metabolism of pimozide seems to be mediated via CYP3A4, although other enzymes may be involved. Evidence for the involvement of CYP3A4 comes from reports of interactions with CYP3A4 inhibitors such as clarithromycin [44, 45]. Pimozide's effects on the QT interval may be indirectly exacerbated by CYP3A4 inhibitors, so such drugs should not be co-administered with pimozide.

Conventional antipsychotics continue to be useful drugs despite their adverse effects and remain the yardstick against which newer drugs are measured (Management focus 6.1).

MANAGEMENT FOCUS 6.1

Conventional antipsychotics	
Absorption	Less than complete when taken orally
Elimination	Hepatic
Plasma half-life	Depends on drug – usually fairly long-acting
Hepatic cytochromes involved	Not clearly determined Probably CYP2D6, CYP3A4 and CYP1A2 (see text)
Hepatic cytochromes affected	May competitively inhibit CYP2D6
Major interactions	Other sedatives; other drugs which prolong QT interval Carbamazepine may reduce levels
Efficacy	Good. Almost all first-episode patients respond Treatment resistance develops Prevent relapse
Adverse-effect profile/ tolerability	Extrapyramidal adverse effects, hyperprolactinaemia, TD, QT prolongation

References

1. Farde L, Wiesel F A, Nordstrom A L, Sedvall G. D_1- and D_2-dopamine receptor occupancy during treatment with conventional and atypical neuroleptics. *Psychopharmacol (Hist Arch)* 1989; 99: S28–S31.

2. Wiesel F A, Farde L, Nordstrom A L, Sedvall G. Central D_1- and D_2-receptor occupancy during antipsychotic drug treatment. *Prog Neuropsychopharmacol Biol Psychiatry* 1990; 14: 759–767.

3. Farde L, Nordstrom A L, Wiesel F A *et al.* Positron emission tomographic analysis of central D_1 and D_2 dopamine receptor occupancy in patients treated with classical neuroleptics and clozapine. Relation to extrapyramidal side effects. *Arch Gen Psychiatry* 1992; 49: 538–544.

4. Xiberas X, Martinot J L, Mallet L *et al.* Extrastriatal and striatal D_2 dopamine receptor blockade with haloperidol or new antipsychotic drugs in patients with schizophrenia. *Br J Psychiatry* 2001; 179: 503–508.

5. Taylor D. Low dose typical antipsychotics – a brief evaluation. *Psychiatr Bull* 2000; 24: 465–468.

6. Kapur S, Remington G, Jones C *et al.* High levels of dopamine D_2 receptor occupancy with low-dose haloperidol treatment: a PET study. *Am J Psychiatry* 1996; 153: 948–950.

7. Kapur S, Zipursky R, Jones C *et al.* Relationship between dopamine D_2 occupancy, clinical response, and side effects: a double-blind PET study of first-episode schizophrenia. *Am J Psychiatry* 2000; 157: 514–520.

8. Crocker A D, Hemsley K M. An animal model of extrapyramidal side effects induced by antipsychotic drugs: relationship with D_2 dopamine receptor occupancy. *Prog Neuropsychopharmacol Biol Psychiatry* 2001; 25: 573–590.

9. Lieberman J A, Phillips M, Gu H *et al.* Atypical and conventional antipsychotic drugs in treatment-naive first-episode schizophrenia: a 52-week randomized trial of clozapine vs chlorpromazine. *Neuropsychopharmacology* 2003; 28: 995–1003.

10. Lieberman J, Jody D, Geisler S *et al.* Time course and biologic correlates of treatment response in first-episode schizophrenia. *Arch Gen Psychiatry* 1993; 50: 369–376.

11. Robinson D G, Woerner M G, Alvir J M J *et al.* Predictors of treatment response from a first episode of schizophrenia or schizoaffective disorder. *Am J Psychiatry* 1999; 156: 544–549.

12. Miyamoto S, Duncan G E, Marx C E, Lieberman J A. Treatments for schizophrenia: a critical review of pharmacology and mechanisms of action of antipsychotic drugs. *Mol Psychiatry* 2005; 10: 79–104.

13. Thornley B, Rathbone J, Adams C E, Awad G. Chlorpromazine versus placebo for schizophrenia. *Cochrane Database of Systematic Reviews* 2003, issue 2. DOI: 10.1002/14651858. CD000284.

14. Joy C B, Adams C E, Lawrie S M. Haloperidol versus placebo for schizophrenia. *Cochrane Database of Systematic Reviews* 2001, issue 2. DOI: 10.1002/14651858. CD003082.

15. David A, Adams C E, Eisenbruch M *et al.* Depot fluphenazine decanoate and enanthate for schizophrenia. *Cochrane Database of Systematic Reviews* 2004, issue 2. DOI: 10.1002/14651858. CD000307.

16. Quraishi S, David A. Depot haloperidol decanoate for schizophrenia. *Cochrane Database of Systematic Reviews* 1999, issue 1. DOI: 10.1002/14651858. CD001361.

17. Kane J, Honifeld G, Singer J, Meltzer H. Clozapine for the treatment-resistant schizophrenic. A double-blind comparison with chlorpromazine. *Arch Gen Psychiatry* 1988; 45: 789–796.

18. Oosthuizen P, Emsley R A, Turner J, Keyter N. Determining the optimal dose of haloperidol in first-episode psychosis. *J Psychopharmacol* 2001; 15: 251–255.

19. McEvoy J P, Hogarty G E, Steingard S. Optimal dose of neuroleptic in acute schizophrenia. A controlled study of the neuroleptic threshold and higher haloperidol dose. *Arch Gen Psychiatry* 1991; 48: 739–745.

20. Waraich P S, Adams C E, Roque M *et al.* Haloperidol dose for the acute phase of schizophrenia. *Cochrane Database of Systematic Reviews* 2002, issue 2. DOI: 10.1002/14651858. CD001951.

21. Zimbroff D L, Kane J M, Tamminga C A *et al.* Controlled, dose–response study of sertindole and haloperidol in the treatment of schizophrenia. *Am J Psychiatry* 1997; 154: 782–791.

22. Taylor D. Establishing a dose–response relationship for haloperidol decanoate. *Psychiatr Bull* 2005; 29: 104–107.

23. Marques L O, Lima M S, Soares B G O. Trifluoperazine for schizophrenia. *Cochrane Database of Systematic Reviews* 2004, issue 1. DOI: 10.1002/14651858. CD003545.pub2.

24. Sultana A, McMonagle T. Pimozide for schizophrenia or related psychoses. *Cochrane Database of Systematic Reviews* 2000, issue 3. DOI: 10.1002/14651858. CD001949.

25. Sultana A, Reilly J, Fenton M. Thioridazine for schizophrenia. *Cochrane Database of Systematic Reviews* 2000, issue 2. DOI: 10.1002/14651858. CD001944.

26. Dahl S G, Strandjord R E. Pharmacokinetics of chlorpromazine after single and chronic dosage. *Clin Pharmacol Ther* 1977; 21: 437–448.

27. Yeung P K, Hubbard J W, Korchinski E D, Midha K K. Pharmacokinetics of chlorpromazine and key metabolites. *Eur J Clin Pharmacol* 1993; 45: 563–569.

28. Rivera-Calimlim L, Nasrallah H, Strauss J, Lasagna L. Clinical response and plasma levels: effect of dose, dosage schedules, and drug interactions on plasma chlorpromazine levels. *Am J Psychiatry* 1976; 133: 646–652.

29. Froemming J S, Lam Y W, Jann M W, Davis C M. Pharmacokinetics of haloperidol. *Clin Pharmacokinet* 1989; 17: 396–423.

30. Klein M, Cooper T B, Musacchio J M. Effects of haloperidol and reduced haloperidol on binding to sigma sites. *Eur J Pharmacol* 1994; 254: 239–248.

31. Kudo S, Ishizaki T. Pharmacokinetics of haloperidol: an update. *Clin Pharmacokinet* 1999; 37: 435–456.

32. Brockmoller J, Kirchheiner J, Schmider J *et al.* The impact of the CYP2D6 polymorphism on haloperidol pharmacokinetics and on the outcome of haloperidol treatment. *Clin Pharmacol Ther* 2002; 72: 438–452.

33. Perry P J, Miller D D, Arndt S V *et al.* Haloperidol dosing requirements: the contribution of smoking and nonlinear pharmacokinetics. *J Clin Psychopharmacol* 1993; 13: 46–51.

34. Dahl S G. Plasma level monitoring of antipsychotic drugs. Clinical utility. *Clin Pharmacokinet* 1986; 11: 36–61.
35. Volavka J, Cooper T B, Czobor P, Meisner M. Plasma haloperidol levels and clinical effects in schizophrenia and schizoaffective disorder. *Arch Gen Psychiatry* 1995; 52: 837–845.
36. Fitzgerald P B, Kapur S, Remington G *et al.* Predicting haloperidol occupancy of central dopamine D_2 receptors from plasma levels. *Psychopharmacology* 2000; 149: 1–5.
37. Jann M W, Ereshfsky L, Saklad S R. Clinical pharmacokinetics of the depot antipsychotics. *Clin Pharmacokinet* 1985; 10: 315–333.
38. Davis J M, Metalon L, Watanabe M D, Blake L. Depot antipsychotic drugs place in therapy. *Drugs* 1994; 47: 741–773.
39. Altamura A C, Sassella F, Santini A *et al.* Intramuscular preparations of antipsychotics: uses and relevance in clinical practice. *Drugs* 2003; 63: 493–512.
40. Taylor D. Depot antipsychotics revisited. *Psychiatr Bull* 1999; 23: 551–553.
41. McCreadie R G, Heykants J J, Chalmers A, Anderson A M. Plasma pimozide profiles in chronic schizophrenics. *Br J Clin Pharmacol* 1979; 7: 533–534.
42. McCreadie R, Mackie M, Morrison D, Kidd J. Once weekly pimozide versus fluphenazine decanoate as maintenance therapy in chronic schizophrenia. *Br J Psychiatry* 1982; 140: 280–286.
43. Pinder R M, Brogden R N, Swayer R *et al.* Pimozide: a review of its pharmacological properties and therapeutic uses in psychiatry. *Drugs* 1976; 12: 1–40.
44. Flockhart D A, Drici M D, Kerbusch T *et al.* Studies on the mechanism of a fatal clarithromycin–pimozide interaction in a patient with Tourette syndrome. *J Clin Psychopharmacol* 2000; 20: 317–324.
45. Dresser G K, Spence J D, Bailey D G. Pharmacokinetic–Pharmacodynamic consequences and clinical relevance of cytochrome P450 3A4 inhibition. *Clin Pharmacokinet* 2000; 38: 41–57.

7

Benzamides – sulpiride and amisulpride

There are a number of substituted benzamides marketed as therapeutic agents. They include sultopride (an antipsychotic), tiapride (an antidepressant) and metoclopramide (an antiemetic) [1]. Cisapride, another benzamide, was previously used to promote gastrointestinal motility but was withdrawn because of cardiac toxicity. Remoxipride was withdrawn because of an association with blood dyscrasia. In the UK sulpiride and amisulpride are licensed for the treatment of schizophrenia.

Sulpiride

Sulpiride is a racemic mixture of D- and L- enantiomers of N-[(1-ethyl-2-pyrrolidinyl)methyl]-2-methoxy-5-sulfamoylbenzamide (Figure 7.1).

Sulpiride's pharmacological actions are limited to antagonist activity at dopamine D_2 and D_3 receptors; it has no important activity at any other receptors [2]. Human positron emission tomography (PET) studies using a variety of ligands have shown that low or moderate doses of sulpiride (800–1600 mg/day) produce striatal D_2 receptor occupancies of 68–82% [3, 4]. Occupancies at the lower end of this range (assuming adequate clinical efficacy) are consistent with atypical properties and, to some extent, animal experiments with sulpiride support this supposition [2]. It has been suggested that sulpiride may preferentially block presynaptic D_2 receptors at low doses or in the prefrontal cortex [5]. This activity is likely to increase dopaminergic transmission in certain brain

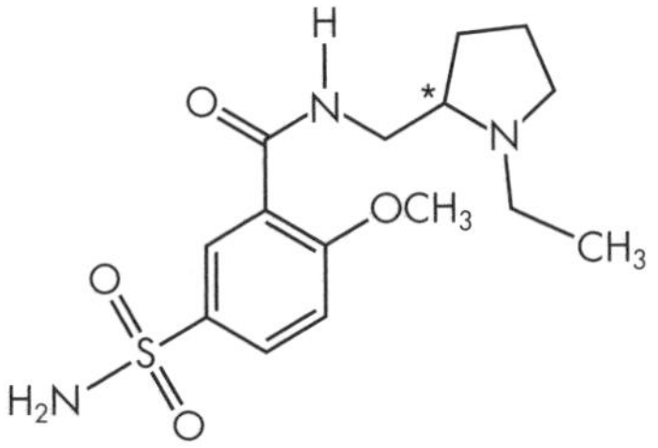

Figure 7.1 Sulpiride. *Chiral centre.

areas and may explain sulpiride's observed antidepressant effects and postulated effects against negative symptoms. At higher doses, it is supposed that postsynaptic D_2 or D_3 antagonism accounts for sulpiride's antipsychotic effects. Sulpiride was originally marketed as an antipsychotic with activity against positive, negative and depressive symptoms of schizophrenia but with a 'lack of association with the development of tardive dyskinesia' (TD) [6]. Some, but not all, of these claims have proved to be correct.

Clinical efficacy

Numerous studies have evaluated the efficacy of sulpiride but trial methods and subject numbers leave something to be desired by today's more exacting standards. Three trials comparing sulpiride (800–1800 mg/day) with chlorpromazine (400–675 mg/day) included fewer than 200 subjects combined but were claimed individually to demonstrate equivalent antipsychotic activity [7–9]. Similarly, two studies with haloperidol (0.5–24 mg/day) as the comparator with sulpiride (100–3200 mg/day) recruited just over 100 subjects in total and claimed to show antipsychotic equivalence [10, 11]. A single, again small ($n = 47$), study appeared to suggest slightly improved outcome with sulpiride – a comparison with the phenothiazine perphenazine (4–32 mg/day) [12]. It would of course be inappropriate to draw conclusions from this one tiny study.

Overall, 18 efficacy studies of the use of sulpiride in various stages of schizophrenia have been conducted and published. In reviewing these studies, the Cochrane collaboration [13] found no evidence for superior efficacy of sulpiride over other antipsychotics in any symptom domain and noted the poor quality of the trials conducted. Other reviewers concur with this conclusion [2], further emphasising that evidence supporting particular efficacy against negative symptoms is limited to a single brief report published in 1987 [14].

Adverse effects

Sulpiride is virtually devoid of sedative properties and is not usually associated with adverse effects related to antagonism of histaminic, cholinergic or alpha-noradrenergic receptors [2, 13]. Adverse effects reported to be associated with sulpiride are linked to the drug's known effects on dopaminergic transmission. Hyperprolactinaemia is a particular problem with sulpiride: it occurs even after the use of minuscule doses

(1–50 mg/day) [15], and gynaecomastia and galactorrhoea were commonly reported in some clinical trials [9] (as they are in clinical practice). There is debate over sulpiride's propensity to cause acute movement disorders. Some studies showed advantages for sulpiride compared with haloperidol [11] but others found no clear differences. Overall, the rate of extrapyramidal reactions may be slightly less than that seen with conventional antipsychotics (52.8% versus 60.5% of patients in trials) [2]. It is more difficult to be sure about sulpiride's association with TD. The manufacturers of sulpiride originally claimed that sulpiride did not cause TD, citing the absence of reports of TD despite sulpiride's use in more than 10 000 Japanese patients [6]. Sulpiride has also been used as a treatment for TD [16]. Nonetheless, cases of both sulpiride-induced TD [17] and tardive dystonia [18] have been reported. Neuroleptic malignant syndrome may also occur with sulpiride [19].

Pharmacokinetics

Sulpiride shows poor oral bioavailability (around 25–30% of a dose), largely, it is thought, because of limited intestinal absorption [20, 21]. It appears to be removed from the body primarily by renal excretion of unchanged drug, with around 90% of an intravenous dose recovered unchanged in the urine [22]. Hepatic metabolism is very limited. Plasma half-life ranges from around 5 to 14 hours. As expected, clearance is markedly reduced and half-life extended in patients with impaired renal function [23]. Plasma sulpiride concentrations shows some correlation with the frequency of extrapyramidal effects [24].

Because sulpiride does not undergo extensive hepatic metabolism, pharmacokinetic drug interactions are uncommon (Management focus 7.1).

Amisulpride

Amisulpride is chemically similar to sulpiride and differs only in the addition of an amide group and the replacement of the sulphamoyl moiety with an ethylsulphonyl group (Figure 7.2). Its chemical name is 4-amino-N-[(1-ethyl-2-pyrollidinyl) methyl1]-5-(ethylsulphonyl)-2-methoxybenzamide.

Amisulpride is a selective antagonist at dopamine D_2 and D_3 receptors, with almost no activity at serotonergic, histaminergic or muscarinic receptors [25]. Animal experiments suggest that amisulpride has different

MANAGEMENT FOCUS 7.1

Sulpiride	
Absorption	Around 25% of oral dose absorbed
Elimination	Renal
Plasma half-life	5–14 hours
Hepatic cytochromes involved	None
Hepatic cytochromes affected	None
Major interactions	None
Efficacy	At least as effective as a variety of conventional antipsychotics but studies are generally poor
Adverse-effect profile/tolerability	Hyperprolactinaemia (e.g. breast growth, sexual function changes). Acute extrapyramidal effects slightly less common than with conventionals

effects at different dose levels. At low doses amisulpride seems to enhance dopaminergic transmission whereas higher doses block the effects of co-administered dopamine agonists [26]. Experiments with rats suggest that amisulpride may preferentially affect dopamine receptors outside the striatal region and be 'limbic-selective' in its action [27]. Human studies support this observation to some extent: PET studies suggest that, at least at low doses, amisulpride preferentially binds to extrastriatal dopamine receptors [28]. Binding to striatal receptors is plasma concentration-dependent [29] and of a similar magnitude to that seen with conventional antipsychotics – amisulpride doses of 630–1100 mg/day gave striatal

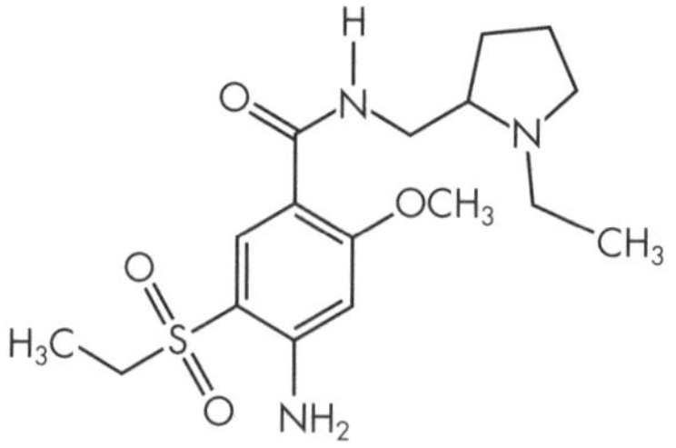

Figure 7.2 Amisulpride.

occupancies of 70–85% in a PET study using ^{76}Br-bromolisuride as the ligand [30]. These data predict high rates of hyperprolactinemia and extrapyramidal side-effects (EPSEs), that is, a typical adverse-effect profile. In fact, although hyperprolactinaemia is seen even after very small doses of amisulpride [31], EPSEs are relatively less often seen [32] – a consequence perhaps of amisulpride's loose binding to striatal receptors [33], which provides a limbic-selective pharmacological profile [28].

Clinical efficacy

There are three major studies of amisulpride's efficacy compared with conventional drugs in acute exacerbations of schizophrenia [34]. A dose-ranging study compared 400, 800 and 1200 mg amisulpride with 16 mg haloperidol in a 4-week trial. There were no clear differences in outcome between any treatment groups. A second short-term study compared 800 mg/day amisulpride with 20 mg/day haloperidol. Efficacy against overall symptoms was similar but amisulpride showed significantly greater improvement on the Positive and Negative Symptom Scale (PANSS) negative subscale. The response rate was also higher in the amisulpride group. A third short-term study compared amisulpride (600–1000 mg/day) with flupentixol (15–25 mg/day). There was some evidence of superior efficacy for amisulpride, although negative symptom response was similar for both drugs. When these results and those of other comparisons of amisulpride and conventional drugs (published and unpublished) are combined in a meta-analysis, amisulpride shows clear therapeutic advantage over older drugs [35].

At least some of this apparent superiority may be a consequence of amisulpride's greater efficacy against negative symptoms. The effect of amisulpride on primary negative symptoms has been evaluated in four trials. A small ($n = 20$) short-term study showed significantly better outcome with amisulpride (50–100 mg/day) than with placebo [36]. A similar study compared amisulpride 100 or 300 mg/day with placebo and also found that amisulpride was relatively more effective against negative symptoms [37]. A 6-month comparison of placebo and 100 mg/day amisulpride gave similar results [38], as did a 12-week study evaluating doses of 50 and 100 mg/day [39]. In all of these studies positive symptoms were either not present or, if present, not affected by amisulpride treatment. This suggests that amisulpride's effect is seen in primary negative symptoms as opposed to secondary symptoms (which occur as a result of positive phenomena).

Amisulpride has also been compared with atypical antipsychotics. Two studies used risperidone as a comparator. In a 6-week comparison [40], amisulpride (800 mg/day) was at least as effective as risperidone (8 mg/day) against both positive and negative symptoms. In a 6-month comparison, amisulpride (400–1000 mg/day) was more effective on some measures than risperidone (4–10 mg/day) but similar on the main outcome of reduction of PANSS score [41]. One further study compared amisulpride (200–800 mg/day) with olanzapine (5–20 mg/day) over 6 months [42]. Clinical outcome was almost identical for the two treatment groups.

Overall, studies show that amisulpride is at least as effective as both conventional and atypical antipsychotics. Its apparent advantages over typical drugs [35] are somewhat unexpected given amisulpride's rather narrow range of pharmacological activity. If indeed this is a fair appraisal of amisulpride's relative efficacy then it may be explained by its particular efficacy against negative symptoms or by therapeutically useful loose binding to postsynaptic dopamine receptors. It is also notable that amisulpride improves cognitive and depressive symptoms in schizophrenia [25].

Adverse effects

Like sulpiride, amisulpride is largely non-sedative and does not cause adverse effects related to receptor activity other than dopamine antagonism. As already mentioned [31], amisulpride readily induces hyperprolactinaemia and related symptoms of galactorrhoea and gynaecomastia occur fairly frequently – at least as often as with haloperidol [25]. Frequency of EPSEs is less with amisulpride than with conventional drugs but similar to risperidone and olanzapine [42, 43] (although comparisons with risperidone used high doses of this drug). EPSEs are clearly dose-related with amisulpride: at least one symptom occurred in 31, 42, 45 and 55% of patients given 100, 400, 800 and 1200 mg/day respectively in a trial where haloperidol 16 mg/day caused EPSEs in 58% of subjects [44]. To some extent these observed rates do fit with known receptor-binding activity of amisulpride but also suggest some protection against EPSEs, perhaps because of limbic selectivity. TD does occur after longer-term treatment with amisulpride, although its incidence is thought to be less than with conventional drugs [43]. Neuromalignant syndrome has also been reported [45], albeit rarely. Amisulpride appears not to affect cardiac rhythm and has a low potential for weight gain and diabetes [25].

Pharmacokinetics

Amisulpride shows an oral bioavailability of around 50% of an ingested dose, has a plasma half-life of approximately 12 hours and is largely renally excreted [46]. The rate and extent of amisulpride oral absorption is increased by ethanol [47] but amisulpride does not enhance the cognitive depressant effects of alcohol [46]. Amisulpride is metabolised to a very small extent, producing two inactive metabolites. It appears to have no effect on hepatic enzyme capacity. Plasma levels of amisulpride are linearly associated with dose and average around 400 µg/l in patients taking around 800 mg/day [48]. Plasma levels have not been clearly linked to therapeutic effect and no target range of levels has been defined.

Amisulpride excretion is reduced in the elderly (as might be expected) [47, 48]. Co-administered lithium also decreases amisulpride excretion to a small extent: plasma levels rise by about 30% [49]. Amisulpride does not, however, affect lithium excretion [50] and is not known to affect the removal of any other psychotropic drugs [47].

Benzamides are useful, non-sedative antipsychotics which are usually well tolerated and which rarely interact with co-administered drugs (Management focus 7.2).

MANAGEMENT FOCUS 7.2

Amisulpride	
Absorption	50% of oral dose absorbed
Elimination	Renal
Plasma half-life	12 hours
Hepatic cytochromes involved	None
Hepatic cytochromes affected	None
Major interactions	None
Efficacy	At least as effective as conventional and atypical drugs. May have slight advantages over conventionals
Adverse-effect profile/tolerability	Hyperprolactinaemia (breast growth, sexual function changes). Acute extrapyramidal effects dose-related. Incidence of TD may be relatively low

References

1. Peselow E D, Stanley M. Clinical trials of benzamides in psychiatry. *Adv Biochem Psychopharmacol* 1982; 35: 163–164.
2. Caley C F, Weber S S. Sulpiride: an antipsychotic with selective dopaminergic antagonist properties. *Ann Pharmacother* 1995; 29: 152–160.
3. Farde L, Wiesel F A, Halldin C, Sedvall G. Central D_2-dopamine receptor occupancy in schizophrenic patients treated with antipsychotic drugs. *Arch Gen Psychiatry* 1988; 45: 71–76.
4. Farde L, Nordstrom A L, Wiesel F A *et al*. Positron emission tomographic analysis of central D_1 and D_2 dopamine receptor occupancy in patients treated with classical neuroleptics and clozapine. Relation to extrapyramidal side effects. *Arch Gen Psychiatry* 1992; 49: 538–544.
5. Jenner P, Marsden C D. The mode of action of sulpiride as an atypical anti-depressant agent. *Adv Biochem Psychopharmacol* 1982; 32: 85–103.
6. *Dolmatil (Sulpiride)*. London: ER Squibb, 1982.
7. Toru M, Scimazono Y, Miyasaka M *et al*. A double-blind comparison of sulpiride with chlorpromazine in chronic schizophrenia. *J Clin Pharmacol New Drugs* 1972; 12: 221–229.
8. Bratfos O, Haung J O. Comparison of sulpiride and chlorpromazine in psychoses. A double-blind multicentre study. *Acta Psychiatr Scand* 1979; 60: 1–9.
9. Harnryd C, Bjerkebstedt L, Gullberg B *et al*. Clinical evaluation of sulpiride in schizophrenic patients – a double-blind comparison with chlorpromazine. *Acta Psychiatr Scand* 1984; 311: 7–30.
10. Cassano G B, Castrogiovanni P, Conti L, Bonollo L. Sulpiride – an antipsychotic agent: comparative trial vs. haloperidol. *Psychopharmacol Bull* 1977; 13: 41–43.
11. Gerlach J, Behnke K, Heltberg J *et al*. Sulpiride and haloperidol in schizophrenia: a double-blind cross-over study of therapeutic effect, side effects and plasma concentrations. *Br J Psychiatry* 1985; 147: 283–288.
12. Lepola U, Koshinen T, Rimon R *et al*. Sulpiride and perphenazine in schizophrenia. A double-blind clinical trial. *Acta Psychiatr Scand* 1989; 80: 92–96.
13. Soares B G O, Fenton M, Chue P. Sulpiride for schizophrenia (Cochrane review). *Cochrane Library*, issue 4, 2002. Oxford: Update Software.
14. Petit M, Zann M, Lesieur P, Colonna L. The effect of sulpiride on negative symptoms of schizophrenia. *Br J Psychiatry* 1987; 150: 270–271.
15. McMurdo M E, Howie P W, Lewis M *et al*. Prolactin response to low dose sulpiride. *Br J Clin Pharmacol* 1987; 24: 133–137.
16. Gerlach J, Casey D E. Sulpiride in tardive dyskinesia. *Acta Psychiatr Scand Suppl* 1984; 311: 93–102.
17. Achiron A, Zoldan Y, Melamed E. Tardive dyskinesia induced by sulpiride. *Clin Neuropharmacol* 1990; 13: 248–252.
18. Miller L G, Jankovic J. Sulpiride-induced tardive dystonia. *Move Disord* 2004; 5: 83–84.
19. Kashihara K, Ishida K. Neuroleptic malignant syndrome due to sulpiride. *J Neurol Neurosurg Psychiatry* 1988; 51: 1109–1110.
20. Wiesel F A, Alfredsson G, Ehrnebo M, Sedvall G. The pharmacokinetics of intravenous and oral sulpiride in healthy human subjects. *Eur J Clin Pharmacol* 1980; 17: 385–391.

21. Bressolle F, Bres J, Faure-Jeantis A. Absolute bioavailability, rate of absorption, and dose proportionality of sulpiride in humans. *J Pharm Sci* 1992; 81: 26–32.

22. Bres J, Bressolle F. Pharmacokinetics of sulpiride in humans after intravenous and intramuscular administrations. *J Pharm Sci* 1991; 80: 1119–1124.

23. Bressolle F, Bres J, Mourad G. Pharmacokinetics of sulpiride after intravenous administration in patients with impaired renal function. *Clin Pharmacokinet* 1989; 17: 367–373.

24. Alfredsson G, Bjerkenstedt L, Edman G *et al*. Relationships between drug concentrations in serum and CSF, clinical effects and monoaminergic variables in schizophrenic patients treated with sulpiride or chlorpromazine. *Acta Psychiatr Scand* 1984; 311: 49–74.

25. Coukell A J, Spencer C M, Benfield P. Amisulpride: a review of its pharmacodynamic and pharmacokinetic properties and therapeutic efficacy in the management of schizophrenia. *CNS Drugs* 1996; 6: 237–256.

26. Scatton B, Claustre Y, Cudennec A *et al*. Amisulpride: from animal pharmacology to therapeutic action. *Int Clin Psychopharmacol* 1997; 12: S29–S36.

27. Schoemaker H, Claustre Y, Fage D *et al*. Neurochemical characteristics of amisulpride, an atypical dopamine D_2/D_3 receptor antagonist with both presynaptic and limbic selectivity. *J Pharmacol Exp Ther* 1997; 280: 83–97.

28. Bressan R A, Erlandsson K, Jones H M *et al*. Is regionally selective D_2/D_3 dopamine occupancy sufficient for atypical antipsychotic effect? An *in vivo* quantitative [^{123}I] epidepride SPET study of amisulpride-treated patients. *Am J Psychiatry* 2003; 160: 1413–1420.

29. Vernaleken I, Siessmeier T, Buchholz H G *et al*. High striatal occupancy of D_2-like dopamine receptors by amisulpride in the brain of patients with schizophrenia. *Int J Neuropsychopharmacol* 2004; 7: 421–430.

30. Martinot J L, Paillere-Martinot M L, Poirier M F *et al*. *In vivo* characteristics of dopamine D_2 receptor occupancy by amisulpride in schizophrenia. *Psychopharmacology (Berl)* 1996; 124: 154–158.

31. Wetzel H, Wiesner J, Hiemke C, Benkert O. Acute antagonism of dopamine D_2-like receptors by amisulpride: effects on hormone secretion in healthy volunteers. *J Psychiatr Res* 1994; 28: 461–473.

32. Curran M P, Perry C M. Spotlight on amisulpride in schizophrenia. *CNS Drugs* 2002; 16: 207–211.

33. Kapur S, Seeman P. Does fast dissociation from the dopamine D_2 receptor explain the action of atypical antipsychotics? A new hypothesis. *Am J Psychiatry* 2001; 158: 360–369.

34. Freeman H L. Amisulpride compared with standard neuroleptics in acute exacerbations of schizophrenia: three efficacy studies. *Int Clin Psychopharmacol* 1997; 12: S11–S17.

35. Davis J M, Chen N, Glick I D. A meta-analysis of the efficacy of second-generation antipsychotics. *Arch Gen Psychiatry* 2003; 60: 553–564.

36. Paillere-Martinot M L, Lecrubier Y, Martinot J L, Aubin F. Improvement of some schizophrenic deficit symptoms with low doses of amisulpride. *Am J Psychiatry* 1995; 152: 130–134.

37. Boyer P, Lecrubier Y, Puech A J *et al*. Treatment of negative symptoms in schizophrenia with amisulpride. *Br J Psychiatry* 1995; 166: 68–72.

38. Loo H, Poirier-Littre M F, Theron M *et al*. Amisulpride versus placebo in the medium-term treatment of the negative symptoms of schizophrenia. *Br J Psychiatry* 1997; 170: 18–22.

39. Danion J M, Werner R, Fleurot O *et al*. Improvement of schizophrenia patients with primary negative symptoms treated with amisulpride. *Am J Psychiatry* 1999; 156: 610–616.

40. Peuskens J, Bech P, Moller H J *et al*. Amisulpride vs. risperidone in the treatment of acute excerbations of schizophrenia. Amisulpride study group. *Psychiatry Res* 1999; 88: 107–117.

41. Sechter D, Peuskens J, Fleurot O *et al*. Amisulpride vs. risperidone in chronic schizophrenia: results of a 6-month double-blind study. *Neuropsychopharmacology* 2002; 27: 1071–1081.

42. Mortimer A, Martin S, Loo H, Peuskens J. A double-blind, randomised comparative trial of amisulpride versus olanzapine for 6 months in the treatment of schizophrenia. *Int Clin Psychopharmacol* 2004; 19: 63–69.

43. Rein W, Coulouvrat C, Dondey-Nouvel L. Safety profile of amisulpride in short- and long-term use. *Acta Psychiatr Scand* 2000; 101: 23–27.

44. Puech A, Fleurot O, Rein W. Amisulpride, an atypical antipsychotic, in the treatment of acute episodes of schizophrenia: a dose-ranging study vs. haloperidol. *Acta Psychiatr Scand* 1998; 98: 65–72.

45. Atbasoglu E C, Ozguven H D, Can Saka M, Goker C. Rhabdomyolsis and coma associated with amisulpride: a probable atypical presentation of neuroleptic malignant syndrome. *J Clin Psychiatry* 2004; 65: 1724–1725.

46. Rosenzweig P, Canal M, Patat A *et al*. A review of the pharmacokinetics, tolerability and pharmacodynamics of amisulpride in healthy volunteers. *Hum Psychopharmacol* 2002; 17: 1–13.

47. McKeage K, Plosker G L. Amisulpride: a review of its use in the management of schizophrenia. *CNS Drugs* 2004; 18: 933–956.

48. Bergemann N, Kopitz J, Kress K R, Frick A. Plasma amisulpride levels in schizophrenia or schizoaffective disorder. *Eur Neuropsychopharmacol* 2004; 14: 245–250.

49. Bergemann N, Kress K R, Abu-Tair F *et al*. Increase in plasma concentrations of amisulpride after receiving co-medication with lithium. *Pharmacopsychiatry* 2005; available online at: www.thieme-connect.com/ejournals/toc/pharmaco/doi.10.1055/s-2005-862621.

50. Canal M, Legangneux E, Van Lier J J *et al*. Lack of effect of amisulpride on the pharmacokinetics and safety of lithium. *Int J Neuropsychopharmacol* 2003; 6: 103–109.

8

Clozapine – a unique antipsychotic

Clozapine is an unusual drug in a number of ways. It is the only anti-psychotic that has been shown conclusively to be more effective than other antipsychotics [1]; it very rarely causes the extrapyramidal side-effects (EPSEs) common to all other conventional antipsychotics and it is one of a handful of drugs to be reintroduced having first been withdrawn because of serious adverse effects. Clozapine is also the only psychotropic to be used under strict guidance from company-run monitoring schemes.

The success of clozapine as a treatment for schizophrenia has also substantially altered long-held biochemical theories of this disorder and forced a beneficial change in research strategies for the discovery and development of new antipsychotics. This chapter is a relatively in-depth study of this unique drug.

Development

Clozapine is [8-chlor-11-(4-methyl-1-piperazinyl)-5H-dibenzo[1,4]diazepine], a dibenzodiazepine derivative (Figure 8.1). The compound was first synthesised and patented in 1960 [2] and was originally predicted to have antidepressant properties [3]. It was soon found, however, that clozapine was an effective antipsychotic [4]. It was also noted that clozapine appeared not to produce any EPSEs. Clozapine was said to be non-'neuroleptic' (in the true sense of the word: literally, 'neurone-seizing') in that it did not cause extrapyramidal effects or induce apathy and lack of volition [3]. However, many psychiatrists at that time considered EPSEs to be a prerequisite of antipsychotic activity and so clozapine did not initially gain favour. Clozapine was eventually marketed in parts of northern Europe some years later and subsequently shown conclusively to be an effective antipsychotic in the first double-blind trial of the drug [5]. Clinical experience with the drug later confirmed both its efficacy and its unique lack of EPSEs. Clozapine thus became the first effective marketed 'atypical', that is, non-neuroleptic, antipsychotic.

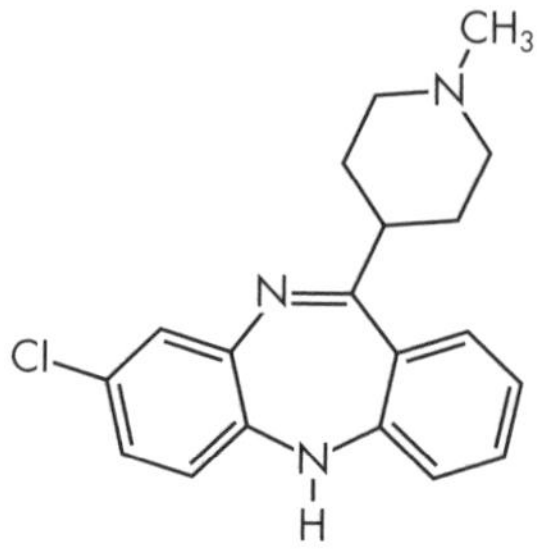

Figure 8.1 Chemical structure of clozapine.

Clozapine use increased until 1975 when reports of blood dys-crasia associated with the drug were confirmed. Of 1500–2000 patients treated with clozapine in Finland, 18 developed, within 107 days of starting clozapine, 'severe blood disorder': eight of these patients died from complications resulting from agranulocytosis [6]. A centralised system of recording cause of death in Finland enabled this rare occur-rence to be linked to the use of clozapine. Clozapine was withdrawn from the market and was later shown to be associated with an incidence of agranulocytosis of up to 2% [7].

Clozapine continued to be used on a named-patient basis (that is, by special request to, and agreement with, the manufacturer) in a number of countries throughout the late 1970s and the 1980s. Interest began to grow in clozapine's 'atypical' nature and its pharmacology was intensively investigated. In addition, the results of several studies [8, 9] suggested that the efficacy of clozapine might be superior to traditional antipsychotics. Clozapine's full potential was eventually conclusively demonstrated by Kane *et al.* in 1988 [10]; these authors showed that the drug was more effective than chlorpromazine in the treatment of antipsychotic-resistant schizophrenia (see below). Since then, clozapine has been marketed in many countries and its superior efficacy observed in clinical practice and confirmed by numerous trials [11]. Within 4 years of reintroduction, around 750 000 people worldwide had received clozapine [12].

Efficacy

Treatment with standard antipsychotics is helpful in around 80% of first-episode patients suffering from schizophrenia [13]. Up to 20% do not respond to drug treatment despite high doses. Many of those who do respond suffer residual symptoms, especially debilitating negative symptoms. Positive psychotic symptoms such as hallucinations and thought disorder may also persist. The standard or typical antipsychotics are now held to have broadly equal efficacy in schizophrenia and to differ only in side-effect profile.

In 1988, Kane *et al.*'s study of clozapine in refractory schizophrenia [10] showed for the first time that not all antipsychotics had equal efficacy. Kane *et al.* studied a cohort of 319 schizophrenic inpatients who had failed to respond to at least three different antipsychotics and had a long history of poor functioning. Subjects were first given placebo for 2 weeks and then a 6-week trial of high-dose haloperidol (with benztropine). Thirty-three of 309 patients given haloperidol responded (5 patients), became uncooperative or violated the study protocol and were removed from the study. Another 18 dropped out during the first placebo period or during the subsequent week-long placebo run-in. Eventually, 126 subjects were randomised to receive clozapine (up to 900 mg/day) and 142 to chlorpromazine (up to 1800 mg/day). After 6 weeks of treatment 30% of clozapine-treated subjects were found to have responded, compared with only 4% of those given chlorpromazine. (A 'response' was defined as a 20% reduction in Brief Psychiatric Rating Scale (BPRS) score.)

This seminal study showed that clozapine could bring relief to patients who had been refractory to standard neuroleptic treatment for many years. Previously, this large subgroup of patients with schizophrenia had been considered beyond the reach of conventional therapy. Another remarkable observation was that both positive and negative symptoms were substantially improved – an effect not previously seen with standard antipsychotics. These results were unusually impressive (in that these patients had, at least in the recent past, remained unchanged by any of numerous drug treatments) and they provoked a response from the licensing authorities which eventually led to the introduction of clozapine to many countries.

Kane *et al.*'s study also suggested that the improvement seen in response to clozapine might continue after 6 weeks: graphs of overall response were still rising at the 6-week endpoint. In 1989, Meltzer and co-workers [14] published results of a longer-term study which confirmed this suggestion. Fifty-one treatment-resistant schizophrenic patients received clozapine for a mean duration of 10.3 months. At 12 months, 60.8% of subjects had shown at least a 20% decrease in BPRS. Improvement in both positive and negative symptoms was again noted. Only 45.2% of those patients who eventually responded had responded after 6 weeks. Many patients only reached 20% reduction in

BPRS after 3 or 6 months, and some only after 9 or 12 months. Two important inferences were drawn from the study: the first that more than half of treatment-resistant patients could gain benefit from clozapine; the second that 6–12 months of treatment might be necessary to assess response to clozapine fully.

More recent studies have established the efficacy of clozapine in wider populations and disease states. For example, Hong and others [15] compared clozapine and chlorpromazine in Chinese patients diagnosed with refractory schizophrenia. Outcome was remarkably similar to that seen in Kane *et al.*'s original study. Over the 12-week study period 29% of those receiving clozapine showed at least a 20% fall in BPRS compared with none of those receiving chlorpromazine. Clozapine also seems to be effective in treatment-resistant childhood-onset schizophrenia [16], in psychotic bipolar disorder [17] in psychosis associated with borderline personality disorder [18] and in refractory schizophrenia not responding to olanzapine [19].

Clozapine may also be effective against neurocognitive symptoms of schizophrenia [20], having been shown to improve attention, memory, verbal fluency and reaction time in refractory schizophrenia [21]. It may also reduce overall mortality of schizophrenia [22], probably through a reduction in suicidality [23]. The mechanism for this effect is not known and is the subject of wide debate. Evidence for a specific effect on suicidal thoughts and actions has recently come from a large trial showing reduced suicidality compared with olanzapine but in the absence of clear clinical superiority [24].

Pharmacology

For more than three decades the dopamine hypothesis of schizophrenia has been propounded as the basis for drug effect in schizophrenia. As already mentioned, according to this hypothesis the efficacy of antipsychotic drugs is a result of their ability to block central (mesolimbic) dopamine D_2 receptors. Blockade of nigrostriatal D_2 receptors accounts for the EPSEs seen with antipsychotics and these two actions were, of course, long thought to be inseparable: efficacy was considered inexorably to result in EPSEs.

As previously noted, new drugs have been developed in line with the dopamine hypothesis. This has led to the introduction of drugs with a specific site of action (affecting D_2 receptors only) such as amisulpride, sulpiride and pimozide. However, these new drugs are no more effective than other antipsychotics.

The success of clozapine originally cast doubt on the dopamine hypothesis. Clozapine has a complex pharmacology (Table 8.1) – it is an antagonist at dopamine D_1, D_2, D_3 and D_4 receptors as well as at α_1, α_2, 5-hydroxytryptamine$_2$ ($5HT_2$), histamine H_1 and muscarinic receptors [25]. Which of these actions gives clozapine its unique effect is not yet known but several important observations have been made. For example, unlike other antipsychotics, clozapine does not up-regulate D_2 receptors; it only rarely causes extrapyramidal effects and it does not elevate plasma prolactin levels [26]. Positron emission tomography studies have shown that occupancy of striatal D_2 receptors is less with clozapine (48%) than with standard antipsychotics (78%) [27]. This reduced occupancy of D_2 receptors has also been shown in clozapine-treated patients who have a better clinical outcome [28]. Thus it was thought D_2 receptor blockade may not be important to the efficacy of clozapine, and this observation directly challenges the dopamine hypothesis of schizophrenia. However, more recent single photon emission computed tomography studies have suggested that clozapine has preferential antagonistic activity at extrastriatal (i.e. mesolimbic) D_2/D_3 receptors [29, 30].

Other aspects of clozapine's pharmacology have been investigated in an attempt to determine the key to its efficacy. D_1 antagonism, $D_1 + D_2$ antagonism, site-specific (mesolimbic) D_2 blockade and D_4 antagonism have all been put forward as possible candidates [33]. No definitive

Table 8.1 Receptor-binding activity of clozapine (adapted from Moore *et al.* [31] and Kando *et al.* [32])

Receptor	Receptor affinity K_i (nmol/l)
D_1	85
D_2	126
D_3	280
D_4	9
$5HT_{1a}$	875
$5HT_{2a}$	12
$5HT_{2c}$	8
$5HT_3$	170
H_1	6
α_1	7
α_2	8
M_1	1.9
M_2	10
M_3	14
M_4	18

answer has yet been found. Blockade of $5HT_2$ receptors was once accepted as being at least partly responsible for the low incidence of extrapyramidal effects seen with clozapine [34]. (The two neuronal systems appear to be closely interconnected.) Now, even this theory is in doubt after it was shown that $5HT_{2a}$ receptor blockade was not related to therapeutic effects [35] and that clozapine-induced 5HT blockade did not protect against dopamine-related effects of haloperidol [36]. In contrast, variation in coding for certain 5HT receptor genes seems to predict response to clozapine [37], suggesting a crucial role for these receptors.

Such is the uncertainty surrounding clozapine's activity that virtually all of its pharmacological effects have been suggested as the key to its efficacy in schizophrenia at some time [26]. At one time most promise came from the theory that clozapine exerts its effect via blockade of D_4 receptors: D_4 receptor numbers are increased in schizophrenia [38] and clozapine is a potent antagonist at D_4 receptors [39]. There are several subtypes of D_4 receptors and clozapine was thought to exert its effect by acting at one or more of these [40]. Failure of D_4 antagonist drugs in clinical trials eventually led to the rejection of this theory. Research has now begun to concentrate on clozapine's effect on glutamatergic systems: its exact interaction with glutamate receptors is yet to be fully elucidated but clozapine seems able to antagonise some of the psychotomimetic effects of the glutamate antagonist phencyclidine [41], presumably via interaction with N-methyl-D-aspartate receptors [42].

Investigation of clozapine's pharmacology has already advanced our understanding of the biochemical basis of schizophrenia. Many potentially fruitful theories have been developed. (For discussion of these theories, see Bigliani and Pilowsky [43] and Kapur and Seeman [44].) Along with these new theories have come new 'atypical' drugs which have been developed, not by adherence to the dopamine hypothesis, but by mimicking some or all of clozapine's pharmacological activity. The first of these drugs to be marketed was risperidone (Janssen), a $5HT_2/D_2$ antagonist, which was followed by others such as olanzapine (Lilly), quetiapine (Zeneca) sertindole (Lundbeck), amisulpride (Sanofi) and aripiprazole (BristolMyersSqibb).

Adverse effects

As already mentioned, clozapine only very rarely gives rise to movement disorders. However, clozapine causes a wide range of other adverse effects which are largely a result of its diverse pharmacology (Adverse-effects focus 8.1).

ADVERSE-EFFECTS FOCUS 8.1

Adverse effects of clozapine

Adverse effect	Time course	Pharmacological action involved
Sedation	First 4 weeks. May persist, but usually wears off	Histamine, H_1 antagonism, α_1 receptor antagonism
Hypersalivation	First 4 weeks. May persist, but usually wears off. Often very troublesome at night	Unclear; may have agonist activity at one or other cholinergic receptors
Constipation	Usually persists	Muscarinic antagonism
Hypotension	First 4 weeks	α_1 receptor antagonism
Tachycardia	First 4 weeks, but often persists	Unclear
Weight gain	Usually during the first year of treatment	Possibly related to blockade of H_1 and $5HT_{2c}$ receptors
Fever	First 3 weeks	Unclear
Seizures	May occur at any time	Dose-related: incidence 4.4% above 600 mg/day [45]. May also be dose-related (see later). Mechanism not clear
Nausea	First 6 weeks	Unclear
Neutropenia/ Agranulocytosis	First 18 weeks (but may very rarely occur after this time)	Unclear, but possibly drug-induced abnormal immunological response [46]
Impaired glucose tolerance	Any time	Unclear [47]

Pharmacokinetics and interactions

Clozapine, when given orally as tablets, reaches peak plasma concentration after around 3 hours and has a plasma half-life which averages 6 hours after a single dose [48]. Plasma half-life in multiple dosing is longer, averaging around 14 hours [49]. There is extensive variation in pharmacokinetics between individuals [50] and perhaps even within individuals over time [51]. Clozapine clearance appears to be lower in females and in older patients [52]. Extent of oral absorption varies substantially according to formulation but may be as high as 60% [49, 50].

Metabolism

Using evidence gained mainly from experiments in animals, Jann *et al.* [53] concluded that clozapine undergoes hepatic metabolism to form clozapine N-oxide, desmethyl-clozapine and other hydroxyl metabolites. Clozapine N-oxide is readily reduced to clozapine *in vitro* [54] and this reaction is assumed to take place *in vivo*. Desmethylclozapine (norclozapine) is more stable and more toxic than clozapine against haematopoietic stem cells [55]. Clozapine may also be hepatically converted to a protein-reactive metabolite [54, 56]. Thus there are four major products of primary clozapine metabolism: (1) desmethylclozapine; (2) clozapine N-oxide; (3) hydroxylated metabolites; and (4) a protein-reactive metabolite (Figure 8.2). These compounds are further metabolised via epoxide formation, sulphation and glucuronidation (Flanagan R J, personal communication). The ratios of concentrations of primary metabolites vary considerably [53, 54] but conversion to desmethylclozapine is undoubtedly the major route of metabolism [53, 54, 56].

Clozapine is metabolised by the cytochrome P450 system [53, 56] but there is some confusion over which of the subtypes of this group of enzymes is (or are) responsible. Fischer *et al.* [57] found that clozapine was readily bound by the active site of cytochrome P450IID6 (CYP2D6) in human liver microsomes *in vitro*. Clozapine was also metabolised by this enzyme *in vitro* but not to desmethylclozapine or the N-oxide. The authors concluded that clozapine was metabolised *in vivo* by CYP2D6 and that genetic variation in the function of this enzyme might explain the wide variation in clozapine plasma levels seen. However, in a small human volunteer study, Dahl *et al.* [58] showed no difference in clozapine metabolism between poor metabolisers of debrisoquine (a marker for CYP2D6) and extensive metabolisers.

A similar study [59] used caffeine as a marker for cytochrome P450IA2 (CYP1A2) function and showed that the function of this enzyme correlated with clozapine clearance. It was concluded that clozapine was 'to a major extent metabolised by CYP1A2'. The role of CYP1A2 has been confirmed *in vitro* by Pirmohamed *et al.* [54], who identified the enzyme as that responsible for the conversion of clozapine to desmethylclozapine and discounted any role for CYP2D6. Arranz and others [60] have also found that response to clozapine is not related

Clozapine

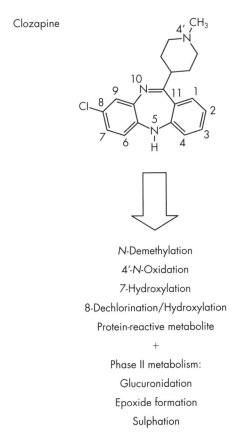

N-Demethylation

4′-N-Oxidation

7-Hydroxylation

8-Dechlorination/Hydroxylation

Protein-reactive metabolite

+

Phase II metabolism:

Glucuronidation

Epoxide formation

Sulphation

Figure 8.2 Clozapine metabolism.

to CYP2D6 phenotype and inferred that CYP2D6 is not the major enzyme responsible for the metabolism of clozapine (although the basis for this inference is somewhat illogical since there is no firm evidence, for example, that D_2 receptor polymorphisms are related to clozapine response [61]). In addition, another small human study [62] has shown that an individual's expression of CYP2D6 does not affect clozapine clearance.

An *in vitro* study [63] found that CYP1A2 was responsible for the conversion of clozapine to norclozapine and CYP3A4 for conversion to N-oxide. These results were supported by experiments using CYP1A2-null mice [64] which showed substantially reduced metabolism via demethylation compared with normally bred mice. In turn, Ozdemir and colleagues [65], in a study of schizophrenic patients, found that clozapine plasma levels were closely correlated with CYP1A2 activity as indicated by a caffeine test. Also, there is a case in the literature of failure to respond to clozapine because of unusually high CYP1A2 activity [66].

Against these observations are the *in vitro* findings of Linnet and Olesen [67] who showed, using fluvoxamine as a metabolic probe, that the cytochromes 2C19 and 3A4 should each account for about 35% of the oxidative metabolism of clozapine and 1A2 about 10%. A later similar study suggested that 2C19 might account for 50% of clozapine demethylation [68]. These findings have yet to be fully explained and have caused consternation amongst world experts in the field [69]. The divergence in opinion may be a function of different *in vivo* affinities and metabolic capacities of the cytochrome enzymes involved: certain cytochromes may have the functional ability to metabolise clozapine when exposed to it *in vitro*, but may not affect clozapine *in vivo* because of inadequate exposure to the drug in normal human distribution.

With clozapine, ethnic differences in metabolism have been noted for Caucasians compared with Chinese patients [70, 71]. Differences in response to clozapine have been reported in Korean-Americans and Caucasians [72], differences that may have been a result of different pharmacokinetics, pharmacodynamics, or both [61]. At present, too little is known of racially determined cytochrome function for these observed differences to contribute to the understanding of clozapine's metabolism.

In contrast, drug interaction studies do inform understanding. The drug interactions described below to a large extent lend credence to the central role of CYP1A2 but some implicate CYP2D6 or other enzymes, while some rather confuse current understanding and demand further investigation. Co-administered interacting drugs may have a profound effect on clozapine therapy: drugs that induce enzymes responsible for clozapine metabolism may reduce efficacy; those that inhibit these enzymes may give rise to clozapine toxicity.

Pharmacokinetic interactions

Smoking

Cigarette smoke contains polycyclic aromatic hydrocarbons that are potent inducers of CYP1A2 [73]. Smokers might then be expected to have lower plasma clozapine levels than their non-smoking counter-parts. Some workers have shown such a difference [74, 75] while others [76] have not (the magnitude of cigarette consumption necessary to induce CYP1A2 activity has not been determined and this may explain these discrepancies). A case report has described the occurrence of clozapine-induced seizures in a man who abruptly stopped smoking [77]. In addition, a prospective study of 11 patients who stopped smoking found an average increase in plasma levels of 71.9% (or 443 ng/mL on average) [78]. Interestingly, a small prospective open study (55 smokers; 15 non-smokers) has suggested that smokers may respond better to clozapine than non-smokers and clozapine may reduce smoking frequency [79]. In this study, smoking behaviour was assessed by observation of number of cigarettes smoked; by type and brand of cigarette; and by measurement of expired carbon monoxide.

Fluvoxamine

The selective serotonin reuptake inhibitor (SSRI) fluvoxamine is a potent inhibitor of CYP1A2 [80] and so might be predicted to interact with clozapine. Dramatic increases in plasma clozapine levels (sometimes with corresponding increases in adverse effects) have indeed been described in several case reports [81–83] where fluvoxamine and clozapine have been co-administered. These observations were confirmed in a 30-subject prospective study where clozapine plasma levels increased 1.7–6.0-fold after 14 days [84]. A second study (n = 16) showed up to sixfold increases in plasma levels over 4 weeks [85]. *In vitro* studies have provided rather different results. For example, Chang and co-workers [86] showed only modest *in vitro* inhibition of clozapine metabolism by fluvoxamine but substantial *in vivo* effects. Olesen and Linnet [68] suggested that fluvoxamine's observed *in vitro* effects on cytochromes predict that inhibition of cytochromes CYP1A2, CYP2C9 and CYP2D6 is responsible for the observed effects *in vivo*. In fact, some workers contend that CYP2C19 is the primary metabolic enzyme for clozapine oxidation [86].

Caffeine

As already mentioned, caffeine, a substrate for CYP1A2, can be used as a marker of the enzyme's activity. A case of adverse interaction between caffeine and clozapine has been reported [87]. The patient described suffered drowsiness and sialorrhoea while taking clozapine (as tablets) and caffeine (coffee and chocolate). Cessation of caffeine intake engendered a fall in plasma clozapine levels from 1500 to 630 ng/mL. Competitive inhibition of CYP1A2 was the presumed mechanism of interaction.

Erythromycin

The macrolide antibiotic erythromycin is an inhibitor of both CYP1A2 and cytochrome P450 3A (CYP3A) [88]. As an inhibitor of CYP1A2, erythromycin would be expected to increase clozapine levels if given concomitantly. One case of adverse interaction has been described [89]: the introduction of erythromycin-induced seizures and an apparent increase in clozapine plasma concentrations.

Anticonvulsants

The known association between clozapine and seizures often leads to the prophylactic or remedial prescribing of anticonvulsant drugs. Phenytoin is sometimes co-prescribed with clozapine. It is a potent enzyme-inducer which is thought to increase the activity of cytochrome P450 3A4 (CYP3A4) [90] and CYP1A2 [88], amongst others. Two cases of apparent phenytoin-induced reduction in clozapine plasma levels have been described [91]. In both patients, plasma clozapine levels fell dramatically (by 65–85%) and psychotic symptoms worsened.

Carbamazepine is also a potent enzyme-inducer but it is rarely used in clozapine therapy because it may cause neutropenia. The elevation of plasma clozapine levels after carbamazepine withdrawal has been reported in 2 patients [92]. Adverse effects were not described. Carbamazepine is thought to be an inducer of CYP3A4 and perhaps other cytochrome enzymes [93]. It may affect CYP1A2 since it has been reported to decrease plasma levels of theophylline [94], which is primarily metabolised by CYP1A2 [80].

Existing data on the effect of valproate co-administration on clozapine plasma levels are contradictory. Centorrino *et al.* [95] in a study of 11 patients found that valproate was associated with a small but significant increase in clozapine plasma levels. It did not, however, affect the concentration of clozapine analytes (i.e. primary metabolites) in total. A case of apparent increase in clozapine plasma concentrations has also been reported [96]. The patient suffered sedation and confusion which resolved when valproate was withdrawn and returned after it was reinstituted. In contrast, a study of 7 patients [97] demonstrated that valproate brought about a 15% decrease in clozapine concentrations and a 65% decrease in norclozapine levels. This potential interaction requires further investigation. No clear mechanism for the interaction has been elucidated or proposed and this may reflect the fact that little is known about the effect of valproate on cytochrome function.

Cimetidine

Cimetidine is a non-selective inhibitor of cytochrome enzymes [98]. An interaction between cimetidine and clozapine has been reported [99]. In this case, clozapine and norclozapine serum levels increased markedly after the addition of cimetidine 800 mg/day and the patient experienced vomiting and severe light-headedness on standing. Serum levels returned to 'normal' after cimetidine was switched to ranitidine. The authors suggested that the interaction described was due to cimetidine's 'reported cytochrome P-450 inhibitory effect'.

Risperidone

Risperidone is metabolised by CYP2D6 to 9-hydroxyrisperidone [100] but is not thought to inhibit any cytochrome enzymes. An adverse pharmacokinetic interaction with clozapine would therefore not be expected. However, there have been two case reports of such an interaction described in the literature. In the first [101], clozapine levels nearly doubled after the addition of low-dose (2 mg/day) risperidone but no increase in adverse effects was noted. In the second [102], the addition of risperidone 2 mg/day provoked an increase in clozapine levels from 829 to 1800 ng/mL, while norclozapine levels fell from 1384 to 980 ng/mL. Again, no adverse effects were reported.

In both reports, the authors, assuming that clozapine is metabolised by CYP2D6, proposed competitive inhibition of this enzyme as the cause of the interaction. This might seem unlikely, given that clozapine is thought to be primarily metabolised by CYP1A2. However, there is no evidence to suggest that risperidone is an inhibitor of CYP1A2 and so the mechanism for this interaction is unclear.

Selective serotonin reuptake inhibitors

The SSRIs fluvoxamine (see above), fluoxetine, paroxetine and sertraline are known to inhibit a variety of cytochrome enzymes [80] but only fluvoxamine has any effect of CYP1A2 [103]. Nevertheless, fluoxetine has been shown substantially to increase levels of clozapine and total clozapine analytes in a study of 6 patients [95]. In an extension of this early work, Centorrino and co-workers [104] demonstrated that fluoxetine, paroxetine and sertraline were all associated with increased plasma levels of clozapine and norclozapine. Moreover, the risk of very high plasma clozapine levels (> 1000 ng/mL) was much greater when these drugs were co-administered.

The authors averred that inhibition of CYP2D6 by SSRIs might account for the observed interaction (all are CYP2D6 inhibitors) but noted that the drugs did not induce a change in clozapine/norclozapine ratio. This might imply inhibition of a metabolic step distal to clozapine N-dealkylation, that is, inhibition of secondary metabolism. Later studies have suggested that paroxetine [84] and sertraline [105] have no effect on clozapine metabolism.

A fifth SSRI, citalopram, has minimal effect on CYP2D6 [80].

Grapefruit juice

Clozapine pharmacokinetics seem not to be affected by the co-administration of grapefruit juice, an inhibitor of CYP3A4 in the gut wall. Two publications report the absence of effect of grapefruit juice on clozapine pharmacokinetics: one a 15-patient prospective study [106] and one a single-subject evaluation [107].

Metabolism of clozapine – conclusion and clinical implications

Clozapine appears to be primarily metabolised by CYP1A2: several studies have indicated this and known inhibitors or inducers of CYP1A2 enzyme have been reported to affect plasma clozapine levels profoundly. The role of CYP2D6 is difficult to establish. Studies appear to show that it is not important to the primary human metabolism of clozapine but some inhibitors of the enzyme have definitively been shown to increase plasma levels of clozapine and its primary metabolites, perhaps by inhibiting a step in secondary metabolism. The role of CYP3A4 in clozapine metabolism remains unclear but most evidence suggests that it has no more than a minor role. CYP2C9 may also play a part in clozapine metabolism but its exact role is not clear.

The lack of certainty about the metabolism of clozapine is a product of two factors. First, techniques for identifying cytochromes have only become available in the past 10 or 15 years and so methods for determining functional changes are somewhat rudimentary. Second, there is clearly a difference between *in vitro* cytochrome capacity to metabolise and *in vivo* function. This difference may reflect *in vivo* cytochrome affinity and capacity which are, of necessity, functionally interdependent on hepatic exposure to clozapine. For example, a cytochrome may be shown to metabolise clozapine *in vitro* but *in vivo* clozapine may not reach this cytochrome's site of action.

There are important practical implications of these conclusions. Clozapine should in theory not be co-administered with the interacting drugs listed here. In addition drugs with which an interaction might be predicted should also be avoided where possible. These include inducers of CYP1A2 (e.g. barbecued food), inhibitors of CYP1A2 (e.g. ciprofloxacin), and direct inhibitors of CYP2D6 (e.g. haloperidol, quinidine). There are also a great many drugs metabolised by CYP2D6 which, like risperidone, may competitively inhibit the enzyme and reduce clozapine clearance (Pharmacokinetics focus 8.1). Further investigation of the role of different cytochromes in the metabolism clozapine is clearly needed.

PHARMACOKINETICS FOCUS 8.1

Pharmacokinetic interactions with clozapine

Interacting drug	Effect on clozapine plasma levels	Proposed mechanism	Comments
Caffeine	Increased	Competitive inhibition of CYP1A2	
Carbamazepine	Decreased	Induction of CYP1A2?	No direct evidence that interaction involves 1A2
Cimetidine	Increased	Inhibition of cytochrome P450 (?1A2)	Non-selective cytochrome inhibitor
Erythromycin	Increased	Inhibition of CYP1A2	Also inhibits CYP3A
Fluoxetine	Increased	Inhibition of CYP2D6?	Also inhibits 3A4
Fluvoxamine	Increased	Inhibition of CYP1A2	
Grapefruit juice	No effect	Inhibition of CYP3A4 in gut wall	May also affect CYP1A2
Paroxetine	Increased	Inhibition of CYP2D6?	Some studies suggest no effect
Phenytoin	Decreased	Induction of CYP1A2?	Inhibits other cytochromes
Risperidone	Increased	Competitive inhibition of CYP2D6	

continued overleaf

Management focus (continued)			
Sertraline	Increased	Inhibition of CYP2D6?	Some studies suggest no effect
Tobacco smoke	Decreased	Induction of CYP1A2	Effect not evident in all studies
Valproate	Unclear	Not known	Increase and decrease reported

Clozapine plasma levels

Clozapine is now well known to be an effective treatment for refractory schizophrenia. However, its use is complicated by a variable and delayed response and by a range of troublesome adverse effects. Early practice was usually to increase the dose initially to around 450 mg/day and then by small increments to a maximum of 900 mg/day according to response and tolerability. While this method was often successful, it was also suggested that a better way of optimising the dose of clozapine might be to monitor plasma concentrations of the drug.

If plasma levels were to be useful, they must be difficult to predict simply from the dose given to an individual patient. In an early study, Thorup and Fog [108] investigated the variation in serum levels both between individuals on the same dose and within individuals. In the 11 patients studied, the dose given seemed to have little bearing on the measured plasma level and levels varied widely in some patients, despite a constant dose. This latter anomaly may have been due to changes in intestinal absorption or to erratic compliance. The assay method also appeared to be somewhat inaccurate: a level of 31 ng/mL was measured in a control patient not taking clozapine. Using a different assay method, Bondesson and Lindstrom [109] examined levels in 22 patients and found that dose correlated well with resultant plasma level. Parent drug levels were also well correlated with clozapine's major metabolite, norclozapine. A much larger study [74] of 148 patients again showed a significant but weak ($r = 0.5266$) correlation between dose and serum level. Further analysis revealed that male patients and smokers had significantly lower levels than females and non-smokers respectively. Older patients had higher levels. Haring *et al.* [75], apparently reporting the same study ($n = 148$) with different co-authors and a different analysis of results, established a linear relationship ($r = 0.61$) between dose and serum level. Variation in the relationship was, unsurprisingly, mostly accounted for by age (levels lower in younger patients), smoking (lower in smokers) and gender (lower in males).

Thus, there appears to be a weak but definite relationship between the dose of clozapine and the plasma level which results. Plasma concentrations tend to be lower in younger patients, in males and in smokers. Because of the generally weak correlation between dose and level and the range of influencing factors, it would seem difficult to predict with any precision the plasma level which might be afforded by a given dose. Moreover, as previously discussed, clozapine plasma levels appear to be readily altered by the co-administration of other commonly used drugs: carbamazepine reduces clozapine levels [92] and fluoxetine may greatly increase them [95].

Given that the plasma level cannot accurately be predicted from the dose, it is then important to establish whether levels relate to efficacy or to the severity of adverse effects. In Thorup and Fog's small study [108] there was no correlation between plasma level and therapeutic effect. In a later and larger study of 29 patients, Perry *et al.* [110] established a threshold for response to clozapine of 350 ng/mL. Below this level 22% responded, but above it 64% responded. (The overall low response rate of 37.9% was due to the short (4–8 weeks) trial period.) A follow-up study of the same patients 2½ years later showed that overall response rate had risen to 58% [111]. Five of seven non-responders from the first study became responders after obtaining a level higher than 350 ng/mL. Piscitelli *et al.* [112], in a 6-week trial, compared serum levels to response in 11 adolescents with schizophrenia. A consistent linear relationship between level and response was discovered, although no threshold level was established. In a 4-week study of 48 adults with schizophrenia [113], the threshold level for response was found to be 420 ng/mL – 60% of patients with levels above this responded compared with 8% for those with levels below it. Increasing levels in non-responders above 420 ng/mL greatly improved response. Interestingly, clozapine levels varied 45-fold in patients given the same dose. In a still later study, Kronig *et al.* [114] studied clozapine levels in 45 patients given large doses of clozapine for 6 weeks. No correlation between plasma level and response could be found but a threshold of 350 ng/mL was established for response after 6 weeks of treatment.

One long-term study [76] investigated the relationship between response and serum clozapine levels. Fifty-nine treatment-resistant patients given clozapine for up to 76 months had random clozapine and norclozapine levels taken. Response to clozapine (defined as 20% BPRS reduction) was said to have occurred in 30 patients at 6 months. In these, the dose of clozapine was not significantly different from the dose in non-responders but serum levels of clozapine and norclozapine were significantly higher. A clozapine serum level of 370 ng/mL was said to be the optimum cut-off point to distinguish responders from non-responders, although six of the non-responders had levels above this value and 14 responders had levels below it. Another interesting finding was that clozapine serum levels did not differ between male smokers and non-smokers.

More recent evaluations have done little to confirm the value of plasma level which represents a threshold for response. For example, Vanderzwagg and colleagues [115] found that patients with low plasma levels (50–150 ng/mL) were less likely to respond to clozapine than patients with medium (200–300 ng/mL) or high (350–450 ng/mL) levels. Importantly, response was not significantly different in the medium and high level group, suggesting that the threshold for response might be as low as 200 ng/mL. Conversely, Spina and co-workers [116], in a study of 45 subjects, again suggested that the threshold for response was around 350 ng/mL. However, in a case report [117] response was only seen at levels above 1200 ng/mL.

Most recently, Perry [118] has put forward a level of 504 ng/mL as the threshold for response. This is based on the results of response defined by the use of scales such as the Schedule for the Assessment of Positive Symptoms and the Schedule for Assessment of Negative Symptoms, which are said to be more specific to symptoms of schizophrenia than the BPRS.

Overall, response to clozapine can be said to occur at levels above 200 ng/mL and may be more robustly associated with levels above 350–500 ng/mL.

Plasma clozapine levels appear also to relate to adverse effects. Simpson and Cooper [119] described two cases of seizures occurring in patients with high levels of clozapine. One had no seizures while maintaining a level of 600 ng/mL but suffered a grand mal seizure when the level rose to 1313 ng/mL following an overdose. Another suffered a grand mal seizure after a drug administration error resulted in a clozapine serum level of 2194 ng/mL. Kane et al. [120] discovered that high clozapine levels appeared to be related to lower prolactin levels in two schizophrenic patients given clozapine for up to 15 weeks, although changes in prolactin levels were small. In another tentative study (n = 60) [121], it was found that clozapine-induced tardive dyskinesia (an effect now known to be very rare) was significantly associated with higher clozapine plasma levels (above around 500 ng/mL) although 'contamination' of these observations by the effects of prior antipsychotic treatment cannot be discounted.

Higher clozapine levels also appear to be associated with patho-logical electroencephalogram (EEG) changes. Haring *et al.* [122] found that 15 patients showing EEG changes had a mean clozapine plasma level of 235.7 ng/mL whereas those with a normal EEG (n = 14) had a mean level of only 81.6 ng/mL. Perhaps the most important adverse effect of clozapine is neutropenia; Centorrino *et al.* [123] found that there was no association between the degree of leucopenia caused by clozapine and clozapine or norclozapine plasma levels. An upper limit to the therapeutic range of plasma clozapine levels has not been estab-lished, although Liu *et al.* [124] have suggested a limit of 700 ng/mL. Clearly some adverse effects are related to plasma level but it seems inappropriate to suggest 700 ng/mL as the upper limit of the therapeutic range: adverse effects occur to an important extent below this level. In addition, very much higher levels seem sometimes to be reasonably well tolerated. For example, cases of plasma levels above 3800 ng/mL have been reported (in overdose) [125, 126] where few overt adverse effects were evident. It is also important to note that many adverse effects (sedation, postural hypotension, hypersalivation, for example) reduce over time, presumably without change in plasma level.

In summary, clozapine serum levels are difficult to predict from the dose given and there are many factors that influence the serum level obtained. Short- and long-term studies have shown that the minimum effective concentration is probably between 350 and 500 ng/mL and that there may be a linear relationship between plasma level and response, at least in adolescents. Some of clozapine's adverse effects also appear to be plasma level-related; EEG changes and seizures seem particularly sensitive to rises in serum levels. Clozapine plasma levels can be said to be useful in optimising therapy. A 'therapeutic range' of serum levels has not yet been established but, based on the evidence presented here, it seems wise to recommend that prescribers aim initially for a dose of 450 mg/day and, if there is no response after 6 weeks, serum levels should be measured, and the dose adjusted so that a level of at least 350 ng/mL is obtained. Levels substantially higher than this should be approached very cautiously. Prescribers should expect to need to give higher doses to young patients, males and smokers.

Clozapine in use – patient-monitoring schemes

Because of the risk of fatal agranulocytosis, clozapine has had certain restrictions placed on its use. Clozapine is only licensed for the treat-ment of schizophrenia in patients who are non-responsive to, or intol-erant of, conventional neuroleptics. Patients starting clozapine must also undertake to have regular blood tests which serve to alert the prescriber to any falls in white cell count which might portend agranulocytosis. In the UK, clozapine's manufacturers monitor the use of clozapine through various schemes.

Regulatory requirements dictate that all patients, prescribers and dispensers of clozapine should be registered with a monitoring scheme. Only registered hospital pharmacies may dispense clozapine and even then only under certain conditions. The pharmacist has a key role in ensuring the safe use of clozapine.

Patients have a weekly blood test for the first 18 weeks and then every 2 weeks thereafter up to a year and then monthly blood testing thereafter. Agranulocytosis usually manifests itself in the first 18 weeks of therapy [127]. Blood is taken 3 days before dispensing is due and a full blood count performed by local laboratories or the manufacturer. The results of the tests are then put on to the manufacturer's computer system, to which registered pharmacies have access via dedicated dispensary-based computers. The pharmacist may only dispense clozapine to a patient if a satisfactory blood test result has been received either via the computer system or by post. In some units, local blood tests are used in an emergency and here the pharmacist plays a central role in co-ordinating other hospital departments to ensure continuity of care. Some centres have established clozapine clinics where personnel from several disciplines work together to provide a comprehensive service for clozapine patients.

Manufacturers' information services may also advise on the course of action to take when white cell counts fall. If a patient has an 'amber' result (white cells 3.0–3.5 $\times$ 10^9/L and/or neutrophils 1.5–2.0 $\times$ 10^9/L) then the prescriber is reminded to assess the patient's clinical condition (e.g. signs of infection) and to repeat the blood sample. If a 'red' result is obtained (white cells < 3.0 $\times$ 10^9/L and/or neutrophils < 1.5 $\times$ 10^9/L) the patient stops clozapine treatment immediately and is admitted to hospital for urgent re-sampling. Patients are then precluded from taking clozapine again.

In 1997, the original clozapine-monitoring system had collected records on 12 760 patients treated with clozapine [128]. Three had died as a result of clozapine-induced agranulocytosis but the rate of suicide in these patients was substantially less than expected. The cumulative incidence of agranulocytosis was 0.73% (neutropenia 2.7%), with peak incidence occurring in weeks 6–18 of treatment. The risk of haematological toxicity was higher in elderly patients and in Asian subjects.

Clozapine is uniquely effective in refractory schizophrenia and remains the drug of choice in this condition. Its use is complicated by a wide range of sometimes serious adverse effects (Management focus 8.1).

MANAGEMENT FOCUS 8.1

Clozapine	
Absorption	Variable, incomplete (less than 60%)
Elimination	Hepatic
Plasma half-life	Variable. Up to 33 hours
Hepatic cytochromes involved	CYPIA2, possibly CYP2D6
Hepatic cytochromes affected	None
Major interactions	Plasma levels reduced by smoking, carbamazepine and phenytoin; increased by some SSRIs, valproate, caffeine, cimetidine and erythromycin
Efficacy	Unique efficacy in treatment-resistant schizophrenia. Activity against positive, negative and cognitive symptoms
Adverse-effect profile/tolerability	Strongly sedative, hypersalivation, blood pressure changes, tachycardia, constipation, seizures, neutropenia and agranulocytosis

References

1. Taylor D, Duncan-McConnell D. Refractory schizophrenia and atypical antipsychotics, *J Psychopharmacol* 2000; 14: 409–418.
2. Baldessarini R J, Frankenbrug F R. Clozapine, a novel antipsychotic agent. *N Engl J Med* 1991; 324: 11.
3. Hippius H. The history of clozapine. *Psychopharmacology* 1989; 99: S3–S5.
4. Gross H, Langner E. Das Wirkungsprofil eines chemisch neuartigen Breitbandneuroleptikums der Dibenzodiazepingruppe. *Wien Med Wochenschr* 1966; 116: 814–816.
5. Angst J, Bente D, Berner P. Das klinische Wirkungsbild von clozapine. *Pharmakopsychiatrie* 1971; 4: 200–211.
6. Idaanpaan-Heikkila J, Alhava E, Olkinvora M, Palva I. Clozapine and agranulocytosis. *Lancet* 1975; ii: 611.

7. Fitton A, Heel R C. Clozapine – a review of its pharmacological properties and therapeutic use in schizophrenia. *Drugs* 1990; 40: 722–747.

8. Fischer-Cornelssen K A, Ferner U J. An example of European multicenter trials: multispectral analysis of clozapine. *Psychopharmacol Bull* 1976; 12: 34–39.

9. Claghorn J, Honigfeld G, Abuzzahab F S *et al.* The risks and benefits of clozapine versus chlorpromazine. *J Clin Psychopharmacol* 1987; 7: 377–384.

10. Kane J, Honigfeld G, Singer J, Meltzer H. Clozapine for treatment resistant schizophrenia – a double-blind comparison with chlorpromazine. *Arch Gen Psychiatry* 1998; 45: 789–796.

11. Fleischhacker W W. Clozapine: a comparison with other novel antipsychotics. *J Clin Psychiatry* 1999; 60: 30–34.

12. King D J. The safety of newer and older antipsychotics. *Eur Neuropsychopharmacol* 1994; 4: 220–221.

13. Carpenter W T, Buchanan R W. Schizophrenia. *N Engl J Med* 1994; 330: 681–688.

14. Meltzer H Y, Bastani B, Young Kwon K *et al.* A prospective study of clozapine in treatment-resistant patients: a preliminary report. *Psychopharmacology* 1989; 99 (suppl. 68): 568–572.

15. Hong C J, Chen J Y, Chiu H J *et al.* A double-blind comparative study of clozapine versus chlorpromazine on Chinese patients with treatment-refractory schizophrenia. *Int Clin Psychopharmacol* 1997; 12: 123–130.

16. Turetz M, Mozes T, Toren P *et al.* An open trial of clozapine in neuroleptic-resistant childhood onset schizophrenia. *Br J Psychiatry* 1997; 170: 507–510.

17. Ciapparelli A, Dell'Osso L, Pini S *et al.* Clozapine for treatment-refractory schizophrenia, schizoaffective disorder, and psychotic bipolar disorder: a 24-month naturalistic study. *J Clin Psychiatry* 2000; 61: 5.

18. Chengappa K N, Ebeling T, Kang J S *et al.* Clozapine reduces severe self-mutilation and aggression in psychotic patients with borderline personality disorder. *J Clin Psychiatry* 1999; 60: 477–483.

19. Conley R R, Tamminga C A, Kelly D L *et al.* Treatment-resistant schizophrenic patients respond to clozapine after olanzapine non-response. *Biol Psychiatry* 1999; 46: 73–77.

20. Hagger C, Buckley P, Kenny J T *et al.* Improvement in cognitive functions and psychiatric symptoms in treatment-refractory schizophrenic patients receiving clozapine. *Biol Psychiatry* 1993; 34: 702–712.

21. Sharma T. Cognitive effects of conventional and atypical antipsychotics in schizophrenia. *Br J Psychiatry* 1999; 174: 44–51.

22. Walker A M, Lanza L L, Arellano F, Rothman K J. Mortality in current and former users of clozapine. *Epidemiology* 1997; 8: 671–677.

23. Meltzer H Y, Cola P, Way L *et al.* Cost effectiveness of clozapine in neuroleptic-resistant schizophrenia. *Am J Psychiatry* 1995; 150: 1630–1638.

24. Meltzer H Y, Alphs L, Green A I *et al.* Clozapine treatment for suicidality in schizophrenia. *Arch Gen Psychiatry* 2003; 60: 82–91.

25. Coward D M. General pharmacology of clozapine. *Br J Psychiatry* 1992; 160 (suppl. 17): 5–11.

26. Lieberman J A. Understanding the mechanism of action of atypical antipsychotic drugs. *Br J Psychiatry* 1993; 163 (suppl. 22): 7–18.

27. Farde I, Nordstrom A I. PET analysis indicates atypical dopamine receptor occupancy in clozapine treated patients. *Schizophr Bull* 1992; 16 (suppl. 17): 30–33.

28. Pilowsky L S, Costa D C, Ell P J *et al*. Clozapine, single photon emission tomography and the D_2-receptor blockade hypothesis of schizophrenia. *Lancet* 1992; 340: 199–202.

29. Pilowsky L S, Mulligan R S, Acton P D *et al*. Limbic selectivity of clozapine. *Lancet* 1997; 350: 490–491.

30. Pilowsky L S, Ell P J. Clozapine and dopamine D_2 blockade. *Am J Psychiatry* 2002; 159: 324–325.

31. Moore N A, Calligaro D O, Wong D T *et al*. The pharmacology of olanzapine and other new antipsychotic agents. *Curr Opin Invest Drugs* 1993; 2: 281–299.

32. Kando J C, Shepski J C, Satterlee W. Olanzapine: a new antipsychotic agent with efficacy in the management of schizophrenia. *Ann Pharmacother* 1997; 31: 1325–1334.

33. Fitton A, Benfield P. Clozapine: an appraisal of its pharmacoeconomic benefits in the treatment of schizophrenia. *PharmacoEconomics* 1993; 4: 131–156.

34. Meltzer H Y. The importance of serotonin–dopamine interactions in the action of clozapine. *Br J Psychiatry* 1992; 160 (suppl. 17): 22–29.

35. Travis M J, Busatto G F, Pilowsky L S *et al*. 5-HT_{2A} receptor blockade in patients with schizophrenia treated with risperidone or clozapine. *Br J Psychiatry* 1998; 173: 236–241.

36. Kapur S, Roy P, Daskalakis J *et al*. Increased dopamine D_2 receptor occupancy and elevated prolactin level associated with addition of haloperidol to clozapine. *Am J Psychiatry* 2001; 158: 311–314.

37. Arranz M J, Munro J, Birkett J *et al*. Pharmacogenetic prediction of clozapine response. *Lancet* 2000; 355: 1615–1616.

38. Seeman P, Guan H C, Van Tol H H M. Dopamine D_4-receptors elevated in schizophrenia. *Nature* 1993; 365: 441–444.

39. Van Tol H H M, Bunzow J R, Guan H C *et al*. Cloning of the gene for human D_4-receptor with high affinity for the antipsychotic clozapine. *Nature* 1991; 350: 610–619.

40. Kerwin R W, Pilowsky L, Munro J *et al*. Functional neuroimaging and pharmacogenetic studies of clozapine's action at dopamine receptors. *J Clin Psychiatry* 1994; 55 (suppl. B): 57–62.

41. Tsai G E, Yang P, Chung L C *et al*. D-Serine added to clozapine for the treatment of schizophrenia. *Am J Psychiatry* 1999; 156: 1822–1825.

42. Olney J W, Nuri B, Farber M D. Efficacy of clozapine compared with other antipsychotics in preventing NMDA-antagonist neurotoxicity. *J Clin Psychiatry* 1994; 55: 43–52.

43. Bigliani V, Pilowsky L S. *In vivo* neuropharmacology of schizophrenia. *Br J Psychiatry* 1999; 174: 23–33.

44. Kapur S, Seeman P. Does fast dissociation from the dopamine D_2 receptor explain the action of atypical antipsychotics? A new hypothesis. *Am J Psychiatry* 2001; 158: 360–369.

45. Geibig C B, Marks L W. Treatment of clozapine and molindone induced agranulocytisis with granulocyte colony stimulation factor. *Ann Pharmacother* 1993; 27: 1190–1192.

46. Faber H J, Smit A J, van de Loosdrecht A A. Clozapine induced agranulocytosis: hypothesis on immune-medicated pathogenesis and the role of haematopoietic growth factors. *Netherlands J Med* 1999; 55: 86–87.

47. Mir S, Taylor D. Atypical antipsychotics and hyperglycaemia. *Int Clin Psychopharmacol* 2001; 16: 63–74.

48. Ackenheil M. Clozapine – pharmacokinetic investigations and biochemical effects in man. *Psychopharmacology* 1989; 99: 32–37.

49. Choc M G, Hsuan F, Honigfeld G *et al*. Single vs multiple-dose pharmacokinetics of clozapine in psychiatric patients. *Pharm Res* 1990; 7: 347–351.

50. Guitton C, Abbar M, Kinowski J-M *et al*. Multiple-dose pharmacokinetics of clozapine in patients with chronic schizophrenia. *J Clin Psychopharmacol* 1998; 18: 470–476.

51. Kurz M, Hummer M, Kemmler G *et al*. Long-term pharmacokinetics of clozapine. *Br J Psychiatry* 1998; 173: 341–344.

52. Lane H-Y, Chang Y-C, Chang W-H *et al*. Effects of gender and age on plasma levels of clozapine and its metabolites: analyzed by critical statistics. *J Clin Psychiatry* 1999; 60: 36–40.

53. Jann M W, Grimsley S R, Gray E C *et al*. Pharmacokinetics and pharmacodynamics of clozapine. *Clin Pharmacokinet* 1993; 24: 161–176.

54. Pirmohamed M, Williams D, Madden S *et al*. Metabolism and bioactivation of clozapine by human liver *in vitro*. *J Pharmacol Exp Ther* 1995; 272: 984–990.

55. Gerson S, Arce C, Meltzer H. *N*-Desmethylclozapine: a clozapine metabolite that suppresses haemoporesis. *Br J Haematol* 1994; 86: 555–561.

56. Maggs J L, Williams D, Pirmohamed M, Park B K. The metabolic formation of reactive intermediates from clozapine, a drug associated with agranulocytosis in man. *Am Soc Pharmacol Exp Ther* 1995; 275: 1463–1475.

57. Fischer V, Vogels B, Maurer G *et al*. The antipsychotic clozapine is metabolized by the polymorphic human microsomal and recombinant cytochrome P4502D6. *J Pharmacol Exp Ther* 1992; 260: 1355–1360.

58. Dahl M-L, Llerena A, Bondesson U *et al*. Disposition of clozapine in man: lack of association with debrisoquine and S-mephenytoin hydroxylation polymorphisms. *Br J Clin Pharmacol* 1994; 37: 71–74.

59. Bertilsson L, Carrillo J A, Dahl M-L *et al*. Clozapine disposition covaries with CYP1A2 activity determined by a caffeine test. *Br J Clin Pharmacol* 1994; 38: 471–473.

60. Arranz M J, Dawson E, Shaikh S *et al*. Cytochrome P4502D6 gene type does not determine response to clozapine. *Br J Clin Pharmacol* 1995; 39: 417–420.

61. Masellis M, Basile V S, Özdemir V *et al*. Pharmacogenetics of antipsychotic treatment: lessons learned from clozapine. *Biol Psychiatry* 2000; 47: 252–266.

62. De Leon J, Wedlund P, Ehlers R *et al*. Cytochrome P450–2D6 (CYP2D6) genotype: relationship with clozapine and haloperidol metabolism. *Biol Psychiatry* 1996; 39: 591.

63. Eiermann B, Engel G, Johansson I *et al*. The involvement of CYP1A2 and CYP3A4 in the metabolism of clozapine. *Br J Clin Pharmacol* 1997; 44: 439–453.

64. Aitchison K J, Jann M W, Zhao J H *et al*. Clozapine pharmacokinetics and pharmacodynamics studied with CYP1A2-null mice. *J Psychopharmacol* 2000; 14: 353–359.

65. Ozdemir V, Kalow W, Posner P *et al*. CYP1A2 activity as measured by a caffeine test predicts clozapine and active metabolite norclozapine steady-state concentration in patients with schizophrenia. *J Clin Psychopharmacol* 2001; 21: 398–407.

66. Bender S. Very high cytochrome P4501A2 activity and non-response to clozapine. *Arch Gen Psychiatry* 1998; 55: 1048–1050.

67. Linnet K, Olesen O V. Metabolism of clozapine by ₂DNA-expressed human cytochrome P450 enzymes. *Drug Metab Disposition* 1997; 25: 1379–1382.

68. Olesen O V, Linnet K. Fluvoxamine–Clozapine drug interaction: inhibition *in vitro* of five cytochrome P450 isoforms involved in clozapine metabolism. *J Clin Psychopharmacol* 2000; 20: 35–42.

69. Shader R L, Greenblatt D J. Clozapine and fluvoxamine, a curious complexity. *J Clin Psychopharmacol* 1998; 18: 101–102.

70. Farooq S. Ethnicity and clozapine metabolism. *Br J Psychiatry* 1998; 173: 87.

71. Chong S A. Ethnicity and clozapine metabolism. *Br J Psychiatry* 1998; 172: 97.

72. Matsuda K T, Cho M C, Lin K-M *et al*. Clozapine dosage, serum levels, efficacy, and side-effect profiles: a comparison of Korean-American and Caucasian patients. *Psychopharmacol Bull* 1996; 32: 253–257.

73. Schein J R. Cigarette smoking and clinically significant drug interactions. *Ann Pharmacother* 1995; 29: 1139–1148.

74. Haring C, Meise M, Humpel C *et al*. Dose-related plasma levels of clozapine: influence of smoking behaviour, sex and age. *Psychopharmacology* 1989; 99: S38–S40.

75. Haring C, Fleischhacker W W, Schett P *et al*. Influence of patient-related variables on clozapine levels. *Am J Psychiatry* 1990; 147: 1471–1475.

76. Hasegawa M, Gutierrez-Esteinou R, Way L *et al*. Relationship between clinical efficacy and clozapine concentrations in plasma in schizophrenia: effect of smoking. *J Clin Psychopharmacol* 1993; 13: 383–390.

77. McCarthy R H. Seizures following smoking cessation in a clozapine responder. *Pharmacopsychiatry* 1994; 27: 210–211.

78. Meyer J M. Individual changes in clozapine levels after smoking cessation: results and a predictive model. *J Clin Psychopharmacol* 2000; 21: 569–574.

79. McEvoy J P, Freudenreich O, Wilson W H. Smoking and therapeutic response to clozapine in patients with schizophrenia. *Biol Psychiatry* 1999; 46: 125–129.

80. Taylor D, Lader M. Cytochromes and psychotropic drug interactions. *Br J Psychiatry* 1996; 168: 529–532.

81. Dequardo J R, Roberts M. Elevated clozapine levels after fluvoxamine initiation. *Am J Psychiatry* 1996; 153: 840–841.

82. DuMortier G, Lochu A, Colen De Melo P *et al*. Elevated clozapine plasma concentrations after fluvoxamine initiation. *Am J Psychiatry* 1996; 153: 738–739.

83. Koponen H J, Leinonen E, Lepola U. Fluvoxamine increases the clozapine serum levels significantly. *Eur Neuropsychopharmacol* 1996; 6: 69–71.

84. Wetzel H, Anghelescu I, Szegedi A *et al*. Pharmacokinetic interactions of clozapine with selective serotonin reuptake inhibitors: differential effects of fluvoxamine and paroxetine in a prospective study. *J Clin Psychopharmacol* 1998; 18: 2–9.

85. Fabrazzo M, La Pia S, Monteleone P *et al.* Fluvoxamine increases plasma and urinary levels of clozapine and its major metabolites in a time- and dose-dependent manner. *J Clin Psychopharmacol* 2000; 20: 708–710.

86. Chang W-H, Augustin B, Lane H-Y *et al.* *In-vitro* and *in-vivo* evaluation of the drug–drug interaction between fluvoxamine and clozapine. *Psychopharmacology* 1999; 145: 91–98.

87. Odom-White A, De Leon J. Clozapine levels and caffeine. *J Clin Psychiatry* 1996; 57: 175–176.

88. Slaughter R L, Edwards D J. Recent advances: the cytochrome P450 enzymes. *Ann Pharmacother* 1995; 29: 619–624.

89. Funderberg L G, Vertrees J E, True J E *et al.* Seizure following addition of erythromycin to clozapine treatment. *Am J Psychiatry* 1994; 151: 1840–1841.

90. Bertilsson L, Dahl M-L. Polymorphic drug oxidation. Relevance to the treatment of psychiatric disorders. *CNS Drugs* 1996; 5: 200–223.

91. Miller D D. Effect of phenytoin on plasma clozapine concentrations in two patients. *J Clin Psychiatry* 1991; 52: 23–25.

92. Raitasuo B, Lehtovaara R, Huttunen M O. Carbamazepine and plasma levels of carbamazepine. *Am J Psychiatry* 1993; 150: 169.

93. Levy R H. Cytochrome P450 isoenzymes and antiepileptic drug interactions. *Epilepsia* 1995; 36 (suppl. 5): S8–S13.

94. Rosenberry K R, Defusco C J, Mansmann H C *et al.* Reduced theophylline half-life induced by carbamazepine therapy. *J Paediatr* 1983; 102: 472–474.

95. Centorrino F, Baldessarini R J, Kando J *et al.* Serum concentrations of clozapine and its major metabolites: effects of co-treatment with fluoxetine or valproate. *Am J Psychiatry* 1994; 151: 123–125.

96. Costello L E, Suppes T. A clinically significant interaction between clozapine and valproate. *J Clin Psychopharmacol* 1995; 15: 139–141.

97. Longo L P, Salzman C. Valproic acid effects on serum concentrations of clozapine and norclozapine. *Am J Psychiatry* 1995; 152: 650.

98. Murray M. P450 enzymes – inhibition mechanisms, genetic regulation and effects of liver disease. *Clin Pharmacokinet* 1992; 23: 132–146.

99. Szymanski S, Lieberman J A, Picou D *et al.* A case report of cimetidine-induced clozapine toxicity. *J Clin Psychiatry* 1991; 52: 21–22.

100. Heykants J, Huang M-L, Mannens G *et al.* The pharmacokinetics of risperidone in humans: a summary. *J Clin Psychiatry* 1994; 55 (suppl. 5): 13–17.

101. Tyson S C, Devane C L, Risch S C. Pharmacokinetic interaction between risperidone and clozapine. *Am J Psychiatry* 1995; 152: 1401–1402.

102. Koreen A R, Lieberman J A, Kronig M *et al.* Cross-tapering clozapine and risperidone. *Am J Psychiatry* 1995; 152: 1690.

103. Nemeroff C B, Devane C L, Pollock B G. Newer antidepressants and the cytochrome P450 system. *Am J Psychiatry* 1996; 153: 311–320.

104. Centorrino F, Baldessarini R J, Frankenburg F R *et al.* Serum levels of clozapine and norclozapine in patients treated with selective serotonin re-uptake inhibitors. *Am J Psychiatry* 1996; 153: 820–822.

105. Spina E, Avenoso A, Salemi M *et al.* Plasma concentrations of clozapine and its major metabolites during combined treatment with paroxetine or sertraline. *Pharmacopsychiatry* 2000; 33: 213–217.

106. Lane H-Y, Jann MW, Chang Y-C et al. Repeated ingestion of grapefruit juice does not alter clozapine's steady-state plasma levels, effectiveness, and tolerability. *J Clin Psychiatry* 2001; 62: 812–817.

107. Ozdemir V, Kalow W, Okey A B et al. Treatment-resistance to clozapine in association with ultrarapid CYP1A2 activity and the C→A. Polymorphism in intron 1 of the CYP1A2 gene: effect of grapefruit juice and low-dose fluvoxamine. *J Clin Psychopharmacol* 2001; 21: 603–607.

108. Thorup M, Fog R. Clozapine treatment of schizophrenic patients. *Acta Psychiatr Scand* 1977; 55: 123–126.

109. Bondesson U, Lindstrom L H. Determination of clozapine and its N-demethylated metabolite in plasma by use of gas chromatography-mass spectrometry with single ion detection. *Psychopharmacology* 1988; 95: 472–475.

110. Perry P J, Miller D D, Arndt S V, Cadoret R J. Clozapine and norclozapine plasma concentrations and clinical response of treatment refractory schizophrenic patients. *Am J Psychiatry* 1991; 148: 231–235.

111. Miller D D, Fleming F, Holman T L et al. Plasma clozapine concentrations as a predictor of clinical response: a follow-up study. *J Clin Psychiatry* 1994; 55 (suppl. B): 117–121.

112. Piscitelli S C, Frazier J A, Mckenna K et al. Plasma clozapine and haloperidol concentrations in adolescents with childhood-onset schizophrenia: association with response. *J Clin Psychiatry* 1994; 55 (suppl. B): 94–97.

113. Potkin S G, Bera R, Gulasekaram B et al. Plasma clozapine concentrations predict clinical response in treatment-resistant schizophrenia. *J Clin Psychiatry* 1994; 55 (suppl. B): 133–136.

114. Kronig M H, Munne R A, Szymanski S et al. Plasma clozapine levels and clinical response for treatment-refractory schizophrenic patients. *Am J Psychiatry* 1995; 152: 179–182.

115. Vanderzwaag C, Mcgee M, Mcevoy J P et al. Response of patients with treatment-refractory schizophrenia to clozapine within three serum level ranges. *Am J Psychiatry* 1996; 153: 1579–1583.

116. Spina E, Avenoso A, Facciola G et al. Relationship between plasma concentrations of clozapine and norclozapine and therapeutic response in patients with schizophrenia resistant to conventional neuroleptics. *Psychopharmacology* 2000; 148: 83–89.

117. Trappler B, Kwong V, Leeman C P. Therapeutic effect of clozapine at an unusually high plasma level. *Am J Psychiatry* 1996; 153: 133–134.

118. Perry P J. Therapeutic drug monitoring of atypical antipsychotics. *CNS Drugs* 2000; 13: 167–171.

119. Simpson G M, Cooper T A. Clozapine plasma levels and convulsions. *Am J Psychiatry* 1978; 135: 99–100.

120. Kane J, Cooper T D, Sachar E J et al. Clozapine: plasma levels and prolactin response. *Psychopharmacology* 1981; 73: 184–187.

121. Pollack S, Lieberman J, Kleiner D et al. High plasma clozapine levels in tardive dyskinesia. *Psychopharmacol Bull* 1993; 29: 257–262.

122. Haring C, Neudorfer C, Schwitzer J et al. EEG alterations in patients treated with clozapine in relation to plasma levels. *Psychopharmacology* 1994; 114: 97–100.

123. Centorrino F, Baldessarini R J, Flood J G et al. Relation of leukocyte counts during clozapine treatment to serum concentrations of clozapine and metabolites. *Am J Psychiatry* 1995; 152: 610–612.

124. Liu H C, Chang W H, Wei F C et al. Monitoring of plasma clozapine levels and its metabolites in refractory schizophrenic patients. *Ther Drug Monit* 1996; 18: 200–207.

125. Stevens I, Gaertner H J. Plasma level measurement in a patient with clozapine intoxication. *J Clin Psychopharmacol* 1996; 16: 86–87.

126. Broich K, Heinrich S, Marneros A. Acute clozapine overdose: plasma concentration and outcome. *Pharmacopsychiatry* 1998; 31: 149–151.

127. Krupp P, Barnes P. Leponex associated granulocytopenia: a review of the situation. *Psychopharmacology* 1989; 99: 118–121.

128. Munro J, O'Sullivan D, Andrews C et al. Active monitoring of 12 760 clozapine recipients in the UK and Ireland. *Br J Psychiatry* 1999; 175: 576–580.

9

Risperidone

Chemistry and pharmacology

Risperidone is a benzisoxole derivative developed by Janssen Pharmaceuticals in the 1980s. Its full chemical name is 3-{2-{4-(6-fluoro-1,2-benzisoxazol-3-yl)-1-piperidinyl]ethyl}-6,7,8,9-tetrahydro-2-methyl-4H-pyrido[1,2-a]pyrimidin-4-one (Figure 9.1).

Risperidone is structurally unrelated to any other antipsychotic. It is the ultimate result of a developmental process stretching back to the synthesis of haloperidol and owes much to the foresight of Paul Janssen.

Janssen had also developed ritanserin, a specific 5-hydroxytryptamine$_2$ (5HT$_2$) antagonist, which appeared to reduce the incidence and severity of extrapyramidal adverse effects when added to antipsychotic treatment [1, 2]. Risperidone combined D$_2$ antagonism with 5HT$_2$ antagonism and was predicted to be an effective antipsychotic with a low propensity for extrapyramidal side-effects (EPSEs) on the basis that, pharmacologically, it resembled ritanserin and haloperidol combined [3]. It was also noted that the only known atypical drug at that time, clozapine, was also a 5HT$_2$ antagonist. Interestingly, this line of thinking may well have been flawed: many typical drugs such as chlorpromazine are also 5HT$_2$ antagonists and 5HT$_2$ antagonism may not in fact protect against EPSEs [4].

Risperidone is a very potent antagonist at 5HT$_{2A}$ receptors and a potent antagonist at 5HT$_{2C}$ and dopamine D$_2$ receptors [5]. Its D$_2$ activity *in vitro* is about half that of haloperidol on a molar basis. Other pharmacological activity includes moderate antagonism of histamine H$_1$ and noradrenergic α$_1$ receptors. It has no activity at muscarinic receptors [6].

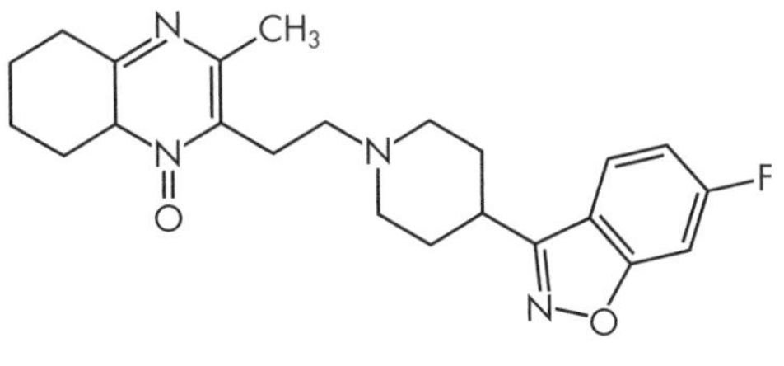

Figure 9.1 Risperidone.

Human positron emission tomography studies show risperidone to have a curiously typical profile. Using ^{11}C-raclopride as the radioactive ligand, striatal D_2 occupancy ranged from 75% to 85% at 6 mg/day and 53–78% on 3 mg/day [7, 8]. In the same studies $5HT_2$ occupancy ranged from 78% to 112%. Extrapyramidal effects occurred in 6 of 7 (first-episode) patients on 6 mg/day [8]. This is somewhat surprising because risperidone shows an atypical profile in animal and humans [6]. One possible explanation is that risperidone differs from typical drugs in the slope of its dose–response curve. Haloperidol shows a near-vertical relationship between dose and striatal occupancy, whereas risperidone's curve tends more to the horizontal [5]. The result of this is that dose titration with risperidone more readily allows separation of therapeutic and adverse effects. It follows that risperidone will appear typical when used in high doses and this is borne out by clinical trials and experience.

Clinical efficacy

There have been three major, randomised, fixed-dose placebo and haloperidol-controlled trials which combined include over 1500 subjects [9–11]. These fixed-dose studies are invaluable in establishing the dose–response relationship in relapsed schizophrenia. In these trials, risperidone 2 mg/day was no more effective than placebo but doses of 4, 6, 8, 10 and 16 mg/day were significantly more effective and no differ-ent from haloperidol 10 or 20 mg/day. Efficacy appeared to be optimal at 4–8 mg/day with response appearing to decline somewhat at higher doses. There was a suggestion that risperidone was more effective than haloperidol in treating negative symptoms. This was also seen in other comparisons with conventional drugs [12, 13] but these findings may in part reflect the high doses of haloperidol and other drugs used (that is, 10 or 20 mg/day).

In first-episode schizophrenia, risperidone (mean dose 3.3 mg/day) is at least as effective as haloperidol (mean dose 2.9 mg/day) while pro-viding better protection against relapse [14]. Risperidone also seems to be more effective than haloperidol in preventing relapse in multi-episode chronic schizophrenia [15].

When results of all studies comparing risperidone and conventional drugs are combined, risperidone shows distinct advantages. Risperidone is more effective than haloperidol in both the short and long term [16] and is more effective against both positive [17] and negative symptoms [18].

Risperidone has also been compared with other atypical anti-psychotics. For example, risperidone and olanzapine have been found to have broadly similar effects in relapsed schizophrenia in formal controlled trials [19, 20] and in analyses of a more naturalistic design [21, 22]. Some differences in outcome have been observed, with one study suggesting better efficacy and tolerability for olanzapine [19] and another suggesting the converse [20]. Rather predictably, these diverse outcomes seem to owe more to the study's sponsor than to any clear clinical differences. Risperidone seems to be as effective as amisulpride [23], clozapine [24], aripiprazole [25] and ziprasidone [26] in relapsed schizophrenia.

In refractory schizophrenia, there is a degree of published evidence to suggest that risperidone is as effective as clozapine [27–29]. However, although risperidone may be slightly more effective than conventional drugs in resistant schizophrenia [28], experience suggests that it has a very limited role in practice. Apparent equivalence with clozapine probably arises as a result of including treatment-intolerant subjects and of using too low a dose of clozapine. In fact the outcome of risperidone/clozapine comparisons is a function of the dose of clozapine: the lower the dose, the more 'equivalent' risperidone is seen to be [30].

As already mentioned, the dose of risperidone itself is an important influence of trial outcome. It is now fairly well accepted that the optimal dose of oral risperidone is somewhere close to 4 mg/day [31–33] and so it follows that studies using lower or higher doses may underestimate the true effect of risperidone. It also follows that, in practice, doses above 4 mg/day should rarely be used.

Risperidone is also available as a long-acting intramuscular injection (RLAI). At doses of 25–75 mg every 2 weeks, RLAI is more effective than placebo [34, 35] and produced the same therapeutic effects as oral risperidone (2–6 mg/day) [36]. The injectable formulation also seems to be effective in the medium term (up to 1 year) [37, 38], although in practice attrition from treatment is quite high [39].

It is not possible to calculate exact dose equivalency for oral/injection risperidone D_2 receptor occupancies range from 25% to 48% for 25 mg/2 weeks, 59–83% for 50 mg/2 weeks and 62–72% for 75 mg/2 weeks [40]. These data suggest that 25–75 mg/2 weeks is equivalent to 2–6 mg/day oral risperidone. However it should be noted that 25 mg/2 weeks is demonstrably effective whereas 2 mg/oral is not.

Adverse effects

Risperidone shows placebo-level incidence of acute movement disorders at oral doses of 2–6 mg/day [33] and intramuscular doses of 25–37.5 mg/2 weeks [41]. Above these doses EPSE frequency gradually increases to a level equivalent to that seen with conventional drugs [12,

33]. At oral doses of 4–8 mg/day, the incidence of EPSEs is similar to other atypical drugs [20, 21, 23, 25].

The incidence of tardive dyskinesia (TD) in people treated only with risperidone is difficult to establish in the absence of controlled studies. An annual incidence of 0.0006% has been put forward [42], but this is undoubtedly a gross underestimate. The year-long relapse prevention study [15] found an incidence of 0.6%/year and there are a good number of risperidone-related cases of TD in the literature [43, 44]. Similarly, neuroleptic malignant syndrome has been fairly frequently reported in relation to risperidone treatment [45–47].

Risperidone usually gives rise to hyperprolactinaemia when used at therapeutic doses [14]. In fact, the prolactogenic effect of risperidone may even exceed that of conventional drugs [14, 48]. The effect is clearly dose-related, with the prevalence of symptoms increasing as the dose increases [49] (see Chapter 15).

Other adverse effects of risperidone are somewhat trivial. Orthostatic hypotension (α_1 effect) is common when treatment is started so the dose should be increased slowly. Moderate weight gain can be expected and there is a tentative link between risperidone and diabetes mellitus (see Chapter 15). Despite moderate activity at H_1 receptors, risperidone tends not to be sedative and may even occasionally cause insomnia, anxiety and agitation.

Pharmacokinetics

Risperidone is hepatically metabolised to four major compounds, of which one – 9-hydroxyrisperidone, the major metabolite – is clinically active, with a receptor activity profile similar to the parent compound [50]. Risperidone itself has a plasma half-life of around 3 hours but the active moiety (parent drug + 9-hydroxyrisperidone) has a plasma half-life close to 20 hours [8, 50]. Pharmacokinetic parameters do not alter substantially when the route of administration changes and oral risperidone shows nearly 100% bioavailability [50].

The metabolism of risperidone to 9-hydroxyrisperidone seems to be controlled by the hepatic cytochrome CYP2D6 [51]. People who are phenotypically poor metabolisers via CYP2D6 tend to tolerate risperidone poorly [52]. The cytochrome CYP3A4 also seems to be involved in risperidone metabolism [51, 53]. Adverse interaction with drugs affecting the function of CYP2D6 or CYP3A4 might be expected but in fact they are uncommon. This is probably because the amount of active moiety changes little when enzyme function changes. Enzyme inhibitors slow conversion to 9-hydroxyrisperidone whereas inducers accelerate the process. The ratio of parent drug to active metabolite changes but the amount of active moiety remains much the same.

Plasma levels of risperidone or the active moiety do not seem to be related to clinical response [54]. In oral dosing (4–9 mg/day) risperidone plasma concentrations ranged from 2 to 78 nmol/l and active moiety levels from 36 to 368 nmol/l (median 11 nmol/l and 137 nmol/l respectively) [54].

Long-acting intramuscular risperidone is a formulation of risperidone incorporated into a copolymer microsphere. Absorption from the injection is delayed for 3–4 weeks after administration. Apparent plasma half-life is 3–6 days [41]. Median steady-state trough levels of active moiety have been measured at 38 nmol/l (25 mg/2 weeks), 67 nmol/l (37.5 mg/2 weeks) and 99 nmol/l (50 mg/2 weeks) [55]. The range of values obtained was very wide with each dose.

Risperidone is a popular, effective antipsychotic which is usually well tolerated. It is the only second generation antipsychotic available as a long-acting injection (Management focus 9.1).

MANAGEMENT FOCUS 9.1

Risperidone	
Absorption	Approaches 100% oral bioavailability
Elimination	Hepatic. Major metabolite, 9-hydroxy risperidone, is active
Plasma half-life	Parent drug 3 hours; active moiety up to 20 hours
Hepatic cytochromes involved	CYP2D6, CYP3A4
Hepatic cytochromes affected	None
Major interactions	Few clinically important pharmacokinetic interactions
Efficacy	Good. At least as effective as conventional drugs and may show some advantages (lower rates of relapse)
Adverse-effect profile/tolerability	Well tolerated. Can initially cause headache, dizziness and agitation. EPSEs rare at low doses. Hyperprolactinaemia very common

References

1. Bersani G, Grispini A, Marini S *et al*. Neuroleptic-induced extrapyramidal side effects: clinical perspectives with ritanserin (R55667), a new selective 5-HT sub(2) receptor antagonist. *Curr Ther Res Clin Exp* 1986; 40: 492–499.

2. Bersani G, Grispini A, Marini S *et al*. 5-HT$_2$ antagonist ritanserin in neuroleptic-induced parkinsonism: a double-blind comparison with orphenadrine and placebo. *Clin Neuropharmacol* 1990; 13: 500–506.

3. Janssen P A, Niemegeers C J, Awouters F *et al*. Pharmacology of risperidone (R64766), a new antipsychotic with serotonin-S$_2$ and dopamine-D$_2$ antagonistic properties. *Am Soc Pharmacol Exp Ther* 1988; 244: 685–693.

4. Den Boer J A, Vahlne J O, Post P *et al*. Ritanserin as add-on medication to neuroleptic therapy for patients with chronic or subchronic schizophrenia. *Hum Psychopharmacol Clin Exp* 2000; 15: 179–189.

5. Leysen J E, Janssen P M F, Megens A A N P, Schotte A. Risperidone: a novel antipsychotic with balanced serotonin–dopamine antagonism, receptor occupancy profile, and pharmacologic activity. *J Clin Psychiatry* 1994; 55: 5–12.

6. He H, Richardson J S. A pharmacological, pharmacokinetic and clinical overview of risperidone, a new antipsychotic that blocks serotonin 5-HT$_2$ and dopamine D$_2$ receptors. *Int Clin Psychopharmacol* 1995; 10: 19–30.

7. Farde L, Nyberg S, Oxenstierna G *et al*. Positron emission tomography studies on D$_2$ and 5-HT$_2$ receptor binding in risperidone-treated schizophrenic patients. *J Clin Psychopharmacol* 1995; 15: 19S–23S.

8. Nyberg S, Eriksson B, Oxenstierna G *et al*. Suggested minimal effective dose of risperidone based on PET-measured D$_2$ and 5-HT$_{2A}$ receptor occupancy in schizophrenic patients. *Am J Psychiatry* 1999; 156: 869–875.

9. Chouinard G, Jones B, Remington G *et al*. A Canadian multicenter placebo-controlled study of fixed doses of risperidone and haloperidol in the treatment of chronic schizophrenic patients. *J Clin Psychopharmacol* 1993; 13: 25–40.

10. Peuskens J. Risperidone in the treatment of patients with chronic schizophrenia: a multi-national, multi-center, double-blind, parallel-group study versus haloperidol. *Br J Psychiatry* 1995; 166: 712–726.

11. Marder S R, Meibach R C. Risperidone in the treatment of schizophrenia. *Am J Psychiatry* 1994; 151: 825–835.

12. Hoyberg O J, Fensbo C, Remvig J *et al*. Risperidone versus perphenazine in the treatment of chronic schizophrenic patients with acute exacerbations. *Acta Psychiatr Scand* 1993; 88: 395–402.

13. Claus A, Bollen J, De Cuyper H *et al*. Risperidone versus haloperidol in the treatment of chronic schizophrenic inpatients: a multicentre double-blind comparative study. *Acta Psychiatr Scand* 1992; 85: 295–305.

14. Schooler N, Rabinowitz J, Davidson M *et al*. Risperidone and haloperidol in first-episode psychosis: a long-term randomised trial. *Am J Psychiatry* 2005; 162: 947–953.

15. Csernansky J G, Mahmoud R, Brenner R. A comparison of risperidone and haloperidol for the prevention of relapse in patients with schizophrenia. *N Engl J Med* 2002; 346: 16–22.

16. Hunter R H, Joy C B, Kennedy E *et al*. Risperidone versus typical antipsychotic medication for schizophrenia. *Cochrane Database of Systematic Reviews* 2003, issue 2. DOI: 10.1002/14651858. CD000440.

17. Glick I D, Lemmens P, Vester-Blokland E. Treatment of the symptoms of schizophrenia: a combined analysis of double-blind studies comparing risperidone with haloperidol and other antipsychotic agents. *Int Clin Psychopharmacol* 2001; 16: 265–274.

18. Carman J, Peuskens J, Vangeneugden A. Risperidone in the treatment of negative symptoms of schizophrenia: a meta-analysis. *Int Clin Psychopharmacol* 1995; 10: 207–213.

19. Tran P V, Hamilton S H, Kuntz A J *et al*. Double-blind comparison of olanzapine versus risperidone in the treatment of schizophrenia and other psychotic disorders. *J Clin Psychopharmacol* 1997; 17: 407–418.

20. Conley R R, Mahmoud R. A randomised double-blind study of risperidone and olanzapine in the treatment of schizophrenia or schizoaffective disorder. *Am J Psychiatry* 2001; 158: 765–774.

21. Ho B C, Miller D, Nopoulos P, Andreasen N C. A comparative effectiveness study of risperidone and olanzapine in the treatment of schizophrenia. *J Clin Psychiatry* 1999; 60: 658–663.

22. Taylor D M, Wright T, Libretto S E. Risperidone compared with olanzapine in a naturalistic clinical study: a cost analysis. *J Clin Psychiatry* 2003; 64: 589–597.

23. Peuskens J, Bech P, Moller H J *et al*. Amisulpride vs. risperidone in the treatment of acute exacerbations of schizophrenia. Amisulpride study group. *Psychiatry Res* 1999; 88: 107–117.

24. Klieser E, Lehmann E, Kinzler E *et al*. Randomized, double-blind, controlled trial of risperidone versus clozapine in patients with chronic schizophrenia. *J Clin Psychopharmacol* 1995; 15: 45S–51S.

25. Potkin S G, Saha A R, Kujawa M J *et al*. Aripiprazole, an antipsychotic with a novel mechanism of action, and risperidone vs placebo in patients with schizophrenia and schizoaffective disorder. *Arch Gen Psychiatry* 2003; 60: 681–690.

26. Hagger C, Mitchell D, Wise A L, Schulz S C. Effects of oral ziprasidone and risperidone on cognitive functioning in patients with schizophrenia or schizoaffective disorder: preliminary data. *Eur Neuropsychopharmacol* 1997; 7: 219–219.

27. Bondolfi G, Dufour H, Patris M *et al*. Risperidone versus clozapine in treatment-resistant chronic schizophrenia: a randomized double-blind study. *Am J Psychiatry* 1998; 55: 499–504.

28. Volavka J, Czobor P, Sheitman B *et al*. Clozapine, olanzapine, risperidone, and haloperidol in the treatment of patients with chronic schizophrenia and schizoaffective disorder. *Am J Psychiatry* 2002; 159: 255–262.

29. Wirshing D A, Marshall B D Jr, Green M F *et al*. Risperidone in treatment-refractory schizophrenia. *Am J Psychiatry* 1999; 156: 1374–1379.

30. Davis J M, Chen N, Glick I D. A meta-analysis of the efficacy of second-generation antipsychotics. *Arch Gen Psychiatry* 2003; 60: 553–564.

31. Williams R. Optimal dosing with risperidone: updated recommendations. *J Clin Psychiatry* 2001; 62: 282–289.

32. Davis J M, Chen N. Dose response and dose equivalent of antipsychotics. *J Clin Psychopharmacol* 2004; 24: 192–208.

33. Ezewuzie N, Taylor D. Establishing a dose–response relationship for oral risperidone in relapsed schizophrenia. *J Psychopharmacol* 2005; 20: 86–90.

34. Lauriello J, McEvoy J P, Rodriguez S *et al.* Long-acting risperidone vs. placebo in the treatment of hospital inpatients with schizophrenia. *Schizophr Res* 2005; 72: 249–258.

35. Kane J M, Eerdekens M, Lindenmayer J P *et al.* Long-acting injectable risperidone: efficacy and safety of the first long-acting atypical antipsychotic. *Am J Psychiatry* 2003; 160: 1125–1132.

36. Chue P, Eerdekens M, Augustyns I *et al.* Comparative efficacy and safety of long-acting risperidone and risperidone oral tablets. *Eur Neuropsychopharmacol* 2005; 15: 111–117.

37. Fleischhacker W W, Eerdekens M, Karcher K *et al.* Treatment of schizophrenia with long-acting injectable risperidone: a 12-month open-label trial of the first long-acting second-generation antipsychotic. *J Clin Psychiatry* 2003; 64: 1250–1257.

38. Lasser R, Bossie C A, Gharabawi G *et al.* Efficacy and safety of long-acting risperidone in stable patients with schizoaffective disorder. *J Affect Disord* 2004; 83: 263–275.

39. Taylor D M, Young C L, Mace S *et al.* Early clinical experience with risperidone long-acting injection: a prospective, 6-month follow-up of 100 patients. *J Clin Psychiatry* 2004; 65: 1076–1083.

40. Gefvert O, Eriksson B, Persson P *et al.* Pharmacokinetics and D_2 receptor occupancy of long-acting injectable risperidone (Risperdal Consta™) in patients with schizophrenia. *Int J Neuropsychopharmacol* 2005; 8: 27–36.

41. Harrison T S, Goa K L. Long-acting risperidone a review of its use in schizophrenia. *CNS Drugs* 2004; 18: 113–132.

42. Tooley P J H, Zuiderwijk P. Drug safety: experience with risperidone. *Adv Ther* 1997; 14: 262–266.

43. Buzan R D. Risperidone-induced tardive dyskinesia. *Am J Psychiatry* 1996; 153: 734–735.

44. Woerner M G, Sheitman B B, Lieberman J A *et al.* Tardive dyskinesia induced by risperidone? *Am J Psychiatry* 1996; 153: 843.

45. Dave M. Two cases of risperidone-induced neuroleptic malignant syndrome. *Am J Psychiatry* 1995; 152: 1233–1234.

46. Sharma R, Trappler B, Ng Y K, Leeman C P. Risperidone-induced neuroleptic malignant syndrome. *Ann Pharmacother* 1996; 30: 775–778.

47. Webster P, Wijeratne C. Risperidone-induced neuroleptic malignant syndrome. *Lancet* 1994; 344: 1228–1229.

48. Shiwach R S, Carmody T J. Prolactogenic effects of risperidone in male patients – a preliminary study. *Acta Psychiatr Scand* 1998; 98: 81–83.

49. Kleinberg D L, Davis J M, De Coster R *et al.* Prolactin levels and adverse events in patients treated with risperidone. *J Clin Psychopharmacol* 1999; 19: 57–61.

50. Heykants J, Huang M L, Mannens G *et al.* The pharmacokinetics of risperidone in humans: a summary. *J Clin Psychiatry* 1994; 55: 13–17.

51. Bork J A, Rogers T, Wedlund P J, de Leon J. A pilot study on risperidone metabolism: the role of cytochromes P450 2D6 and 3A. *J Clin Psychiatry* 1999; 60: 469–476.

52. Kohnke M D, Griese E U, Stosser D *et al.* Cytochrome P450 2D6 deficiency and its clinical relevance in a patient treated with risperidone. *Pharmacopsychiatry* 2002; 35: 116–118.

53. Devane C L, Nemeroff C B. An evaluation of risperidone drug interactions. *J Clin Psychopharmacol* 2001; 21: 408–416.

54. Spina E, Avenoso A, Facciola G. Relationship between plasma risperidone and 9-hydroxyrisperidone concentrations and clinical response in patients with schizophrenia. *Psychopharmacology* 2001; 153: 238–243.

55. Castberg I, Spigset O. Serum concentrations of risperidone and 9-hydroxy-risperidone after administration of the long-acting injectable form of risperidone evidence from a routine therapeutic drug monitoring service. *Ther Drug Monit* 2005; 27: 103–106.

10

Olanzapine

Chemistry and pharmacology

Olanzapine is a thienobenzodiazepine compound that is structurally similar to quetiapine and clozapine (Figure 10.1). Animal experiments with olanzapine show results consistent with atypicality in humans [1, 2]. Olanzapine has a broad range of receptor activities, including potent blockade of 5-hydroxytryptamine-2a ($5HT_{2a}$), $5HT_{2c,}$ histamine H_1, muscarine M_1 and α_1 receptors with less potent activity at dopamine D_1, D_2, D_4 and α_2 receptors [3, 4].

Early studies of olanzapine's *in vivo* activity suggested low striatal D_2 activity with extensive blockade of $5HT_2$ receptors [5, 6]. In fact, olanzapine induces near saturation of $5HT_2$ receptors at only 5 mg/day [7]. Later studies revealed a dose-dependent effect for olanzapine on striatal D_2 receptors – occupancy rates of around 80% appear to be afforded by doses of 30–40 mg/day [8, 9].

Preliminary data suggested that olanzapine is a potent antagonist at cortical D_2 receptors [4, 5]. Conversely, striatal D_2 antagonism is known to predict acute extrapyramidal effects: as discussed earlier, typical neuroleptics typically show 70–80% or higher occupancy of striatal D_2 receptors. Olanzapine's relatively weak activity at these receptors at lower therapeutic doses is consistent with its low incidence of extrapyramidal side-effects (EPSEs).

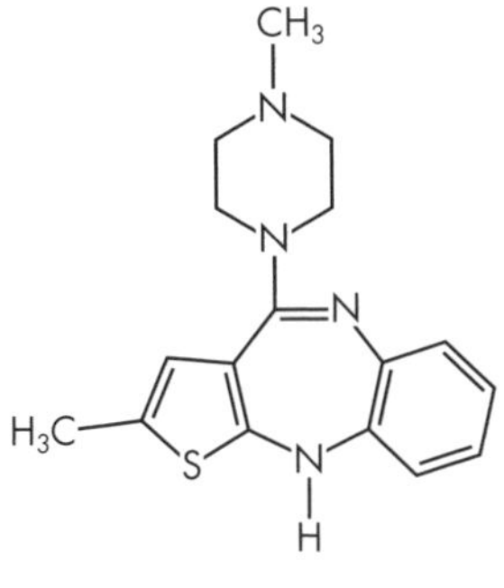

Figure 10.1   Olanzapine structure.

As previously noted, the pathology of schizophrenia may involve a number of neurotransmitter systems in addition to dopaminergic symptoms. On this basis, olanzapine's wide receptor activity (as with clozapine) was initially expected to provide therapeutic benefits. Debate continues today as to whether olanzapine's clinical effects have matched its early theoretical promise and whether multiple receptor activity confers therapeutic advantages.

Efficacy

Clinical efficacy studies

Early studies evaluated doses ranging from 1 to 30 mg/day [10]. Later double-blind, randomised, controlled studies in large sample groups give a more complete view of olanzapine's therapeutic potential.

Combining the results of these well-conducted studies allows several conclusions to be drawn. Olanzapine can be seen to be at least as effective as haloperidol in the short-term treatment of schizophrenia. Some studies also show advantages for olanzapine. For example, negative symptoms appear to respond better to olanzapine than to haloperidol. This is thought to be a direct therapeutic effect of olanzapine [11] rather than an indirect effect on secondary negative symptoms.

This superiority is best evidenced by the results of a large and scientifically robust trial which allowed free titration of doses of haloperidol or olanzapine between 5 and 20 mg/day [12]. Differences shown in such a trial are unlikely to be due to chance. Note also, however, the failure to show superiority in the treatment of positive symptoms. If no difference in effect can be shown in such a large trial, then true differences are likely to be small or non-existent.

Another notable finding of this study was olanzapine's beneficial effect on depressive symptoms, as shown on the Montgomery–Asberg Depression Rating Scale. Again, this is considered to be a direct mood-elevating effect of the drug [13]. (Improvements in mood can be indirectly engendered by treating positive or negative symptoms or by reducing EPSEs.)

Long-term extensions of trials [14] usually demonstrate a statistically significant advantage for olanzapine over haloperidol in maintaining remission. No published trial has yet compared olanzapine with depot medication in response maintenance.

In a medium-term study of olanzapine and risperidone, olanzapine appeared to have some important advantages [15]. It was shown to be more effective on one measure of negative symptom severity (Schedule for Assessment of Negative Symptoms) and in overall response rate, defined as a 40% reduction in Positive and Negative Symptom Scale score. Response maintenance was again better with olanzapine over the full trial period. It should be noted that the findings of this study have been heavily criticised on grounds of inappropriate dosing (that is, high doses of risperidone) and use of *post hoc* analyses [16, 17] and fiercely defended [18], largely on the basis that free titration of doses was allowed.

A later comparison of the two drugs gave very different results [19]. Using lower doses of risperidone, this trial suggested that risperidone was more effective than olanzapine on some efficacy measures while being equally well tolerated.

Other analyses of patients in larger olanzapine trials have been conducted. For example, olanzapine has been shown to be effective in subgroups of patients with first-episode psychosis [20] and schizoaffective disorder [21]; olanzapine also seems more effective than haloperidol in maintenance treatment of schizophrenia [14].

Refractory schizophrenia

Olanzapine is licensed for the initial and maintenance treatment of schizophrenia. Although not explicitly stated, this indication can be said to include patients with schizophrenia who have failed to respond to one or more antipsychotics – so-called treatment-refractory schizophrenia. The *British National Formulary* [22] stated for several years that atypical antipsychotics 'may be effective in patients refractory to other treatments'. Partly because of this and partly because of assumptions made about the drug (largely based on its pharmacological and chemical similarities to clozapine), olanzapine was and, to a lesser extent, still is widely used in clinical practice for the poorly responsive patient. A review of olanzapine's effectiveness in this area is therefore pertinent.

Some early studies appeared to show worthwhile efficacy for olanzapine. In some cases, this may have been a result of including treatment-intolerant patients [23] or of including less severely resistant patients [24]. Where clearly and severely resistant patients were studied [25] olanzapine showed no effect. Moreover, in a study of outpatients switched from clozapine to olanzapine [26] more than three-quarters deteriorated, with many requiring hospitalisation. Against this are the findings of a double-blind comparison with clozapine which suggested that olanzapine was 'not inferior' [27]. These last findings go against the author's clinical experience and are in clear contrast to other findings described above. In practice, olanzapine shows no clear benefit in true refractory schizophrenia and clozapine is frequently observed to be effective when olanzapine has failed.

At present olanzapine has no clear role in treatment-refractory schizophrenia, although high-dose treatment (> 25 mg/day) perhaps needs further investigation in randomised controlled trials. Augmentation of olanzapine with sulpiride, for example [28], is also worthy of further, more careful evaluation, as is the use of olanzapine in patients intolerant of clozapine [29].

Olanzapine and other conditions

The use of olanzapine has been evaluated in other areas of mental illness. It appears to be as effect as haloperidol in cannabis-induced psychosis [30] and more effective than placebo in the treatment of mania [31] and in maintaining response in bipolar disorder [32] (both licensed indications). Olanzapine may also be effective in rapid tranquillisation [33], obsessive-compulsive disorder [34] and in the treatment of tardive dyskinesia (TD) [35]. Many of these studies have been driven by the manufacturer's need to extend licensed indications of olanzapine. The large majority have been funded by the manufacturers.

Safety and tolerability

The basic pharmacology of olanzapine predicts a low incidence of EPSEs and hyperprolactinaemia, but with a potential for sedation (H_1 antagonism), hypotension (α_1 antagonism) and anticholinergic effects. Clinical trials and clinical practice largely support these suppositions.

EPSEs occurred much less frequently than with haloperidol in all clinical trials [10]. In the largest study of olanzapine [12], mean scores on two assessment scales (Simpson–Angus Scale and Barnes Akathisia Scale) fell in patients given olanzapine and new symptoms emerged in fewer than 15% of olanzapine-treated patients. In clinical practice, EPSEs are very rarely seen when olanzapine is given at licensed doses.

Small and transient prolactin level elevations have been detected in patients given olanzapine [12] but symptoms are not usually noted. In practice, symptomatic hyperprolactinaemia is extremely rare. Indeed, the vast majority of patients show gradual improvement in prolactin-related symptoms when switched from typical drugs to olanzapine.

Sedation is often reported by patients taking olanzapine. In trials, 'somnolence' is usually experienced by around a quarter of subjects on olanzapine. In practice, sedation is frequently observed but it is usually short-lived. A very few patients find the sedative effects of olanzapine intolerable. Others, particularly those with agitation or anxiety, find the sedative effects beneficial.

Despite olanzapine's alpha-blocking activity, hypotension is a rare event and is not related to dose-dependent dizziness seen with olanzapine [10]. Since introduction there have been no reports of orthostatic hypotension in the literature. In practice, first-dose hypotension is very occasionally seen, although severe symptoms are very uncommon. Clinicians have observed that using starting doses recommended by the manufacturer reduces substantially the risk of hypotension.

Anticholinergic effects are sometimes experienced by patients taking olanzapine. Of these, only constipation and dry mouth are seen with any regularity and then in only a small proportion of patients [36].

Adverse effects seen with olanzapine but not easily predicted by its pharmacology include weight gain, changes in liver enzyme levels and blood disorders. Weight gain with olanzapine averages around 2 kg over 6 weeks [12] and around 4 kg over 28 weeks (and using a higher starting dose (15 mg/day) than is routinely recommended [15]). In the latter study, weight gain was more severe with olanzapine than with risperidone.

Liver function tests do occasionally show minor abnormalities caused by olanzapine (about 13% of subjects in trials [10]), but these are asymptomatic and transient. One case of agranulocytosis (a potentially fatal reduction in plasma neutrophils) has been reported with olanzapine [37], and low neutrophil counts are occasionally observed [10, 38]. In addition, low neutrophil counts were significantly more common with olanzapine (4.3%) than with risperidone (0.6%) in a comparative trial [15].

In clinical trials, olanzapine appeared not to alter seizure threshold, but olanzapine-related seizures have latterly been reported [39].

Olanzapine seems not to be associated with electrocardiogram changes [40] but now has a clear association with impaired glucose tolerance and diabetes [41, 42].

Tardive dyskinesia

Tollefson and co-workers [43] investigated rates of emergent TD in over 900 subjects given olanzapine or haloperidol. After around 200 days of exposure to these drugs, persistent TD was observed in 1.0% of patients on olanzapine and 4.6% of these on haloperidol – a statistically and clinically significant difference. In addition, cases of olanzapine-induced improvement in TD have been reported [44].

Later, a longer-term (2.6 years) comparison of patients treated with olanzapine or haloperidol was reported [45]. In this study, observed 1-year risk of TD was 7.45% with haloperidol and 0.52% with olanzapine. This apparent low incidence of TD is supported by the dearth of case reports in the literature, although there is not a complete absence of such reports [46] and there is a possibility of publication bias (that is, the failure to publish all suspected cases).

Pharmacokinetics

Metabolism

The pharmacokinetic properties of olanzapine have been reviewed by Kando *et al.* [10]. Olanzapine has a plasma elimination half-life of around 33 hours, which allows once-daily dosing. Four hepatic enzymes are involved in its metabolism – the cytochromes CYP1A2, CYP2D6, and CYP3A4, and flavin-containing mono-oxygenase (FMO) [47]. The major routes of metabolism (Figure 10.2) appear to be to 7-hydroxyolanzapine (via CYP1A2), N-desmethylolanzapine (also via CYP1A2) and to 4-N-oxideolanzapine (via FMO) with a minor route to 2-hydoxyolanzapine (via CYP2D6) [47]. Lower clearance rates are seen in women, the elderly and non-smokers (smoking induces CYP1A2). Combinations of these factors demand lower starting doses of olanzapine. Clearance rates are slightly increased by some enzyme-inducers, such as carbamazepine, but dose adjustments are not thought to be necessary. Olanzapine itself has little effect on the function of hepatic cytochromes [48].

Olanzapine is available as standard tablets, a fast-disintegrating tablet [49], an intramuscular injection [50] and as an extemporaneous (that is, individually prepared) liquid [51]. Oral absorption is usually no higher than 60%, mainly because of extensive first-pass metabolism [10].

Pharmacokinetic interactions

The importance of CYP1A2 in the metabolism of olanzapine has been confirmed by studies and case reports of interactions. For example, carbamazepine, an inducer of CYP1A2 (and CYP3A4) has been shown to increase olanzapine clearance by 44% [52]. The co-administration of

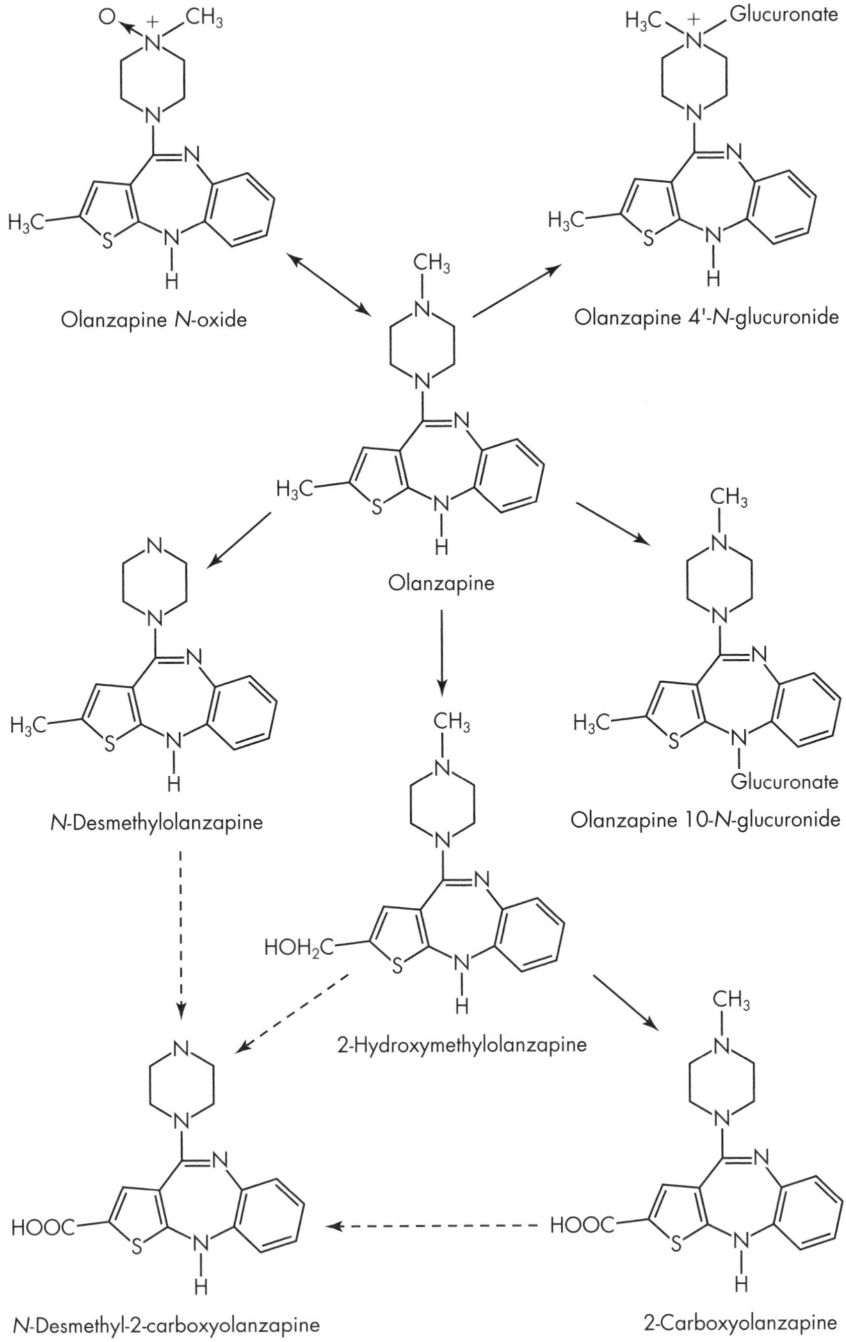

Figure 10.2 Metabolism of olanzapine.

fluvoxamine, an inhibitor of CYP1A2, appeared to increase several-fold plasma levels of olanzapine [53]. A similar interaction has been reported when ciprofloxacin was added to olanzapine treatment [54]. Ciprofloxacin is also an inhibitor of CYP1A2.

Olanzapine pharmacokinetics appear not to be altered by imipramine [55], a drug known to inhibit CYP2D6, but plasma levels may be increased by co-administration of fluoxetine [56], effectively an inhibitor of CYP2D6 and CYP3A4.

Olanzapine itself may competitively inhibit haloperidol metabolism [57], although this is less than clear at present.

Olanzapine plasma levels

A handful of studies have been conducted to evaluate the relationship between olanzapine plasma levels and therapeutic or toxic effects.

The earliest study in this area was conducted by Perry and co-workers [58]. Plasma levels (drawn 24 hours post-dose) were taken from 79 inpatients given either 1 or 10 mg olanzapine daily. Response (20% reduction in Brief Psychiatric Rating Scale score) appeared to be weakly related to trough plasma level. Of patients with plasma levels above 9.3 µg/L, 14 were responders and 19 non-responders. Of those with plasma levels below 9.3 µg/lL, 6 were responders and 40 non-responders. Overall, patients were 3.0–8.7 times more likely to respond on some efficacy measure when plasma levels exceeded 9.3 µg/L than when levels were below this value.

A later analysis by the same research team [59] also found an association between plasma olanzapine level and clinical response. In this study, blood samples were taken 12 hours post-dose from 84 patients included in an American clinical trial. Improvement seemed to be associated with a 12-hour plasma level of 23.2 µg/L or above – 52% of subjects with levels above 23.2 µg/L were defined as responders whereas of those with levels below 23.2 µg/L, only 25% responded. Subjects with levels above 23.2 µg/L were 3.35 times (95% confidence intervals 1.23–9.14) more likely to respond than subjects with levels below 23.2 µg/L. The authors also found that the plasma level obtained was linearly related to daily dose:

$$\text{Plasma level (µg/L)} = -5.4 \times 2.1(\text{daily dose})$$

Some variation in plasma level was found to be associated with gender and so two further, more gender-specific relationships were delineated:

Males: Plasma level (µg/L) = (1.708 × daily dose) − 3.704

Females: Plasma level (µg/L) = (3.121 × daily dose) − 3.704

Aravagiri and colleagues [60] reported their observations of plasma level determinations in patients treated with olanzapine in clinical practice. Plasma levels (again from samples drawn 24 hours post-dose) were linearly related to daily dose ($r = 0.6889$, $P = 0.01$). This association was derived from analysis of 103 samples drawn from 7 patients receiving varying doses. Those receiving 10 mg/day had mean levels of 10.0 µg/L; those on 15 mg/day, 19.9 µg/L; and those on 20 mg/day, 25.4 µg/L. (Patients receiving 10 mg/day had a mean body weight of 92 kg (14 st 8 lb); this might explain the relatively low plasma level.)

Such approximate associations may conceal important factors influencing the plasma level obtained from a given daily dose. For example, Kelly and colleagues [61] found that, although plasma level was linearly related to dose in an individual, levels were significantly higher (63–85% higher) in women than in men receiving the same dose. Also Olesen and Linnet [62] showed that the co-prescription of enzyme inhibitors and enzyme-inducers (specifically carbamazepine) had a significant and substantial effect on olanzapine plasma level. In this latter study, 12-hour post-dose plasma levels ranged from 22 to 146 nmol/L (7–46 µg/L) in 56 patients receiving 5–20 mg/day olanzapine.

These results are remarkably similar to those obtained by the same Danish group [63] and reported some time later. In this analysis, 334 patients were included and about 80% of plasma levels measured were in the range 25–140 nmol/L (8–45 µg/L). Daily doses again ranged from 5 to 20 mg/day for the large majority of patients.

Thus there is some agreement that olanzapine is therapeutic at levels of around 9 mg/L (trough sample) or 23 mg/L (12 hours post-dose) and this is to some extent mirrored by plasma levels obtained in practice (samples being presumably from satisfactorily treated patients). A therapeutic range of 20–40 µg/L has been proposed [64] and levels of above 80 µg/L suggested to be 'toxic'. However, the exact level at which toxicity occurs is obviously dependent upon the individual and is in any case difficult to determine. For example, Bosch and co-workers [65] reported that a patient who ingested 800 mg olanzapine showed a peak plasma level of 200 µg/L and exhibited symptoms of mild somnolence and tachycardia. Conversely, a postmortem study suggested that olanzapine toxicity should be considered at levels about 100 µg/L [66]. In this analysis, postmortem levels averaged 358 µg/L and ranged from 10 to

5200 µg/L. The lowest level thought to be the cause of death was 160 µg/L. There is one confirmed death directly associated with olanzapine (that is, where postmortem examination revealed nothing of note apart from high olanzapine levels) [67]. Here, 600 mg was ingested and the plasma level obtained was 1238 µg/L.

The data presented here give an incomplete picture of the value and relevance of olanzapine plasma levels. Substantially more work needs to be done to establish the true 'therapeutic range' of plasma levels of olanzapine. This work might involve blind randomisation to predetermined plasma level ranges and standardised timing of blood samples.

Olanzapine is very widely prescribed and is usually effective and well tolerated. Metabolic adverse effects are relatively common but this is balanced by a reputation for reliable effectiveness in practice (Management focus 10.1).

MANAGEMENT FOCUS 10.1

Olanzapine	
Absorption	Incomplete, less than 60%
Elimination	Hepatic
Plasma half-life	33 hours
Hepatic cytochromes involved	CYP1A2, CYP2D6, CYP3A4, FMO
Hepatic cytochromes affected	None confirmed. May inhibit haloperidol metabolism
Major interactions	Plasma levels reduced by co-administration of carbamazepine and by smoking. Levels increased by fluvoxamine, ciprofloxacin and possibly other CYP1A2 inhibitors
Efficacy	Good efficacy against positive and negative symptoms. Has antidepressant and antimanic properties. Dubious efficacy in treatment resistance but more effective overall than conventional antipsychotics
Adverse-effect profile/tolerability	Sedation, increased appetite, weight gain, diabetes mellitus, rarely blood dyscrasia and TD. Benign changes in liver function tests fairly common

References

1. Kerwin R, Taylor D. New antipsychotics: a review of their current status and clinical potential. *CNS Drugs* 1996; 6: 71–82.
2. Moore N A, Leander J D, Benvenga M J *et al*. Behavioral pharmacology of olanzapine: a novel antipsychotic drug. *J Clin Psychiatry* 1997; 58 (suppl. 10): 37–44.
3. Moore N A, Calligaro D O, Wong D T *et al*. The pharmacology of olanzapine and other new antipsychotic agents. *Curr Opin Invest Drugs* 1993; 2: 281–299.
4. Stephenson C M E, Pilowsky L S. Psychopharmacology of olanzapine. *Br J Psychiatry* 1999; 174 (suppl. 38): 52–58.
5. Bymaster F P, Rasmussen K, Calligaro D O *et al*. (1997) *In vitro* and *in vivo* biochemistry of olanzapine: a novel, atypical antipsychotic drug. *J Clin Psychiatry* 1997; 58 (suppl. 10): 28–36.
6. Pilowsky L S, Busatto G F, Taylor M *et al*. Dopamine D_2 receptor occupancy *in vivo* by the novel atypical antipsychotic olanzapine – a ^{123}I IBZM single photon emission tomography (SPET) study. *Psychopharmacology* 1996; 124: 148–153.
7. Kapur S, Zipursky R B, Remington G *et al*. 5-HT_2 and D_2 receptor occupancy of olanzapine in schizophrenia: a PET investigation. *Am J Psychiatry* 1998; 155: 921–928.
8. Kapur S, Seeman P. Antipsychotic agents differ in how fast they come off the dopamine D_2 receptors. Implications for atypical antipsychotic action. *J Psychiatry Neurosci* 2000; 25: 161–166.
9. Meisenzahl E M, Dresel S, Frodl T *et al*. D_2 receptor occupancy under recommended and high doses of olanzapine: an iodine-123-iodobenzamide SPECT study. *J Psychopharmacol* 2000; 14: 364–370.
10. Kando J C, Shepski J C, Satterlee W. Olanzapine: a new antipsychotic agent with efficacy in the management of schizophrenia. *Ann Pharmacother* 1997; 31: 1325–1334.
11. Tollefson G D, Sanger T M. Negative symptoms: a path analytic approach to a double-blind, placebo- and haloperidol-controlled clinical trial with olanzapine. *Am J Psychiatry* 1997; 154: 466–474.
12. Tollefson G D, Beasley C M, Tran P V *et al*. Olanzapine versus haloperidol in the treatment of schizophrenia and schizoaffective and schizophreniform disorders: results of an international collaborative trial. *Am J Psychiatry* 1997; 154: 457–465.
13. Tollefson G D, Sanger T M, Lu Y *et al*. Depressive signs and symptoms in schizophrenia: a prospective blinded trial of olanzapine and haloperidol. *Arch Gen Psychiatry* 1998; 55: 250–258.
14. Tran P V, Dellva M A, Tollefson G D *et al*. Oral olanzapine *versus* oral haloperidol in the maintenance treatment of schizophrenia and related psychoses. *Br J Psychiatry* 1998; 172: 499–505.
15. Tran P V, Hamilton S H, Kuntz A J. Double-blind comparison of olanzapine versus risperidone in the treatment of schizophrenia and other psychotic disorders. *J Clin Psychopharmacol* 1997; 17: 407–418.

16. Schooler N R. Double-blind comparison of olanzapine versus risperidone in treatment of schizophrenia and other psychotic disorders. *J Clin Psychopharmacol* 1998; 18: 174–176.

17. Gheuens J, Grebb J A. Double-blind comparison of olanzapine versus risperidone in treatment of schizophrenia and other psychotic disorders. *J Clin Psychopharmacol* 1998; 18: 176–179.

18. Schooler N R. Comments on article by Tran and colleagues, Double-blind comparison of olanzapine versus risperidone in treatment of schizophrenia and other psychotic disorders. *J Clin Psychopharmacol* 1998; 18: 177.

19. Conley R R, Mahmoud R. A randomized double-blind study of risperidone and olanzapine in the treatment of schizophrenia or schizoaffective disorder. *Am J Psychiatry* 2001; 158: 765.

20. Sanger T, Lieberman J, Tohen M *et al*. Olanzapine versus haloperidol treatment in first-episode psychosis. *Am J Psychiatry* 1999; 156: 79–87.

21. Tran P V, Tollefson G D, Sanger T M *et al*. Olanzapine versus haloperidol in the treatment of schizoaffective disorder. *Br J Psychiatry* 1999; 174: 15–22.

22. *British National Formulary 49*. London: British Medical Association, Royal Pharmaceutical Society of Great Britain, 2005.

23. Baldacchino A M, Stubbs J H, Nevison-Andrews D. The use of olanzapine in non-compliant or treatment-resistant clozapine populations in hospital. *Pharm J* 1998; 260: 207–209.

24. Martin J, Gomez J C, Garcia-Bernardo E *et al*. Olanzapine in treatment-refractory schizophrenia: results of an open-label study. The Spanish Group for the Study of Olanzapine in Treatment-Refractory Schizophrenia. *J Clin Psychiatry* 1997; 58: 479–483.

25. Conley R R, Tamminga C A, Bartko J J *et al*. Olanzapine compared with chlorpromazine in treatment-resistant schizophrenia. *Am J Psychiatry* 1998; 155: 914–920.

26. Reinstein M J, Sirotovskaya L A, Chasanov M *et al*. Predictors of treatment response and outcome in psychotic patients switched from clozapine to olanzapine. Poster presented at American Psychiatric Association Annual Conference, June 1998, Toronto, Canada.

27. Tollefson G D, Birkett M A, Kiesler G M *et al*. Double-blind comparison of olanzapine versus clozapine in schizophrenic patients clinically eligible for treatment with clozapine. *Biol Psychiatry* 2001; 49: 52–63.

28. Kotler M, Strous R D, Reznik I *et al*. Sulpiride augmentation of olanzapine in the management of treatment-resistant chronic schizophrenia: evidence for improvement of mood symptomatology. *Int Clin Psychopharmacol* 2004; 19: 23–26.

29. Dossenbach M R K, Beuzen J N, Avnon M *et al*. The effectiveness of olanzapine in treatment-refractory schizophrenia when patients are nonresponsive to or unable to tolerate clozapine. *Clin Ther* 2000; 22: 1021–1034.

30. Berk M, Brook S, Trandafir A I. A comparison of olanzapine with haloperidol in cannabis-induced psychotic disorder: a double-blind randomized controlled trial. *Int Clin Psychopharmacol* 1999; 14: 177–180.

31. Tohen M, Sanger T, Mcelroy S *et al*. Olanzapine versus placebo in the treatment of acute mania. *Am J Psychiatry* 1999; 156: 702–709.

32. Sanger T M, Grundy S L, Gibson P J *et al*. Long-term olanzapine therapy in the treatment of bipolar I disorder: an open-label continuation phase study. *J Clin Psychiatry* 2001; 62: 273–281.

33. Karagianis J L, Dawe I C, Thakur A *et al*. Rapid tranquilization with olanzapine in acute psychosis: a case series. *J Clin Psychiatry* 2001; 62: 12–16.

34. Weiss E L, Potenza M N, MdDougle C J *et al*. Olanzapine addition in obsessive-compulsive disorder refractory to selective serotonin reuptake inhibitors: an open-label case series. *J Clin Psychiatry* 1999; 60: 524–527.

35. Soutullo C A, Keck P E, McElroy S L. Olanzapine in the treatment of tardive dyskinesia: a report of two cases. *J Clin Psychopharmacol* 1999; 19: 100–101.

36. Beasley C M, Tollefson G D, Tran P V *et al*. Olanzapine HGAD study group: olanzapine versus placebo and haloperidol. Acute phase results of the North American Double-blind Olanzapine Trial. *Neuropsychopharmacology* 1996; 14: 111–123.

37. Naumann R, Felber W, Heilemann H *et al*. Olanzapine-induced agranulocytosis. *Lancet* 1999; 354: 566–567.

38. Kodesh A, Finkel B, Lerner A G *et al*. Dose-dependent olanzapine-associated leukopenia: three case reports. *Int Clin Psychopharmacol* 2001; 16: 117–119.

39. Woolley J, Smith S. Lowered seizure threshold on olanzapine. *Br J Psychiatry* 2001; 178: 85–86.

40. Czekalla J, Beasley C M, Dellva M A *et al*. Analysis of the QTc interval during olanzapine treatment of patients with schizophrenia and related psychosis. *J Clin Psychiatry* 2001; 62: 191–198.

41. Mir S, Taylor D. Atypical antipsychotics and hyperglycaemia. *Int Clin Psychopharmacol* 2001; 16: 63–74.

42. Sernyak M J, Leslie D L, Alarcon R D *et al*. Association of diabetes mellitus with use of atypical neuroleptics in the treatment of schizophrenia. *Am J Psychiatry* 2002; 159: 561–566.

43. Tollefson G D, Beasley C M, Tamura R N *et al*. Blind, controlled, long-term study of the comparative incidence of treatment-emergent tardive dyskinesia with olanzapine or haloperidol. *Am J Psychiatry* 1997; 154: 1248–1254.

44. O'Brien J, Barber R. Marked improvement in tardive dyskinesia following treatment with olanzapine in an elderly subject. *Br J Psychiatry* 1998; 172: 186.

45. Beasley C, Dellva M, Tamura R *et al*. Randomised double-blind comparison of the incidence of tardive dyskinesia in patients with schizophrenia during long-term treatment with olanzapine or haloperidol. *Br J Psychiatry* 1999; 174: 23–30.

46. Dunayevich E, Strakowsk S M. Olanzapine-induced tardive dystonia. *Am J Psychiatry* 1999; 156: 1662.

47. Ring B J, Binkley S N, Vandenbranden M *et al*. *In vitro* interaction of the antipsychotic agent olanzapine with human cytochromes P450 CYP2C9, CYP2C19, CYP2D6 and CYP3A. *J Clin Psychopharmacol* 1996; 41: 181–186.

48. Ring B J, Catlow J, Lindsay T J *et al*. Identification of the human cytochromes P450 responsible for the *in vitro* formation of the major oxidative metabolites of the antipsychotic agent olanzapine. *J Pharmacol Exp Ther* 1996; 276: 658–667.

49. Chue P, Jones B, Taylor C C, Dickson R. Dissolution profile, tolerability, and acceptability of the orally disintegrating olanzapine tablet in patients with schizophrenia. *Can J Psychiatry* 2002; 47: 771–774.

50. Jones B, Taylor C C, Meehan K. The efficacy of a rapid-acting intramuscular formulation of olanzapine for positive symptoms. *J Clin Psychiatry* 2001; 62 (suppl. 2): 22–24.

51. Harvey E J, Flanagan R J, Taylor D M. The preparation and stability of a liquid olanzapine preparation for oral administration in hospitals. *Pharm J* 2000; 265: 275–276.

52. Lucas R A, Gilfilan D J, Bergstrom R F. A pharmacokinetic interaction between carbamazepine and olanzapine: observations on possible mechanism. *Eur J Clin Psychopharmacol* 1998; 54: 639–643.

53. De Jong J, Hoogenboom B, van Troostwijk L D, de Haan L. Interaction of olanzapine with fluvoxamine. *Psychopharmacology (Berl)* 2001; 155: 219–220.

54. Markowitz J S, DeVane C L. Suspected ciprofloxacin inhibition of olanzapine resulting in increased plasma concentration. *J Clin Psychopharmacol* 1999; 19: 288–291.

55. Callaghan J T, Cerimele B J, Kassahun K J et al. No clinically significant interaction between olanzapine and imipramine. *J Clin Psychopharmacol* 1997; 37: 971–978.

56. Nelson L A, Swartz C M. Melancholic symptoms during concurrent olanzapine and fluoxetine. *Ann Clin Psychiatry* 2000; 12: 167–170.

57. Gomberg R F. Interaction between olanzapine and haloperidol. *J Clin Psychopharmacol* 1999; 19: 272–273.

58. Perry P J, Sanger T, Beasley C. Olanzapine plasma concentrations and clinical response in acutely ill schizophrenic patients. *Clin Psychopharmacol* 1997; 17: 472–477.

59. Perry P J, Lund B C, Sanger T, Beasley C. Olanzapine plasma concentrations and clinical response: acute phase results of the North American Olanzapine Trial. *J Clin Psychopharmacol* 2001; 21: 14–20.

60. Aravagiri M, Ames D, Wirshing W C et al. Plasma level monitoring of olanzapine in patients with schizophrenia: determination by high-performance liquid chromatography with electrochemical detection. *Ther Drug Monit* 1997; 19: 307–313.

61. Kelly D L, Conley R R, Richardson C M et al. Adverse effects and laboratory parameters of high-dose olanzapine vs. clozapine in treatment-resistant schizophrenia. *Ann Clin Psychiatry* 2003; 15: 181–186.

62. Olesen O V, Linnet K. Olanzapine serum concentrations in psychiatric patients given standard doses: the influence of comedication. *Ther Drug Monit* 1999; 21: 87–90.

63. Linnet K, Olesen O V. Monitoring of serum olanzapine during antipsychotic treatment. *Ugeskr Laeger* 2000; 162: 4802–4805.

64. Rao M L, Hiemke C, Grasma der K, Bauman P. Olanzapine: pharmacology, pharmacokinetics and therapeutic drug monitoring. *Fortschr Neurol-Psychiatr* 2001; 69: 510–570.

65. Bosch R F, Baumbach A, Bitzer M, Erley C M. Intoxication with olanzapine. *Am J Psychiatry* 2000; 157: 304–305.

66. Robertson M D, McMullin M M. Olanzapine concentrations in clinical serum and postmortem blood specimens – when does therapeutic become toxic? *J Forens Sci* 2000; 42: 418–421.
67. Stephens B G, Coleman D E, Baselt R C. Olanzapine-related fatality. *J Forens Sci* 1998; 43: 1252–1253.

11

Quetiapine

Chemistry and pharmacology

Quetiapine is a dibenzothiazepine derivative which bears some structural resemblance to olanzapine and clozapine (Figure 11.1). Its full chemical name is 2-(2-[4-(dibenzo[b, f][1,4]thiazen-11-yl)piperazin-1-yl]ethoxy) ethanol. Quetiapine has also been known as ICI 204,636 and as Seroquel, which later became its trade name. Other dibenzo-thiazepines are metiapine and clothiapine, neither of which has seen widespread use despite being developed over 30 years ago.

Quetiapine is an antagonist at dopamine D_2, 5-hydroxytryptamine$_2$, adrenergic α_1 and histamine H_1 receptors but is virtually devoid of anticholinergic activity [1, 2]. Animal experiments with quetiapine were predictive of antipsychotic activity with a low risk of extrapyramidal side-effects (EPSEs) or hyperprolactinaemia [3].

Quetiapine is a weak dopamine D_2 agonist with *in vitro* activity at these receptors of a similar magnitude to clozapine [1, 4]. In humans, occupancy of striatal D_2 receptors by quetiapine is extremely low – less than 20% (12 hours post-dose) in one positron emission tomography (PET) study using ^{11}C-raclopride as the D_2 ligand [5]. However, in this study occupancy seemed to be very time-sensitive: in 2 patients occupancies of 58% and 64% were observed when quetiapine plasma levels were near their peak [5]. This fairly rapid decline in striatal D_2 occupancy has been observed in other PET studies using ^{11}C-raclopride and ^{11}C-N-methylspiperone as ligands [6, 7]. A further complication to such

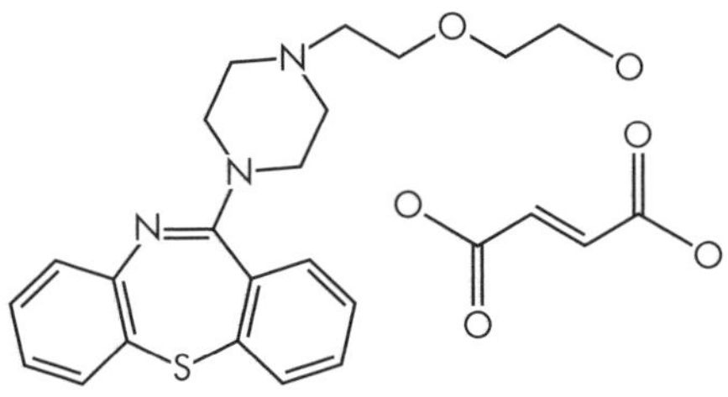

Figure 11.1   Quetiapine fumarate.

investigations is the proposed loose-binding characteristics of quetiapine. It has been suggested that occupancy studies of drugs such as quetiapine and clozapine are in the main part dependent on the relative infinities of the ligands and the drug under evaluation. Notably, it seems occupancy estimates do vary with concentration of ligand, probably because quetiapine and clozapine are so readily displaced from their binding sites [8]. This loose binding may also explain the rapid deterioration sometimes seen in patients whose treatment is abruptly stopped.

Clinical efficacy

Three placebo-controlled studies established the efficacy of quetiapine in acute relapsed schizophrenia [9–11]. In each of these studies, quetiapine showed efficacy against both positive and negative symptoms. Doses of quetiapine ranged from 75 to 750 mg/day but only doses of 150 mg/day or greater were seen to be effective. In the only fixed-dose study [10] the effect of 150 mg/day could not be distinguished from 750 mg/day. However, other studies have suggested that the optimal dose of quetiapine is above 250 mg/day [9] and perhaps above 400 mg/day [12].

Quetiapine has also been compared with conventional antipsychotics. In a 6-week comparison, chlorpromazine (mean dose 384 mg/day) and quetiapine (407 mg/day) showed similar efficacy against positive and negative symptoms [13]. More subjects responded to quetiapine (65%) than to chlorpromazine (52%). In a similar but larger study using haloperidol 8 mg/day as a comparator, quetiapine again showed equivalent efficacy [14]. Both of these active comparator studies included subjects showing acute exacerbation of chronic schizophrenia who were, for the most part, treatment-responsive. A further study compared the effects of quetiapine 600 mg/day and haloperidol 20 mg/day in patients with a history of limited or partial response to antipsychotics [15]. Overall outcome was similar for the two drugs except that more people given quetiapine responded than did those on haloperidol (52.2% versus 38.0%). This is the only published study to suggest that quetiapine has a role to play in treatment-resistant schizophrenia.

Oddly, although quetiapine has been compared with other atypical antipsychotics, none of these studies has been published in full. Brief abstracts of these trials' results suggest that quetiapine has similar efficacy to risperidone and olanzapine [4].

Quetiapine appears to be effective in first-episode schizophrenia [7], in which it appears to improve cognitive functioning [16]. Quetiapine is only licensed for twice-daily use but some studies show once-daily administration to be fairly well tolerated and effective [7, 17].

Adverse effects

Quetiapine is fairly frequently associated with sedation or somnolence (H_1 and α_1 effects), orthostatic hypertension on initiation (α_1 effect) and mild tachycardia (average increase in heart rate 7 beats/minute) [18–20]. Quetiapine is not normally associated with antimuscarinic effects such as dry mouth or constipation. In clinical trials the frequency of movement disorder and hyperprolactinaemia was indistinguishable from placebo [9–11] and significantly lower than with chlorpromazine [13] or haloperidol [14]. In practice, EPSEs and symptoms related to hyper-prolactinaemia are not observed.

Despite the observed placebo-level frequency of EPSEs quetiapine is occasionally linked to dopamine-related disorders such as neuro-malignant syndrome [21, 22] and motor tics [23]. There are very few data on quetiapine's association with tardive dyskinesia [4] but, given the near absence of acute EPSEs with the drug, its incidence is expected to be low (see Chapter 14). Weight gain is fairly often seen with quetia-pine but is usually limited. Short-term trials suggested that weight increases of more than 2 kg (more than 4 lb) might be expected [18], but a longer-term study indicated that this level of weight change was not sustained [24]. The reasons for this are not clear. In practice quetia-pine is considered to be a drug with a low potential for substantial weight gain. Quetiapine may increase the risk of diabetes mellitus, although there is some uncertainty about this (see Chapter 15).

Seizures are very rarely reported in association with quetiapine treatment [25], although the drug generally seems to have no effect on electroencephalogram parameters [26]. Risk of seizure is probably extremely small. Other rare adverse effects include lens opacities (seen only in experimental dogs given large doses; no firm association in humans), mild hypothyroidism and benign changes in hepatic enzyme function [18, 19]. Quetiapine may also prolong the cardiac QT interval to a small extent, although this is controversial. QT interval is usually cited as a corrected value (QTc) because heart rate influences the width or duration of the electrocardiogram complex. Various correction factors may be used (Bazett's, Fridericia's) to account for heart rate and, because quetiapine does alter heart rate, the method of correction is important. Quetiapine prolongs QT interval using some correction methods but does not do so with others [20]. To date, there is no evidence that quetiapine increases the risk of arrhythmia and there is said to be no relationship between quetiapine and sudden cardiac death [18].

Pharmacokinetics

Quetiapine is rapidly absorbed following oral administration and peak plasma levels are reached after only 1–2 hours [27]. Bioavailability is not known [4]. Food reduces quetiapine absorption to a small extent [28]. Quetiapine is approximately 83% bound to serum proteins and has a terminal half-life of around 7 hours [27].

Quetiapine is hepatically metabolised to several (more than 10) molecules, of which two are thought to have pharmacological activity [28]. Rate of metabolism and other pharmacokinetic parameters appear to be unaltered by ethnicity, gender, body weight, cigarette smoking, renal impairment or adolescence [27–30]. Hepatic impairment may reduce quetiapine metabolism [30].

The hepatic enzyme CYP3A4 is chiefly responsible for oxidative metabolism of quetiapine. Quetiapine does not however inhibit the activity of this or any other cytochrome enzyme [27, 31]. Quetiapine clearance can be expected to be increased by co-administration of CYP3A4-inducers such as phenytoin and carbamazepine. Thioridazine also increases quetiapine metabolism, although the mechanism involved

MANAGEMENT FOCUS 11.1

Quetiapine	
Absorption	Unknown
Elimination	Hepatic
Plasma half-life	7 hours
Hepatic cytochromes involved	CYP3A4
Hepatic cytochromes affected	None
Major interactions	Plasma levels may be reduced by carbamazepine Plasma levels increased by thioridazine
Efficacy	Good efficacy against positive and negative symptoms. No clear efficacy advantages over conventional drugs. No role in treatment-resistant schizophrenia
Adverse-effect profile/tolerability	Mild sedation, initial orthostatic hypertension, tachycardia, weight gain, possibly diabetes mellitus and QT prolongation

is not known [32]. Quetiapine metabolism may be inhibited by CYP3A4 inhibitors such as ketoconazole and erythromycin [28]. Co-administration of risperidone, imipramine, fluoxetine and cimetidine does not affect quetiapine pharmacokinetics [27, 28, 32].

Quetiapine is an effective and well-tolerated antipsychotic which is not associated with symptomatic hyperprolactinaemia and rarely causes EPSEs (Management focus 11.1).

References

1. Saller C F, Salama A I. Seroquel: biochemical profile of a potential atypical antipsychotic. *Psychopharmacology* 1993; 112: 285–292.
2. Goldstein J M, Arvanitis L A. ICI 204,636 (Seroquel): a dibenzothiazepine atypical antipsychotic. Review of preclinical pharmacology and highlights of phase II clinical trials. *CNS Drug Rev* 1995; 1: 50–73.
3. Fulton B, Goa K L. ICI-204,636: an initial appraisal of its pharmacological properties and clinical potential in the treatment of schizophrenia. *CNS Drugs* 1995; 4: 68–78.
4. Cheer S M, Wagstaff A J. Quetiapine: a review of its use in the management of schizophrenia. *CNS Drugs* 2004; 18: 173–199.
5. Kapur S, Zipursky R, Jones C *et al*. A positron emission tomography study of quetiapine in schizophrenia. *Arch Gen Psychiatry* 2000; 57: 553–559.
6. Gelvert O, Bergstrom M, Langstrom B *et al*. Time course of central nervous dopamine D_2 and 5-HT$_2$ receptor blockade and plasma drug concentrations after discontinuation of quetiapine (Seroquel) in patients with schizophrenia. *Psychopharmacology* 1998; 135: 119–126.
7. Tauscher-Wisniewski S, Kapur S, Tauscher J *et al*. Quetiapine: an effective antipsychotic in first-episode schizophrenia despite only transiently high dopamine-2 receptor blockade. *J Clin Psychiatry* 2002; 63: 992–997.
8. Seeman P, Tallerico T. Rapid release of antipsychotic drugs from dopamine D_2 receptors: an explanation for low receptor occupancy and early clinical relapse upon withdrawal of clozapine or quetiapine. *Am J Psychiatry* 1999; 156: 876–884.
9. Small J G, Hirsch S R, Arvanitis L A. Quetiapine in patients with schizophrenia: a high and low dose double-blind comparison with placebo. *Arch Gen Psychiatry* 1997; 54: 549–557.
10. Arvanitis L A, Miller B G and the Seroquel Trial 13 Study Group. Multiple fixed doses of 'Seroquel' (quetiapine) in patients with acute exacerbation of schizophrenia: a comparison with haloperidol and placebo. *Biol Psychiatry* 1997; 42: 233–246.
11. Borison R L, Arvanitis L A, Miller B G. The US Seroquel Study Group. ICI 204,636, an atypical antipsychotic: efficacy and safety in a multicenter, placebo-controlled trial in patients with schizophrenia. *J Clin Psychopharmacol* 1996; 16: 158–169.
12. Small J G, Kellams J J, Kolar M C. Relationship between quetiapine dose and efficacy. *Eur Neuropsychopharmacol* 2002; 12: 277.
13. Peuskens J, Link C G G. A comparison of quetiapine and chlorpromazine in the treatment of schizophrenia. *Acta Psychiatr Scand* 1997; 96: 265–273.

14. Copolov D L, Link C G G, Kowalcyk B. A multicentre, double-blind, randomised comparison of quetiapine (ICI 204,636, 'Seroquel') and haloperidol in schizophrenia. *Psychol Med* 2000; 30: 95–105.

15. Emsley R A, Raniwalla J, Bailey P J, Jones A M. A comparison of the effects of quetiapine ('Seroquel') and haloperidol in schizophrenic patients with a history of and a demonstrated, partial response to conventional antipsychotic treatment. *Int Clin Psychopharmacol* 2000; 15: 121–131.

16. Good K P, Kiss I, Buiteman C *et al*. Improvement in cognitive functioning in patients with first-episode psychosis during treatment with quetiapine: an interim analysis. *Br J Psychiatry* 2002; 181: S45–S49.

17. Chengappa K N, Parepally H, Brar J S *et al*. A random-assignment, double-blind, clinical trial of once- vs twice-daily administration of quetiapine fumarate in patients with schizophrenia or schizoaffective disorder: a pilot study. *Can J Psychiatry* 2003; 48: 187–194.

18. Dev V, Raniwalla J. Quetiapine: a review of its safety in the management of schizophrenia. *Drug Safety* 2000; 23: 295–307.

19. Garver D L. Review of quetiapine side effects. *J Clin Psychiatry* 2000; 61: 31–33.

20. Nasrallah H A, Tandon R. Efficacy, safety, and tolerability of quetiapine in patients with schizophrenia. *J Clin Psychiatry* 2002; 63: 12–20.

21. Sing K J, Ramaekers G M G I, Van Harten P N. Neuroleptic malignant syndrome and quetiapine. *Am J Psychiatry* 2002; 159: 149–150.

22. Stanley A K, Hunter J. Possible neuroleptic malignant syndrome with quetiapine. *Br J Psychiatry* 2000; 176: 497.

23. Huang S H, Lai T J, Tsai S J. A case report of quetiapine-related tic-like symptoms. *J Clin Psychiatry* 2002; 63: 1184–1185.

24. Brecher M, Rak I W, Melvin K, Jones A M. The long-term effect of quetiapine (Seroquel) monotherapy on weight in patients with schizophrenia. *Int J Psychiatry Clin Pract* 2000; 4: 287–291.

25. Hedges D W, Jeppson K G. New-onset seizure associated with quetiapine and olanzapine. *Ann Pharmacother* 2002; 36: 437–439.

26. Wetzel H, Szegedi A, Hain C H *et al*. Seroquel (ICI 204 636), a putative 'atypical' antipsychotic, in schizophrenia with positive symptomatology: results of an open clinical trial and changes of neuroendocrinological and EEG parameters. *Psychopharmacology* 1995; 119: 231–238.

27. DeVane C L, Nemeroff C B. Clinical pharmacokinetics of quetiapine: an atypical antipsychotic. *Clin Pharmacokinet* 2001; 40: 509–522.

28. Nemeroff C B, Kinkead B, Goldstein J. Quetiapine: preclinical studies, pharmacokinetics, drug interactions, and dosing. *J Clin Psychiatry* 2002; 63: 5–11.

29. Thyrum P T, Wing Y W, Yeh C. Single-dose pharmacokinetics of quetiapine in subjects with renal or hepatic impairment. *Prog Neuropsychopharmacol Biol Psychiatry* 2000; 24: 521–533.

30. McConville B J, Arvanitis L A, Thyrum P T *et al*. Pharmacokinetics, tolerability, and clinical effectiveness of quetiapine fumarate: an open-label trial in adolescents with psychotic disorders. *J Clin Psychiatry* 2000; 61: 252–260.

31. Grimm S W, Stams K R, Bui K. *In vitro* prediction of potential metabolic drug interactions for Seroquel. *Schizophr Res* 1997; 24: 198.

32. Potkin S G, Thyrum P T, Gustavo A *et al*. The safety and pharmacokinetics of quetiapine when co-administered with haloperidol, risperidone, or thioridazine. *J Clin Psychopharmacol* 2002; 22: 121–130.

12

Ziprasidone

Chemistry and pharmacology

Ziprasidone (formerly CP88,059-1) is a benzothiazolylpiperazine compound which is structurally unrelated to any available antipsychotic drug [1]. It is available in most western countries, with the exception of the UK. Its chemical structure is as shown in Figure 12.1.

Ziprasidone has high affinity for dopamine D_2, 5-hydroxytryptamine $(5HT)_{2a}$, $5HT_{2c}$ and $5HT_{1d}$ receptors, moderate affinity for α_1 and H_1 receptors and very low activity at α_2, $5HT_3$, $5HT_4$ and M_1 (muscarinic) receptors [1–3]. It is distinguished from other atypical antipsychotics by a somewhat different *in vitro* binding profile (see below) and by markedly different activity on some neuronal functions. It is a potent *agonist* at $5HT_{1A}$ receptors [1, 4], an activity which is thought to predict anxiolytic or antidepressant activity [2]. Ziprasidone is also an inhibitor of the neuronal reuptake of serotonin and noradrenaline (norepinephrine) (actions also predictive of antidepressant activity) with similar *in vitro* potency to amitriptyline [5]. Also, ziprasidone has potent activity at $5HT_{1d}$ receptors and so may inhibit serotonin release. This action has also been suggested as being predictive of antidepressant activity. In addition, ziprasidone has a very high $5HT_{2A}/D_2$ receptor-binding ratio [3], a property which is thought to indicate a low potential

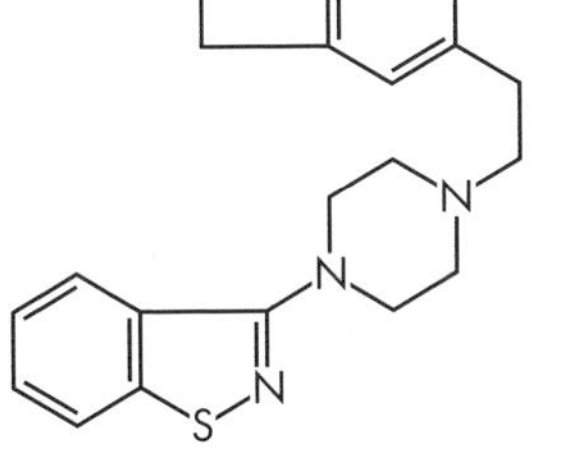

Figure 12.1 Ziprasidone – 5-(2-(4-(1,2-benzisothiazol-3-yl)piperazinyl)ethyl)-6-chloro-1,3-dihydro-2(1H)-indole-2-one.

for extrapyramidal side-effects (EPSEs). Finally, ziprasidone's effects at H_1 and $5HT_{2c}$ receptors are theoretically consistent with weight gain, although this seems not to be borne out in practice (see later).

Ziprasidone appears to be a fairly potent D_2 antagonist. Using ^{11}C-raclopride as a specific D_2 receptor ligand, a single dose of 40 mg ziprasidone produced 77% occupancy [3]. Two further positron emission tomography studies [6], using ^{11}C-raclopride as a D_2 ligand and ^{18}F-setoperone as a $5HT_2$ ligand, essentially confirmed *in vitro* observations of a high $5HT_2/D_2$ ratio of activity. A dose of 40 mg twice daily was predicted to provide $5HT_2$ occupancies of 80–90% while at the same time affording D_2 occupancies of 45–75%. This preferential effect *in vivo* on $5HT_2$ receptors is theoretically consistent with a low incidence of EPSEs, although, as previously discussed, there is debate over the importance of $5HT_2$ antagonism in EPSE frequency and severity.

Another important consideration, and one that is thought to affect changes in negative symptoms, is *in vivo* activity in the prefrontal cortex. Drugs which promote dopamine release in this area are thought to improve negative symptoms. Both ziprasidone and clozapine have been shown to promote dopamine release in rat prefrontal cortex [7]. This seems at least partly to be mediated via $5HT_{1a}$ agonism (clozapine is a partial agonist).

Animal behavioural studies indirectly indicate that ziprasidone affords potent *in vivo* D_2 blockade in rats (it suppresses amfetamine-induced hyperactivity and apomorphine-induced stereotypy) along with relatively more potent effects on $5HT_2$ receptors (it suppresses quizapine-induced head-twitching at lower doses) [8]. Ziprasidone, like risperidone, is much less potent in inducing catalepsy and decreasing spontaneous locomotion [1].

Clinical efficacy

An early dose-ranging clinical study of ziprasidone in schizophrenia and schizoaffective disorder [9] suggested that ziprasidone 160 mg/day was as effective as haloperidol 15 mg/day, as assessed using the Brief Psychiatric Rating Scale (BPRS) and Clinical Global Impression (CGI) scale. However, lower doses of ziprasidone (4, 10, 40 mg/day) were shown not to be effective.

Another 28-day study [10] in a similar patient group compared two doses of ziprasidone (40 and 120 mg/day) with placebo. Only the higher dose of ziprasidone was shown to be superior (BPRS, CGI) to placebo. Differences in the treatment of negative symptoms assessed by the Scale for Assessment of Negative Symptoms were not significant, but ziprasidone 120 mg/day did appear effective in treating depressive symptoms (evaluated using BPRS anxiety–depression cluster – a rather crude measure).

Another trial compared two doses of ziprasidone (80 and 160 mg/day) with placebo over 6 weeks [11]. Both doses of ziprasidone were found to be superior to placebo overall (BPRS, CGI) and in the treatment of negative symptoms (Positive and Negative Symptom Scale (PANSS) negative subscale). Results for the higher dose of ziprasidone were numerically but not significantly superior to the lower dose. Ziprasidone was statistically superior to placebo on most measures after only 7 days. Using the Montgomery–Asberg Depression Rating Scale, ziprasidone 160 mg/day was found to be effective in treating depressive symptoms in those patients showing clinically significant depression at baseline.

Ziprasidone is also more effective than placebo in schizoaffective disorder [12]. Compared with other atypical drugs, ziprasidone fares well. It is at least as effective as olanzapine in schizophrenia, with fewer metabolic effects [13], and at least as effective as risperidone with advantages in terms of extrapyramidal effects and hyperprolactinaemia [14].

The longest ziprasidone trial completed to date is a 52-week evaluation of three doses (40, 80, 160 mg/day) of ziprasidone compared with placebo in stable patients with moderate to severe negative symptoms [15]. All doses of ziprasidone were superior to placebo in relapse prevention, in the treatment of negative symptoms (PANSS) from 16 weeks onwards, and in improving overall functioning (Global Assessment of Functioning [16]) (at 52 weeks). There were no differences between active treatments.

A medium-term active comparator study has also been published [17]. Ziprasidone (80–160 mg/day) was compared with haloperidol (5–15 mg/day) over 28 weeks. Few clear differences between treatments were uncovered, but there were significantly more negative symptom 'responders' in the ziprasidone group (48%) than in the haloperidol group. (Response was defined as a 20% fall in PANSS negative subscale.) Both treatments were broadly effective.

Only one small study has evaluated the effect of ziprasidone on cognitive function [18] – a known deficit in schizophrenia, partly improved by drugs such as clozapine. In this study, subject numbers were too small to allow meaningful conclusions to be drawn, but more recent analyses confirm ziprasidone's positive effects on cognition [19]. Ziprasidone is probably effective in mania, with one large study showing clear superiority for ziprasidone over placebo [20].

The pharmacology of ziprasidone is predictive of anxiolytic activity in humans. One study compared oral doses of ziprasidone 20 mg, diazepam 10 mg and placebo given 3 hours before dental surgery [21]. Using a self-evaluation scale for anxiety, diazepam was superior to placebo and ziprasidone at 1 hour, but ziprasidone (not diazepam) was superior to placebo at 3 hours. Investigator ratings confirmed the rapid onset of activity with diazepam with a slower onset for ziprasidone. Diazepam was significantly more sedative than ziprasidone, but ziprasidone could not be distinguished from placebo in this respect. Ziprasidone is now fairly widely used as an augmenting agent in anxiety spectrum disorders [22].

Ziprasidone is unusual amongst atypical antipsychotics in that a parenteral preparation of it has been evaluated in the treatment of acute psychosis. A simple intramuscular (IM) injection of ziprasidone mesylate has been investigated in a number of studies.

A large ($n = 132$) open study [23] compared IM ziprasidone (10 mg initially, then 5–20 mg q.d.s.) with IM haloperidol (2.5 mg initially, then 5–10 mg q.d.s.) given for 3 days followed by 4 days of oral therapy. Ziprasidone produced a numerically greater reduction in scores for BPRS and CGI by the last day of IM therapy, but no significant differences in efficacy were noted.

IM antipsychotics are often used in the short term to control problem behaviours as much as for their antipsychotic activity. However, rating scales such as the BPRS and Nurses' Observation Scale for Inpatient Evaluation [24] are not specific measures of behavioural disturbance and are thus not ideal measures of acute response to IM antipsychotics. In addition, many rating scales are readily affected by the degree of sedation provoked by IM antipsychotics. Sedation, particularly if severe, is usually not desirable or necessary, but is essentially a byproduct of the use of many drugs.

The Behavioural Activity Rating Scale (BARS) [25] was developed to evaluate changes in behavioural activity. This is a seven-point scale, ranging from profound sedation (1 = 'difficult or unable to rouse') through to profound agitation (7 = 'violent, requires restraint'). The aim of treatment is to reduce scores to a level of 4 (= 'quiet and awake (normal level of activity)') or just below. Several studies using BARS have shown IM ziprasidone to be at least as effective as IM haloperidol [26].

Other published data suggest IM ziprasidone is broadly effective in psychotic agitation [27] and specifically effective in exacerbations of schizophrenia [28]. Data from 483 patients and healthy volunteers have been used to estimate population pharmacokinetics of IM ziprasidone [29]. Plasma levels obtained appear to be dose-related and affected in a linear fashion by body weight and body surface area. Age, gender, renal function and liver function seem not to affect to an important extent the pharmacokinetic parameters of IM ziprasidone.

Population pharmacokinetics indicate that peak plasma levels are obtained within 30 minutes of injection of IM ziprasidone, with steady state being reached within 1 day following repeated administration [30]. Measured plasma half-life ranges from 3.8 hours on the first day of treatment to 10.4 hours on the third day, although accumulation does not occur [30].

Adverse effects and tolerability

Acute EPSEs (parkinsonism, dystonia and akathisia) are commonly seen with typical antipsychotics and obviously have an important effect on patient morbidity. These adverse effects are decidedly unpleasant and may of course adversely contribute to negative symptom severity.

With ziprasidone, EPSEs are rarely seen. For example, an early study [9] showed that the higher dose of ziprasidone (160 mg/day) did not worsen EPSEs from baseline (Simpson–Angus Scale) and overall anticholinergic use was lower with ziprasidone (15%) than with haloperidol (53%). A later study revealed a similar low liability for EPSEs: only 3 of 47 patients receiving ziprasidone 120 mg/day reported EPSEs (although 9 received benztropine) and neither dose of ziprasidone differed significantly from placebo on measures for EPSEs [10]. Other studies of oral ziprasidone do not differ markedly in their observations of EPSEs. Acute EPSEs are also uncommon with parenteral ziprasidone.

Only the year-long study [15] is valuable in assessing ziprasidone's influence on tardive dyskinesia (TD). While emergence of TD was not evaluated, all doses of ziprasidone showed either small reductions in Abnormal Involuntary Movement Scale scores from baseline, or no change. Similar results were reported in the 28-week study [17]. This simply provides a signal that ziprasidone may be associated with low rates of TD. However, TD has been reported to occur in a few cases as a result of exposure only to ziprasidone [31].

Ziprasidone has not been associated in any study with adverse effects related to hyperprolactinaemia. In studies where prolactin levels were measured, ziprasidone either did not elevate prolactin [15] or did so minimally and transiently only at 160 mg/day [9]. In practice, symptoms of hyperprolactinaemia are only very rarely reported [32].

Symptomatic hypotension (e.g. involving dizziness or postural effects) is a dose-limiting adverse effect of many antipsychotics, both typical and atypical. Some atypicals (e.g. risperidone and quetiapine) require careful dose titration, largely because of the risk of hypotensive episodes. Ziprasidone has only moderate activity at α_1 receptors and hypotension is only infrequently reported. Postural hypotension was apparently not observed in the year-long study of ziprasidone [15]. With IM ziprasidone, postural hypotension is also rarely observed.

Ziprasidone appears not to cause clinically important weight gain. Pooled analysis [33] indicates that mean weight gain with ziprasidone at 10 weeks is 0.04 kg and a systematic review [34] suggested that ziprasidone has the lowest risk of inducing weight gain compared with other atypicals.

These results rather go against expectations for a drug with H_1 and $5HT_{2c}$ activity, but are nevertheless compelling.

Ziprasidone appears not to be firmly associated with any bio-chemical or haematological abnormalities. Very infrequently, changes in liver function tests [10, 19] are observed, with results returning to normal on discontinuation. Many studies reported no laboratory abnormalities and, overall, withdrawals caused by such abnormalities were at a very low rate. In practice, liver function tests are rarely changed.

Changes in blood counts have not been associated with ziprasidone. No symptomatic laboratory abnormalities of any type have been observed.

Ziprasidone has a moderate effect on the cardiac QT interval [35], although this seems not to affect its safety: arrhythmia has not been reported [36]. This effect on QT interval has lead to ziprasidone not being marketed in some countries, including the UK. However, the absence of any effect on weight and plasma lipids [37] may mean that ziprasidone is associated with a relatively low cardiovascular risk [36].

Pharmacokinetics

Ziprasidone shows a plasma half-life of 3.2–10 hours in healthy males [3, 38]. Time to peak plasma level is quite long, at around 4–5 hours, but steady-state levels are attained after 1–3 days [38, 39] and peak-to-trough concentration ratio ranges from 2 to 5 in twice-daily dosing [38]. The results of a small-scale trial in elderly and young healthy volunteers

[39] suggest that gender and age have a clinically unimportant effect on ziprasidone pharmacokinetics.

Administration of food, however, has an important effect on ziprasidone absorption. Absorption is doubled by the presence of food, providing an absolute bioavailability of around 60% [1, 3]. These observations have led to the establishment of a standard twice-daily-with-food dosing regimen in males and females of all ages.

In humans, ziprasidone is metabolised to ziprasidone sulphoxide and then to ziprasidone sulphone – reactions which appear to be catalysed by the hepatic cytochrome CYP3A4 [40]. Other enzymes appear not to be involved in ziprasidone metabolism. Ziprasidone does not inhibit cytochromes CYP3A4 or CYP2D6 [40] to a clinically important extent and so pharmacokinetic interactions involving these enzymes are not expected.

Neither renal impairment [41] nor mild to moderate hepatic impairment [42] appears to have an important effect on ziprasidone pharmacokinetics. Hepatic impairment does extend plasma half-life by around 2 hours [42], but renal impairment of any severity has essentially no effect on elimination half-life. This is to be expected, since only 1% of a given dose of ziprasidone is excreted unchanged.

Ziprasidone metabolites appear to have little clinical activity [43], although this needs confirming in human *in vivo* studies.

As already mentioned, ziprasidone appears not to inhibit the activity of CYP3A4 or CYP2D6. Ziprasidone is therefore unlikely to affect plasma levels of co-administered drugs metabolised by these enzymes. Prospective studies have also shown that ziprasidone does not affect to an important degree the pharmacokinetics of co-administered combined oral contraceptives [44] or to any degree the clearance of lithium [45].

Of course, another major consideration is the potential effects of co-administered drugs on the pharmacokinetic profile of ziprasidone. Inducers (e.g. carbamazepine) or inhibitors (e.g. norfluoxetine, nefazodone) of CYP3A4 might be expected to alter the metabolism of ziprasidone. However, the CYP3A4 inhibitor cimetidine had only a marginal effect on ziprasidone pharmacokinetics in a prospective trial (half-life increased from 3.81 to 3.93 hours: not significant) [46]. This might indicate that ziprasidone has alternative routes of metabolism when CYP3A4 is inhibited. In the same trial [46], the co-administration of the antacid Maalox delayed time to peak plasma level by 3 hours (8 versus 11 hours).

In vitro experiments [40] indicate that ziprasidone has little effect on the cytochromes CYP1A2, CYP2C9 or CYP2C19. If these properties are reflected in humans, interactions involving these enzymes are unlikely.

Ziprasidone is very highly (> 99%) protein-bound and this may lead to pharmacokinetic interactions, albeit short-lived ones, with other highly bound drugs. The occurrence and importance of this type of reaction are yet to be clearly determined.

Ziprasidone is an effective and well-tolerated antipsychotic with anxiolytic and antidepressant actions. Regulatory concerns over potential for cardiac toxicity have probably limited clinical use (Management focus 12.1).

MANAGEMENT FOCUS 12.1

Ziprasidone	
Absorption	60% when taken with food
Elimination	Hepatic
Plasma half-life	3.2–10 hours
Hepatic cytochromes involved	CYP3A4
Hepatic cytochromes affected	None
Major interactions	CYP3A4-inducers (e.g. carbamazepine) may reduce plasma levels; inhibitors (e.g. fluoxetine, ketoconazole) may increase levels. Antacids reduce rate of absorption
Efficacy	As effective as conventional drugs. Efficacy against positive and negative symptoms. Has anxiolytic, antidepressant and antimanic properties. No role in refractory schizophrenia
Adverse-effect profile/tolerability	Mildly sedative, rarely causes extrapyramidal side-effects or tardive dyskinesia. QT prolongation occurs but is of unknown clinical significance

References

1. Tandon R, Harrigan E, Zorn S H. Ziprasidone: a novel antipsychotic with unique pharmacology and therapeutic potential. *J Serotonin Res* 1997; 4: 159–177.
2. Leysen J E, Janssen P M F, Heylen L *et al.* Receptor interactions of new antipsychotics: relation to pharmacodynamic and clinical effects. *Int J Psychiatry Clin Pract* 1998; 2: S3–S17.

3. Davis R, Markham A. Ziprasidone. *CNS Drugs* 1997; 8: 153–159.

4. Sprouse J S, Reynolds L S, Braselton J P *et al.* Comparison of the novel antipsychotic ziprasidone with clozapine and olanzapine: inhibition of dorsal raphe cell firing and the role of 5-HT$_{1A}$ receptor activation. *Neuropsychopharmacology* 1999; 21: 622–631.

5. Gunn K P, Zorn S H, Heym J. Ziprasidone: preclinical profile of a new antipsychotic agent. *Schizophr Res* 1997; 24: 204.

6. Miceli J J, Gunn K P, Rubin R H *et al.* 5HT$_2$ and D$_2$ receptor occupancy of ziprasidone in healthy volunteers. *Schizophr Res* 1997; 24: 178.

7. Lu Y, Zorn S H, Schmidt A W, Rollema H. Comparison of the novel antipsychotic ziprasidone with clozapine and olanzapine: effects on dopamine release in rat prefrontal cortex and dorsolateral striatum. *Soc Neurosci Abstr* 1997; 23: 1031.

8. Seeger T F, Seymour P A, Schmidt A W *et al.* Ziprasidone (CP-88,059): a new antipsychotic with combined dopamine and serotonin receptor antagonist activity. *J Pharmacol Exp Ther* 1995; 275: 101–113.

9. Goff D C, Posever T, Herz L *et al.* An exploratory haloperidol-controlled dose-finding study of ziprasidone in hospitalized patients with schizophrenia or schizoaffective disorder. *J Clin Psychopharmacol* 1998; 18: 296–304.

10. Keck P Jr, Buffenstein A, Ferguson J *et al.* Ziprasidone 40 and 120 mg/day in the acute exacerbation of schizophrenia and schizoaffective disorder: a 4-week placebo-controlled trial. *Psychopharmacology (Berl)* 1998; 140: 173–184.

11. Daniel D G, Zimbroff D L, Potkin S G *et al.* Ziprasidone 80 mg/day and 160 mg/day in the acute exacerbation of schizophrenia and schizoaffective disorder: a 6-week placebo-controlled trial. Ziprasidone Study Group. *Neuropsychopharmacology* 1999; 20: 491–505.

12. Keck P E Jr, Reeves K R, Harrigan E P *et al.* Ziprasidone in the short-term treatment of patients with schizoaffective disorder: results from two double-blind, placebo-controlled, multicenter studies. *J Clin Psychopharmacol* 2001; 21: 27–35.

13. Simpson G M, Glick I D, Weiden P J *et al.* Randomized, controlled, double-blind multicenter comparison of the efficacy and tolerability of ziprasidone and olanzapine in acutely ill inpatients with schizophrenia or schizoaffective disorder. *Am J Psychiatry* 2004; 161: 1837–1847.

14. Addington D E, Pantelis C, Dineen M *et al.* Efficacy and tolerability of ziprasidone versus risperidone in patients with acute exacerbation of schizophrenia or schizoaffective disorder: an 8-week, double-blind, multicenter trial. *J Clin Psychiatry* 2004; 65: 1624–1633.

15. Arato M, O'Connor R, Meltzer H Y *et al.* A 1-year, double-blind, placebo-controlled trial of ziprasidone 40, 80 and 160 mg/day in chronic schizophrenia: the Ziprasidone Extended Use in Schizophrenia (ZEUS) study. *Int Clin Psychopharmacol* 2002; 17: 207–215.

16. American Psychiatric Association. *Diagnostic and Statistical Manual of Mental Disorders*, 3rd edn revised (DSM-III-R). Washington, DC: American Psychiatric Association, 1987.

17. Hirsch S R, Kissling W, Bauml J *et al.* A 28-week comparison of ziprasidone and haloperidol in outpatients with stable schizophrenia. *J Clin Psychiatry* 2002; 63: 516–523.

18. Hagger C, Mitchell D, Wise A L, Schulz S C. Effects of oral ziprasidone and risperidone on cognitive functioning in patients with schizophrenia or

schizoaffective disorder: preliminary data. *Eur Neuropsychopharmacol* 1997; 7 (suppl. 2): S219.

19. Keck P E Jr, Versiani M, Potkin S *et al.* Ziprasidone in the treatment of acute bipolar mania: a three-week, placebo-controlled, double-blind, randomized trial. *Am J Psychiatry* 2003; 160: 741–748.

20. Harvey P D. Ziprasidone and cognition: the evolving story. *J Clin Psychiatry* 2003; 64: 33–39.

21. Wilner K D, Anziano R J, Johnson A C *et al.* The anxiolytic effect of the novel antipsychotic ziprasidone compared with diazepam in subjects anxious before dental surgery. *J Clin Psychopharmacol* 2002; 22: 206–210.

22. Crane D L. Ziprasidone as an augmenting agent in the treatment of anxiety-spectrum disorders. *CNS Spectr* 2005; 10: 176–179.

23. Brook S, Lucey J V, Gunn K P. Intramuscular ziprasidone compared with intramuscular haloperidol in the treatment of acute psychosis. Ziprasidone I.M. Study Group. *J Clin Psychiatry* 2000; 61: 933–941.

24. Honigfeld G, Gillis R D, Klett C J. Nurses' Observation Scale for Inpatient Evaluation: a new scale for measuring improvement in chronic schizophrenia. *J Clin Psychol* 1965; 21: 65–71.

25. Swift R H, Harrigan E P, Cappelleri J C *et al.* Validation of the Behavioural Activity Rating Scale (BARS): a novel measure of activity in agitated patients. *J Psychiatr Res* 2002; 36: 87–95.

26. Daniel D G, Zimbroff D L, Swift R H, Harrigan E P. The tolerability of intramuscular ziprasidone and haloperidol treatment and the transition to oral therapy. *Int Clin Psychopharmacol* 2004; 19: 9–15.

27. Preval H, Klotz S G, Southard R, Francis A. Rapid-acting IM ziprasidone in a psychiatric emergency service: a naturalistic study. *Gen Hosp Psychiatry* 2005; 27: 140–144.

28. Brook S, Walden J, Benattia I *et al.* Ziprasidone and haloperidol in the treatment of acute exacerbation of schizophrenia and schizoaffective disorder: comparison of intramuscular and oral formulations in a 6-week, randomized, blinded-assessment study. *Psychopharmacology (Berl)* 2005; 178: 514–523.

29. Tensfeldt T, Miceli J, Kuye O. The population pharmacokinetics of intramuscular ziprasidone in healthy volunteers and schizophrenic patients. *Eur Neuropsychopharmacol* 1998; 8 (suppl. 2): S239.

30. Miceli J, Preskorn S, Wilner K. Pharmacokinetics of intramuscular ziprasidone in schizophrenic patients: population pharmacokinetic modelling. *Eur Psychiatry* 1998; 13: S304–S305.

31. Keck M E, Muller M B, Binder E *et al.* Ziprasidone-related tardive dyskinesia. *Am J Psychiatry* 2004; 161: 175–176.

32. Ramadan M, Khan A, Preskorn S. D_2-blockade and possible ziprasidone-induced galactorrhea. *Int Clin Psychopharmacol* 2005; 20: 113–114.

33. Allison D B, Mentore J L, Moonseong H. Antipsychotic-induced weight gain: a comprehensive research synthesis. *Am J Psychiatry* 1999; 156: 1686–1696.

34. Taylor D M, McAskill R. Atypical antipsychotics and weight gain – a systematic review. *Acta Psychiatr Scand* 2000; 101: 416–432.

35. Harrigan E P, Miceli J J, Anziano R *et al.* A randomized evaluation of the effects of six antipsychotic agents on QTc, in the absence and presence of metabolic inhibition. *J Clin Psychopharmacol* 2004; 24: 62–69.

36. Taylor D. Ziprasidone in the management of schizophrenia: the QT interval issue in context. *CNS Drugs* 2003; 17: 423–430.

37. Kingsbury S J, Fayek M, Trufasiu D *et al.* The apparent effects of ziprasidone on plasma lipids and glucose. *J Clin Psychiatry* 2001; 65: 347–349.

38. Miceli J J, Hansen R A, Johnson A C, Wilner K D. Single and multiple dose pharmacokinetics of ziprasidone in healthy males. *Pharm Res* 1995; 12 (suppl. 9): S392.

39. Tensfeldt T G, Wilner K D, Baris B *et al.* Steady-state pharmacokinetics of ziprasidone in healthy elderly and young volunteers. *Biol Psychiatry* 1997; 42: 42S.

40. Prakash C, Kamel A, Cui D *et al.* Identification of the major human liver cytochrome P450 isoform(s) responsible for the formation of the primary metabolics of ziprasidone and prediction of possible drug interactions. *Br J Clin Pharmacol* 2000; 49: 35S–42S.

41. Aweeka F, Jayesekara D, Horton M *et al.* The pharmacokinetics of ziprasidone in subjects with normal and impaired renal function. *Br J Clin Pharmacol* 2000; 49: 27S–33S.

42. Everson G, Lasseter K C, Anderson K E *et al.* The pharmacokinetics of ziprasidone in subjects with normal and impaired hepatic function. *Br J Clin Pharmacol* 2000; 49: 21S–26S.

43. Honigfeld G, Gillis R D, Klett C J. NOSIE-30: a treatment-sensitive ward behaviour scale. *Psychol Rep* 1966; 19: 180–182.

44. Muirhead G J, Holt P R, Oliver S *et al.* The effect of ziprasidone on steady-state pharmacokinetics of a combined oral contraceptive. *Eur Neuropsychopharmacol* 1996; 6 (suppl. 3): 38.

45. Apseloff G, Mullet D, Wilner K D *et al.* The effects of ziprasidone on steady-state lithium levels and renal clearance of lithium. *Br J Clin Pharmacol* 2000; 49: 61S–64S.

46. Wilner K D, Hansen R A, Folger C J, Geoffroy P P. The pharmacokinetics of ziprasidone in healthy volunteers treated with cimetidine or antacid. *Br J Clin Pharmacol* 2000; 49: 57S–60S.

13

Aripiprazole

Chemistry and pharmacology

Aripiprazole is a partial agonist at dopamine D_2 receptors [1] (Figure 13.1). This means that aripiprazole binds to D_2 receptors and prevents attachment of endogenous dopamine but at the same time stimulates D_2 receptors (but to a lesser degree than by dopamine itself). When aripiprazole occupies 100% of D_2 receptors the overall effect is to reduce receptor-mediated activity by around 70% [1].

The action of partial agonists is to some extent dependent upon the prevailing intensity of neurotransmitter function. For example, where there is a high level of dopamine production, aripiprazole will act so as to reduce net dopaminergic transmission. Where dopamine activity is low, aripiprazole is likely to act so as to increase dopaminergic transmission. This ability to act as both an antagonist and agonist has theoretical importance because, of course, positive symptoms are thought to be related to excess dopamine and negative symptoms to dopaminergic hypofunction.

Aripiprazole's observed effects on D_2 receptors predict an atypical profile. This is because, as we have seen, typical adverse effects tend to occur only when substantially more than 70% of receptors are blocked by dopamine antagonists [2]. Aripiprazole seems unable to exert an effect functionally equivalent to this level of dopamine receptor antagonism and so typical adverse effects would not be expected. In fact, a positron emission tomography study has confirmed that aripiprazole

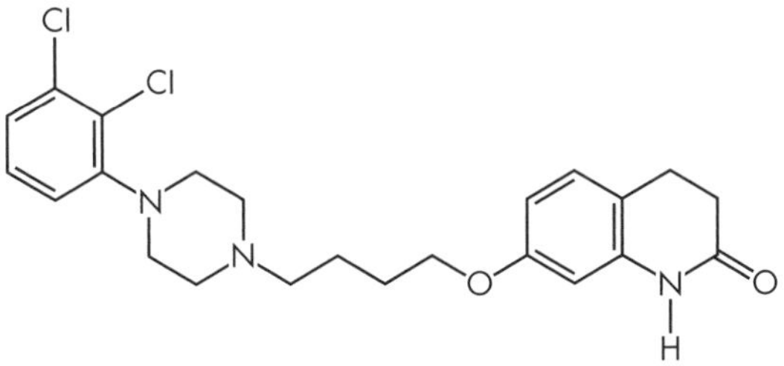

Figure 13.1 Aripiprazole: 7-[4-[4-(2,3-dichlorophenyl)-1-piperazinyl] butoxy]-3,4-dihydrocarbostyril.

does not cause extrapyramidal side-effects (EPSEs), even when 95% of D_2 and D_3 receptors are occupied by the drug [3]. In addition, animal experiments with aripiprazole support the prediction of atypicality in humans [4, 5].

Aripiprazole is a partial agonist at 5-hydroxytryptamine $(5HT)_{1A}$ receptors, an action that may protect against dopamine-medicated adverse effects and provide anxiolytic activity [6]. It is also a potent antagonist at $5HT_{2A}$ receptors and so may, in theory, offer protection against EPSEs. Aripiprazole has only moderate activity at α_1-adrenergic receptors, histamine H_1 receptors and serotonin $5HT_{2C}$ receptors. So, a low incidence of (respectively) postural hypotension, sedation and weight gain might be predicted [7].

Clinical efficacy

Aripiprazole has been compared with placebo, haloperidol, risperidone and olanzapine in clinical trials lasting from 4 weeks to 1 year.

In an early 4-week study, researchers [8] in a double-blind randomised design compared aripiprazole (5–30 mg/day) with haloperidol (5–30 mg/day) and placebo in acute schizophrenic relapse. Both active treatments were more effective than placebo and similarly effective. Aripiprazole appeared to be no more likely than placebo to induce EPSEs, weight gain, electrocardiogram (ECG) changes or increase in serum prolactin. In a similar but rather larger study [8], fixed doses of aripiprazole (2, 10 and 30 mg/day) were compared with haloperidol 10 mg/day and placebo. All three doses of aripiprazole appeared to be effective but 30 mg/day was clearly the most effective dose. Interestingly, although the study was not powered to reveal differences in negative symptom change, aripiprazole was significantly superior to placebo in this respect. Again, aripiprazole appeared not to be associated with EPSEs, raised prolactin, weight gain or ECG changes. In neither of these two preliminary studies was aripiprazole clearly associated with sedation, insomnia or anticholinergic effects. Combining the results of these studies suggests that even the most frequent apparent adverse effects of aripiprazole occurred at the same frequency as with placebo.

In a third 4-week randomised study [9], two doses of aripiprazole (15 and 30 mg/day) were compared with haloperidol 10 mg/day and placebo. All active treatments were equally effective and significantly more effective than placebo. Neither dose of aripiprazole was associated with EPSEs, increased prolactin, weight gain or QTc changes.

A fourth 4-week study compared aripiprazole with risperidone in 404 inpatients with acute schizophrenic relapse [10]. Patients were randomly assigned placebo, aripiprazole 20 mg/day, aripiprazole 30 mg/day, or risperidone 6 mg/day. All active treatments were similarly more effective than placebo against positive and negative symptoms. Adverse effects generally did not differ between subject groups except that weight gain was numerically more common in all the active treatment groups and risperidone-treated patients alone showed increases in prolactin ($P < 0.001$) and QTc (statistical analysis not given in every case). None of the active treatments appeared to differ from placebo in observed rates of other adverse effects.

Two long-term comparative studies have also been conducted. Pigott and colleagues [11] compared aripiprazole with placebo over 26 weeks in stable patients with chronic schizophrenia. At trial endpoint, 34% of patients given aripiprazole 15 mg/day had relapsed compared with 57% of those receiving placebo (a statistically and clinically significant difference). Adverse effects reported with aripiprazole did not differ significantly from those reported with placebo. In the second long-term study researchers compared aripiprazole 30 mg/day with haloperidol 10 mg/day in 1294 patients with acute relapse of chronic schizophrenia [12]. Response rate was higher for those receiving aripiprazole (62.5% showed 20% decrease in severity of illness score) than for those receiving haloperidol (54.9% showed 20% decrease; $P = 0.006$). Aripiprazole was also superior in treating negative symptoms and depressive symptoms and in terms of patients remaining on treatment after 1 year (40% versus 27%; $P < 0.01$). The overall incidence of EPSEs was lower in aripiprazole subjects ($P < 0.001$) but the incidence of weight gain and QTc changes was not significantly different between groups.

Two further clinical studies have contributed to the understanding of aripiprazole's therapeutic and adverse effects. In an 8-week study of patients stabilised on typical or atypical antipsychotics, Casey et al. [13] showed that the method of switching to aripiprazole had no effect on outcome. Adverse and therapeutic effects were similar for patients abruptly switched and those cross-titrated. Other workers [14] examined the effects of moderate and high doses of aripiprazole (30–90 mg/day) given for 15 days. Plasma levels of aripiprazole increased proportionately with dose but this did not give rise to significant weight gain or to prolactin or ECG changes. Only akathisia and tachycardia were more common in patients given 90 mg/day. All patients retained a stable clinical profile.

Aripiprazole also seems to be effective in acute mania, as demonstrated in a randomised, placebo-controlled trial in 262 patients with acute bipolar mania [15]. Subjects received either aripiprazole 30 mg/day or placebo for 3 weeks. Aripiprazole was found to be significantly more effective than placebo (40% of subjects responded; 19% with placebo: $P < 0.01$). Aripiprazole and placebo did not differ in respect to the incidence of acute movement disorder or weight gain and discontinuations due to adverse effects were the same (11% of each group). However, some adverse effects were relatively more common in those receiving aripiprazole. These included nausea (23% versus 10%), dyspepsia (22% versus 10%), vomiting (16% versus 5%) and somnolence (20% versus 5%). Akathisia was also more common in those receiving aripiprazole (11% versus 2%). All of these apparent adverse effects appeared to resolve after the first week of treatment.

Adverse effects

Aripiprazole is generally well tolerated and has shown discontinuation rates from trials similar to those with placebo. Aripiprazole appears not to be associated with acute dystonia, parkinsonism [16] or elevated plasma prolactin [17].

From clinical trial data alone it is difficult to determine exactly what adverse effects aripiprazole might be expected to produce (incidence rates were numerically similar to placebo in many trials and, in some others, no statistical analysis is presented). Aripiprazole may be associated with headache, nausea, vomiting, constipation, dyspepsia, orthostatic hypotension, tachycardia, insomnia, somnolence, akathisia and tremor. These effects are seen early in treatment and occur in less than a third of patients. Generally, although not always, the frequency with which adverse effects occurred was similar to that seen with placebo [16]. In practice, both nausea and agitation are problematic in the first week or so of treatment. Aripiprazole has a very low incidence of weight gain and appears not to affect serum cholesterol [18]. ECG changes appear not to occur [19].

Pharmacokinetics

Two studies ($n = 9$ and $n = 11$) have examined acute and chronic pharmacokinetics of aripiprazole in healthy males [20]. Peak plasma levels were obtained 3.4–6.8 hours after single oral administration (2.8–3.8 hours after 14 days) and plasma half-life ranged from 47.4 to 68.1 hours (mean 60 hours). Oral bioavailability is around 90%. Steady-state plasma levels were obtained after 14 days of continual dosing and plasma levels obtained were linearly related to dose given (5–30 mg/day). No clinically significant changes in physical examinations, clinical chemistry or ECG results were observed.

Aripiprazole is metabolised by multiple enzymatic pathways involving the cytochromes CYP2D6 and CYP3A4. Inhibitors of either of these enzymes (quinidine and ketoconazole, respectively) are known to decrease clearance of aripiprazole and to increase aripiprazole plasma levels. Aripiprazole is not metabolised by CYP1A1, CYP1A2, CYP2C9 or CYP2C9 *in vitro* and so interactions with inducers or inhibitors of these enzymes are not expected. Aripiprazole seems not to affect the metabolism of drugs metabolised by CYP2D6, CYP2C9, CYP2C19 and CYP3A4. Aripiprazole appears not to interact with warfarin or omeprazole. In addition, aripiprazole appears not to interact in any way with lithium or valproate [21].

Hepatic impairment seems not to have clinically important effects on aripiprazole metabolism [22] and aripiprazole pharmacokinetics appears not to be influenced by age or gender [23, 24]. Dose adjustment is not necessary in renal impairment: the pharmacokinetics does not differ between healthy volunteers and subjects with severe renal failure. Absorption of aripiprazole appears not to be influenced by food or gastric pH.

Aripiprazole is effective and well tolerated with few adverse effects normally associated with antipsychotics. More trivial adverse effects such as nausea may compromise tolerability in early treatment (Management focus 13.1).

MANAGEMENT FOCUS 13.1

Aripiprazole	
Absorption	Around 90%
Elimination	Hepatic
Plasma half-life	47–68 hours
Hepatic cytochromes involved	CYP2D6 and CYP3A4
Hepatic cytochromes affected	None
Major interactions	Aripiprazole plasma levels increased by inhibitors of CYP2D6 and CYP3A4
Efficacy	Good efficacy in relapsed schizophrenia and mania. Effective as prophylaxis in schizophrenia. Limited evidence for role in refractory schizophrenia

continued overleaf

Management focus (continued)

Adverse-effect profile/tolerability	Early adverse effects include nausea, vomiting, agitation and insomnia. These can be treated with suitable drugs and are, in any case, usually short-lived. Prolactin-neutral; extrapyramidal side-effects are rare. Does not seem to cause weight gain or diabetes

References

1. Burris K D, Molski T F, Xu C *et al.* Aripiprazole, a novel antipsychotic, is a high-affinity partial agonist at human dopamine D_2 receptors. *J Pharmacol Exp Ther* 2002; 302: 381–389.
2. Tauscher J, Küfferle B, Asenbaum S *et al.* Striatal dopamine-2 receptor occupancy as measured with [^{123}I] iodobenzamide and SPECT predicted the occurrence of EPS in patients treated with atypical antipsychotics and haloperidol. *J Psychopharmacol* 2002; 162: 42–49.
3. Yokoi F, Grunder G, Biziere K *et al.* Dopamine D_2 and D_3 receptor occupancy in normal humans treated with the antipsychotic drug aripiprazole (OPC 14597): a study using positron emission tomography and [^{11}C] raclopride. *Neuropsychopharmacology* 2002; 27: 248–259.
4. Hirose T, Uwahodo Y, Yamada S *et al.* Efficacy and favourable side-effect profile of aripiprazole determined in rates with apomorphine-induced stereotypy, catalepsy, and ptosis induction. *Int J Neuropsychopharmacol* 2000; 3: S131.
5. Nakai S, Hirose T, Uwahodo Y *et al.* Diminished catalepsy and dopamine metabolism distinguish aripiprazole from haloperidol or risperidone. *Eur J Pharmacol* 2003; 472: 89–97.
6. Jordan S, Koprivica V, Chen R *et al.* The antipsychotic aripiprazole is a potent, partial agonist at the human 5-HT$_{1A}$ receptor. *Eur J Pharm* 2002; 441: 137–140.
7. McQuade R, Burris K D, Jordan S *et al.* Aripiprazole: a dopamine–serotonin system stabiliser. *Int J Neuropsychopharmacol* 2002; 5: S176.
8. Marder S R, McQuade R D, Stock E *et al.* Aripiprazole in the treatment of schizophrenia: safety and tolerability in short-term, placebo-controlled trials. *Schizophr Res* 2003; 61: 123–136.
9. Kane J M, Carson W H, Saha A R *et al.* Efficacy and safety of aripiprazole and haloperidol versus placebo in patients with schizophrenia and schizoaffective disorder. *J Clin Psychiatry* 2002; 63: 763–771.
10. Potkin S G, Saha A R, Kujawa M J *et al.* Aripiprazole, an antipsychotic with a novel mechanism of action, and risperidone vs placebo in patients with schizophrenia and schizoaffective disorder. *Arch Gen Psychiatry* 2003; 60: 681–690.

11. Pigott T A, Carson W H, Saha A R *et al*. Aripiprazole for the prevention of relapse in stabilized patients with chronic schizophrenia: a placebo-controlled 26-week study. *J Clin Psychiatry* 2003; 64: 1048–1056.

12. Kasper S, Lerman M N, McQuade R D *et al*. Efficacy and safety of aripiprazole vs haloperidol for long-term maintenance treatment following acute relapse of schizophrenia. *Int J Neuropsychopharmacol* 2003; 6: 325–337.

13. Casey D E, Carson W H, Saha A R *et al*. Switching patients to aripiprazole from other antipsychotic agents: a multicenter randomized study. *Psychopharmacology (Berl)* 2003; 66: 391–399.

14. Saha A R, Ali M W, Ingenito G *et al*. Safety and tolerability of aripiprazole at doses higher than 30 mg. *Int J Neuropsychopharmacol* 2002; 5: S185.

15. Keck P E Jr, Marcus R, Tourkodimitris S *et al*. A placebo-controlled, double-blind study of the efficacy and safety of aripiprazole in patients with acute bipolar mania. *Am J Psychiatry* 2003; 160: 1651–1658.

16. Stock E, Marder S R, Saha A R *et al*. Safety and tolerability meta-analysis of aripiprazole in schizophrenia. *Int J Neuropsychopharmacol* 2002; 5: S185.

17. Carson W, Saha A R, Iwamoto T *et al*. Meta-analysis of prolactin effects with aripiprazole. *Int J Neuropsychopharmacol* 2002; 5: S186.

18. McQuade R D, Stock E, Marcus R *et al*. A comparison of weight change during treatment with olanzapine or aripiprazole: results from a randomized, double-blind study. *J Clin Psychiatry* 2004; 18: 47–56.

19. Stock E, Saha A, Brunell R *et al*. Meta-analysis of cardiac safety with aripiprazole. Poster presented at American Psychiatric Association 155th Annual Meeting, May 18–23 2002, Philadelphia, PA, USA.

20. Mallikaarjun S, Salazar D E, Bramer S L. Pharmacokinetics, tolerability, and safety of aripiprazole following multiple oral dosing in normal healthy volunteers. *J Clin Pharmacol* 2004; 44: 179–187.

21. Citrome L, Josiassen R, Bark N *et al*. Pharmacokinetics of aripiprazole and concomitant lithium and valproate. *J Clin Pharmacol* 2005; 45: 89–93.

22. Mallikaarjun S, Tammara B K, Salazar D E *et al*. The effects of hepatic impairment on the pharmacokinetics of aripiprazole. *Clin Pharmacol Ther* 2002; 71: TPII-91.

23. Mallikaarjun S, Ali M W, Salazar D E *et al*. The effects of age and gender on the pharmacokinetics of aripiprazole. *Clin Pharmacol Ther* 2002; 71: TPII-90.

24. Blumer J L, Findling R, Kauffman R *et al*. Pharmacokinetics, tolerability and safety of aripiprazole in children and adolescents with conduct disorder. *Clin Pharmacol Ther* 2002; 71: MPI-3.

14

Antipsychotic-induced movement disorders

Movement disorders, usually described as extrapyramidal side-effects (EPSEs), are a well-recognised companion to psychotic illnesses and schizophrenia. Many lay people, in fact, may have in mind a picture of a typical case of madness or schizophrenia which features a shuffling gait, tremor, slowness of movement and a mask-like face. Others may think of a person who is agitated, restless, unable to keep still and who continually paces up and down in a state of unremitting fretfulness. Both examples serve as lay archetypes of madness but both, as we know, owe more to the drug treatment of schizophrenia than to the condition itself.

In this chapter we examine the main types of movement disorder seen in schizophrenia treated with antipsychotic drugs.

Akathisia

Akathisia is a word of Greek origin meaning 'not to sit'. It is a syndrome closely related to what is now known as restless-leg syndrome and which has been recognised for many centuries. Akathisia was first used as a diagnosis in the early twentieth century, when it was considered variously as psychogenic and organic in origin [1]. It remained a rare diagnosis until neuroleptics were introduced in the 1950s, after which akathisia became increasingly recognised as a major and common adverse effect of antipsychotic treatment.

Akathisia is rather poorly defined and imprecisely distinguished from similar disorders, both psychological and physical. Its symptoms are conventionally divided into two: the subjective and the objective. Subjective symptoms (those the patient feels and reports) include a sensation of inner restlessness, a compulsion to keep moving, unease, anxiety, discomfort, dysphoria, nervousness and apprehension [2]. Patients with akathisia are usually physically unable to maintain a fixed posture when seated or standing but may be able to lie still and sleep. Objective symptoms (those detected by an observer) usually involve the lower limbs and feet. Patients may be observed repeating purposeless movements, such as rocking from foot to foot, pacing, crossing legs, toe-tapping and face-rubbing. A coarse tremor and myoclonic jerks may also be observed [3]. All of these movements seem to be voluntary responses to inner agitation but patients usually have only limited control over them. Most authorities define akathisia as a condition consisting of *both* subjective and objective features and, in so doing, render akathisia both a psychological and physical condition.

The prevalence of akathisia varies according to definitions used and, perhaps more markedly, with antipsychotics prescribed. Studies with conventional drugs reported prevalences ranging from 8 to 68% compared with a range of 0–81% with early atypicals (including the now-withdrawn remoxipride) [4]. Generally, akathisia is much less commonly seen with newer atypical antipsychotics than with conventional drugs, and is rare indeed with clozapine and quetiapine in particular [5]. Akathisia is also seen with other dopamine antagonists such as metoclopramide and amoxapine and, more rarely, with calcium antagonists, selective serotonin reuptake inhibitors (although this is debated) and anticonvulsants [4].

The pathological basis for drug-induced akathisia has never been precisely defined but the condition seems inexorably to be associated with central, postsynaptic dopamine D_2 antagonism [2]. Support for this contention comes from the observation that all potent D_2 antagonists cause akathisia, that dopamine-depleting agents such as reserpine and tetrabenazine cause akathisia, that most drugs that cause akathisia have inhibitory effects of some sort on dopamine systems, and that destruction of mesolimbic dopamine pathways in animals leads to a reduction of attentional capacity. Most studies suggest that the emergence of akathisia is dose-related and is usually the first of the EPSEs to appear in dose-ranging trials (i.e. doses that cause akathisia may not cause other movement disorders but other movement disorders infrequently occur without some akathisia).

Akathisia usually begins to appear within days of beginning an antipsychotic or increasing its dose. The condition frequently becomes chronic if untreated and may worsen and persist on drug withdrawal. Akathisia may then exist in acute, chronic and tardive forms [6]. The prevalence of tardive akathisia is not known but is an extremely unpleasant and difficult-to-treat condition when it occurs [7].

Indeed, the torturous nature of akathisia is readily appreciated and several authors have linked the dysphoric nature of akathisia to suicide and violence. Akathisia caused by high-potency antipsychotics such as haloperidol seems to provoke (in some) suicidal, homicidal and violent behaviour. Data supporting this association came mainly from case reports but more compelling reports have described akathisia-associated violence in controlled, blind trials [8, 9]. More recently, suicidality has been linked to the subjective aspect of akathisia [10]; it appears that the unpleasant sensations of akathisia provoke suicidal behaviour, as might be expected.

Effective treatment of akathisia (or its minimisation) is a clinical imperative if we are to avoid harming the patient and precipitating treatment discontinuation or refusal. In most cases, akathisia resolves on switching to an atypical antipsychotic. However, some patients show a good clinical response to conventional drugs and it may be desirable for this treatment to continue. Some patients experience akathisia on atypical drugs such as risperidone, olanzapine, amisulpride and aripiprazole [5, 11]. Remedial measures may thus be necessary in an important number of patients.

The mainstay of treatment for drug-induced akathisia is propranolol, which has been shown in a double-blind trial to be moderately effective in reducing both subjective and objective features of akathisia [12]. Doses range from 30 to 80 mg/day and response seems to occur in the first few days of treatment. Other beta-blockers are not effective, either because they do not enter the brain in sufficient concentration or because they lack propranolol's unique action on serotonin systems [13]. Antagonism of 5-hydroxytryptamine ($5HT$)$_2$ receptors is thought to increase dopaminergic activity and so may oppose dopamine-blocker effects, leading to akathisia. There is support for the use of a variety of $5HT_2$ antagonists in akathisia: mianserin, ritanserin, cyproheptadine and trazodone all seem to reduce symptoms levels without worsening psychosis [14, 15]. Other potential treatments include anticholinergic drugs (which seem to be effective where akathisia occurs alongside parkinsonism [16]) and benzodiazepines such as lorazepam and clonazepam [13]. In practice, akathisia is usually treated initially with propranolol and then with further agents added.

Pseudoparkinsonism

Many antipsychotic drugs, particularly conventional or typical drugs, give rise to symptoms similar to those seen in Parkinson's disease (pseudoparkinsonism: Adverse-effects focus 14.1). The prevalence of pseudoparkinsonism in those receiving conventional antipsychotics may reach 75% [17]. In those taking atypical drugs the prevalence of such symptoms is generally less than 20% [5]. Interestingly, the baseline for pseudoparkinsonism in schizophrenia is not zero: symptoms of Parkinson's disease are seen in around 15% of never-medicated people with

Pseudoparkinsonism – symptoms	
Bradykinesia	Slow movements (shuffling gait, soft/weak voice)
Hypokinesia	The absence of purposeful movements (reduced arm swing, masklike expression)
Tremor	Usually coarse or fine hand tremor seen when arms outstretched or when writing Less commonly – pill-rolling tremor
Rigidity	Increased tone of limb and trunk muscles Often results in ratchet-like restriction of movement (cogwheel rigidity). Less often, sustained restriction to movement (leadpipe rigidity)
Others	Drooling, constipation

schizophrenia [18]. Symptoms of drug-induced parkinsonism usually emerge within a few days of starting the offending drug but may emerge slowly over several weeks.

Pseudoparkinsonism seems to occur as a result of a disturbance of the relative balance of influences of dopamine and acetylcholine in the basal ganglia. In Parkinson's disease dopaminergic neurones are destroyed and cholinergic innervation is allowed relative prominence. In antipsychotic-related pseudoparkinsonism, dopaminergic transmission is blocked by the antagonistic actions of these drugs at postsynaptic dopamine receptors. Symptoms seem only to occur when an antipsychotic drug blocks more than 78% of striatal D_2 receptors [19] and the threshold for these effects is higher than that for therapeutic effects [20], even with conventional drugs [21, 22]. However, for conventional drugs it is very difficult to separate therapeutic and parkinsonism effects in everyday practice [23].

Drug-induced pseudoparkinsonism is usually treated today by switching to a drug less likely to be associated with such effects. Parkinson-like effects are almost never seen with clozapine, quetiapine, olanzapine, ziprasidone and aripiprazole and only seen with higher doses of risperidone and amisulpride [5, 24]. Where switching antipsychotics is not practical for any reason, anticholinergic drugs such as trihexyphenidyl and procyclidine are effective, but not without their own adverse effects [16]. With most drugs, deleterious effects on memory and other cognitive functions are apparent [25, 26] and peripheral effects troublesome.

Dystonia

Dystonia is a sustained or repeated involuntary muscular contraction which results in abnormal posture or movement (Adverse-effects focus 14.2). Dystonia is often painful and debilitating. It is seen in up to 40% of those receiving conventional antipsychotics, and is particularly prevalent in younger patients [27]. Other risk factors include male gender and prior dystonic reaction [28]. Symptoms usually appear within a few days of starting treatment (or increasing dose) and typically involve muscles of the head and neck.

ADVERSE-EFFECTS FOCUS 14.2

Acute dystonia – symptoms and syndromes [16, 28, 29]	
Blepharospasm	Sustained eye closure
Oculogyric spasm	Rotation of eyes, leaving only sclera visible
Grimacing	
Trismus	Contraction of masticatory muscles
Dysarthria	Speaking difficulties
Dysphagia	Swallowing difficulties
Torticollis	Dystonic distortion of the neck
Opisthotonos	Distortion of neck, head and trunk
Abnormal gait	

Drug-induced dystonia seems to have the same biochemical cause as other extrapyramidal symptoms: dopamine receptor blockade. Acute dystonia is most common with high-potency conventional neuroleptics, less common with low-potency conventional drugs and not at all common with atypical agents [28]. Dystonia usually presents suddenly and requires urgent treatment, especially where spasm of laryngeal muscles induces stridor. Intramuscular treatment with procyclidine or biperiden is usually given and is effective [16, 28].

Neuroleptic malignant syndrome

Neuroleptic malignant syndrome (NMS) is a rare but serious disorder closely related to, or part of, the drug-induced extrapyramidal syndrome (Adverse-effects focus 14.3). Precise diagnosis is difficult because many of the symptoms of NMS occur in patients treated with antipsychotics and because there is overlap in symptom spectrum between NMS and other conditions such as heat exhaustion, lethal catatonia, malignant hyperthermia and anticholinergic intoxication. Estimates of the incidence of NMS are, as a consequence, rather approximate and range from 0.02% to 3.23%/year of studied population [30]. Symptoms usually develop insidiously and sometimes abruptly after initiating an antipsychotic or after a dose increase.

The main signs and symptoms are fever (> 38°C), rigidity and elevated creatine phosphokinase concentration. Full diagnostic criteria are given in Adverse-effects focus 14.3. Other signs and symptoms may include sialorrhoea, myoclonus, various dystonias, metabolic acidosis, respiratory arrest, raised liver enzymes and electrolyte disturbances [30–32].

ADVERSE-EFFECTS FOCUS 14.3

NMS – diagnostic criteria [30, 31]	
Major manifestations	Fever
	Rigidity
	Raised creatine phosphokinase
Minor manifestations	Tachycardia
	Abnormal blood pressure
	Tachypnoea
	Altered consciousness
	Diaphoresis
	Leukocytosis

Three major, or two major and four minor, manifestations suggest high probability of NMS. Raised creatine phosphokinase is often considered to be diagnostic of NMS but is actually found in 10% of patients on antipsychotics [33].

Established risk factors for the development of NMS include mental retardation and psychomotor agitation [34], recent antipsychotic dose increase or use of intramuscular medication [30, 34], genetic polymorphism of the D_2 receptor gene [35] and withdrawal of anticholinergic agents [36]. NMS seems to occur with all types of antipsychotics, including atypicals [37], although incidence is probably highest with high-potency conventional drugs such as haloperidol [30, 31]. Close monitoring of temperature, creatine phosphokinase and autonomic function may decrease the incidence of full-blown NMS [38].

The pathogenesis of NMS remains uncertain but almost certainly involves dopamine receptor antagonism [39]. Dopamine blockade in the hypothalamus impairs thermoregulation and can lead to hyperthermia; dopamine blockade in the corpus striatum may induce muscular rigidity and thermogenesis. These two actions may combine in predisposed individuals to produce the syndrome of NMS.

Treatment of NMS is not normally attempted in psychiatric institutions but usually involves supportive measures such as cooling and the use of dopamine agonists (e.g. bromocriptine) and muscle relaxants (dantrolene) [30].

Tardive dyskinesia

Tardive dyskinesias (TDs) are late-appearing involuntary movements occurring in people receiving long-term dopamine antagonist drugs. Symptoms typically begin with worm-like (vermicular) movements of the tongue and develop to include more severe involuntary movements of muscles of the face, neck, trunk and limbs (Adverse-effects focus 14.4). Once developed, symptoms may be partly or sometimes wholly irreversible.

Symptoms of TD tend to vary in severity and, particularly in the early stages, may disappear completely for days at a time. Diagnosis of TD is therefore partly dependent on the presence of persistent symptoms

ADVERSE-EFFECTS FOCUS 14.4

TD – symptoms [40]	
General	
Choreiform movements	Rapid, jerking muscular contractions
Athetoid movements	Slow, sinuous muscular spasm
Rhythmic movements	Repeated, purposeless movements (stereotypies)

, atypi......
tency conventi.... **examples**
....ion (fly-catching)
; of temperature, creatine p....
decrease the incidence of full-blow...

(usually for at least 4 weeks). In clinical trials, TD is only usually diagnosed when dyskinesias are observed to be present at two assessment visits at least 2 weeks apart. Symptoms may be complicated by tardive dystonia (commonly neck and trunk dystonias) [41] and tardive akathisia, with symptoms similar to acute akathisia but which do not remit on antipsychotic withdrawal [42] (Case study 14.1).

CASE STUDY 14.1

Diane

Diane was a 32-year-old Caucasian woman with a 15-year history of schizophrenia. She was first treated with haloperidol 6 mg/day. After 2 years' treatment she developed subtle vermicular tongue movements which were first noticed by her mother. Haloperidol was gradually withdrawn but 6 weeks later Diane relapsed and was readmitted to hospital. Risperidone was started and continued at a dose of 4 mg/day.

Over the next several years Diane remained psychologically well but developed increasingly severe involuntary movements. She now suffers from frequent facial dystonias, retrocollis and opisthotonus. Arm movements are erratic and only partially controlled and walking is unsteady. On walking, involuntary arm movements increase in severity and frequency. At rest, Diane exhibits 'piano-playing' finger dyskinesias. Voluntary control over limb movements is severely impaired.

These symptoms are severely debilitating and socially embarrassing. Diane has recently been switched to quetiapine 600 mg/day with no effect. She has previously tried tetrabenazine, vitamin E and propranolol, with limited and short-lived success. She currently takes clonazepam 1 mg every other day, which is effective to some extent. Clozapine is being considered.

Various evaluations of the incidence and prevalence of TD have been made but all should be considered approximate given the variable nature of TD and difficulties with precise diagnosis. Incidence estimates range from 3.9 to 8.7%/year (higher still in elderly patients) and prevalence estimates from 17.5 to 35.1% of populations treated with antipsychotic drugs [40]. Part of the variation in estimates is a result of different antipsychotics used but, as with other movement disorders, the background rate is not zero. For example, a controversial study of never-medicated Indian schizophrenia patients found a prevalence of apparent TD of 38% [43].

Since the definition of TD includes in it the chronic use of antipsychotics, it is not surprising that long-term dopamine blockade has been put forward as the pharmacological basis for TD. It is hypothesised that long-term dopamine blockade in the striatum leads to dopamine receptor hypersensitivity, which in turn leads to a loss of voluntary control over various aspects of motor movement [40, 44]. Support for this theory comes from the observations that symptoms of TD seem only to occur with chronic administration of dopamine antagonists, that dopamine agonists given acutely cause similar dyskinesia, that withdrawing antipsychotics can worsen or reveal TD and that TD may be improved by increasing the dose of antipsychotic.

This dopamine hypersensitivity theory may be rather optimistically simplistic and even just plain optimistic: some postmortem studies show no increase in striatal dopamine receptor numbers in patients dying with TD [45].

Other theories have been developed to explain the development of TD. Gamma-aminobutyric acid (GABA) function seems to be both inhibited and induced by dopamine enervation – the action depending on the location in the brain. TD may result from decreased GABA function in the striatum induced by dopamine hypersensitivity in inhibitory dopaminergic neurones [44]. It has also been postulated that TD arises as a result of overstimulation of encephalin receptors [46] or because of high activity of free radicals [47]. All of the hypotheses so far mentioned inform treatment options for TD, as we will see later.

One of the peculiarities of TD is that it seems not to occur in some people despite decades of antipsychotic consumption whilst in others it appears after only a few months. Several predisposing factors for TD have been noted. These include age, male gender, being non-white, prominent negative symptoms, poor response at first episode, early EPSEs (particularly tremor and akathisia), longer duration of antipsychotic treatment and larger cumulative antipsychotic dose [48–52]. There is also a possibility of a genetic susceptibility to TD but studies of dopamine receptor genes [53], hepatic cytochrome enzymes [54] and monoamine-metabolising enzymes [55] have proved negative. Smoking is also a risk factor for TD and may result from nicotine's ability to increase synthesis and release of dopamine in the striatum [56].

With the introduction of atypical antipsychotics in the 1990s it was hoped that the wider use of these drugs would bring about an overall reduction in the incidence and prevalence of TD. On a superficial level this hope has been realised: on the author's first visit to a psychiatric institution in 1986, he met 6 or 7 residents in the smoking room of the hospital (an anteroom to the hospital entrance!), each of whom had pronounced orofacial dyskinesias; today, it is unusual to see psychiatric inpatients with such pronounced TD. To some extent, trial data bear out this impression of a reduction in the prevalence of TD, or at least a lower incidence of TD with newer antipsychotics. Possibly the most robust analysis of this phenomenon is a comparison of emergent TD with olanzapine and haloperidol in patients enrolled into randomised controlled trials of the drugs. After around 9 months' treatment, 9 of 197 (4.6%) haloperidol-treated subjects had persistent TD as compared with only 7 of 707 (1.0%) olanzapine-treated patients [57]. An extension of this study suggested the yearly incidence of TD to be 7.45% with haloperidol and 0.52% with olanzapine [58]. A more recent review of 11 1-year studies of emergent TD found the mean yearly incidence in adults to be 0.8% compared with an incidence of 5.4% with haloperidol [59]. In older patients with borderline TD at onset of treatment, 6-month incidence was found to be 24.1% with atypicals and 44.9% with conventional drugs [60].

Thus two outcomes are revealed by these studies – atypicals have a lower risk of TD but they may also cause or worsen TD, albeit at a low rate. It is noteworthy that TD does occur in people taking atypical drugs, even weak dopamine antagonists such as clozapine [61] and quetiapine [62]. However it is worth considering what the background rate of TD might be in such patients if untreated. It is possible that the low incidence of TD with atypical drugs represents active suppression of 'natural-occurring' movement disorders in schizophrenia.

A further consideration is the question of dose. We know that cumulative dose of conventional drugs is a risk factor for TD. This suggests that low-dose conventional drugs may also, like atypicals, be less often associated with TD. However, this seems not to be the case: first-episode subjects given an average of 1.68 mg/day haloperidol showed a first-year incidence of TD of 12.3% [63]; older patients given an average of 68.4 mg/day chlorpromazine equivalent were found to have a 3-month incidence of 5.9% [64].

The treatment of TD is to some extent based on theories of the pathogenesis of the condition and partly on serendipitous findings. A good example of the latter route is the use of clozapine. Prior to its widespread use it was usual to treat TD with successive increases in antipsychotic dose which supposedly brought about increased striatal dopamine blockade. Switching to clozapine, a weak dopamine antagonist, essentially reduces striatal blockade but is effective in reducing symptoms of TD in up to half of those treated [65]. This seems to be a true direct therapeutic effect since symptoms gradually subside after starting clozapine and do not re-emerge on continuation. The pharmacological basis for this effect is unclear but may have its origins in clozapine's relatively stronger binding at D_1 receptors [66]. Other weak dopamine (D_2) antagonists such as quetiapine seem to have similar therapeutic effects [67, 68], as do other atypical drugs [69, 70]. Other treatments for TD are listed in Management focus 14.1.

MANAGEMENT FOCUS 14.1

Treatment of TD		
Treatment	**Action**	**Reference**
Tetrabenazine	Dopamine antagonist Inhibits dopamine release	71, 72
Vitamin E	Free radical scavenger (uncertain efficacy)	73, 74
Benzodiazepines	GABA agonists (uncertain efficacy but widely used)	75
Naltrexone	Opiate (encephalin) antagonist	76

Assessing movement disorder severity

A number of rating scales are available for evaluating drug-induced movement disorders. The most commonly used are the Barnes Akathisia Scale [77], the Simpson–Angus Scale (for parkinsonism and dystonia) [78] and the Abnormal Involuntary Movement Scale for tardive dyskinesia [79]. These scales are included in the Appendix.

References

1. Sachdev P. The development of the concept of akathisia: a historical overview. *Schizophr Res* 1995; 16: 33–45.
2. Sachdev P, Loneragan C. The present status of akathisia. *J Nerv Ment Dis* 1991; 179: 381–391.
3. Braude W M, Barnes T R E, Gore S M. Clinical characteristics of akathisia. *Br J Psychiatry* 1983; 143: 139–150.
4. Sachdev P. The epidemiology of drug-induced akathisia: part I. Acute akathisia. *Schizophr Bull* 1995; 21: 431–449.
5. Tarsy D, Baldessarini R J, Tarazi F I. Effects of newer antipsychotics on extrapyramidal function. *CNS Drugs* 2002; 16: 23–45.
6. Sachdev P. The epidemiology of drug-induced akathisia: part II. Chronic, tardive and withdrawal states. *Schizophr Bull* 1995; 21: 451–461.

7. Dufresne R L, Wagner R L. Antipsychotic-withdrawal akathisia versus antipsychotic-induced akathisia. *J Clin Psychiatry* 1988; 49: 435–438.

8. Shaw E D, Mann J J, Weiden P J *et al.* A case of suicidal and homicidal ideation and akathisia in a double-blind neuroleptic crossover study. *J Clin Psychopharmacol* 1986; 6: 196–197.

9. Herrera J N, Sramek J J, Costa J F *et al.* High potency neuroleptics and violence in schizophrenia. *J Nerv Ment Dis* 1988; 176: 558–561.

10. Atbaşağlu E C, Schultz S K, Andreasen N C. The relationship of akathisia with suicidality and depersonalization among patients with schizophrenia. *J Neuropsychiatry Clin Neurosci* 2001; 13: 336–341.

11. Taylor D M. Aripiprazole: a review of its pharmacology and clinical use. *Int J Clin Pract* 2003; 57: 49–54.

12. Adler L, Angrist B, Peselow E *et al.* A controlled assessment of propranolol in the treatment of neuroleptic-induced akathisia. *Br J Psychiatry* 1986; 149: 42–45.

13. Miller C H, Fleischhacker W W. Managing antipsychotic-induced acute and chronic akathisia. *Drug Safety* 2000; 22: 73–81.

14. Maidment I. Use of serotonin antagonists in the treatment of neuroleptic-induced akathisia. *Psychiatr Bull* 2000; 24: 348–351.

15. Stryjer R, Strous R D, Bar F *et al.* Treatment of neuroleptic-induced akathisia with the 5-HT_{2A} antagonist trazodone. *Clin Neuropharmacol* 2003; 26: 137–141.

16. Barnes T R E, McPhillips M A. Antipsychotic-induced extrapyramidal symptoms. *CNS Drugs* 1996; 6: 315–330.

17. Mamo D C, Sweet R A, Keshavan M S. Managing antipsychotic-induced parkinsonism. *Drug Safety* 1999; 20: 269–275.

18. McCreadie R G, Srinivasan T N, Padmavati R, Thara R. Extrapyramidal symptoms in unmedicated schizophrenia. *J Psychiatr Res* 2005; 39: 261–266.

19. Kapur S, Zipursky R, Remington G. Relationship between dopamine D_2 occupancy, clinical response, and side effects: a double-blind PET study of first-episode schizophrenia. *Am J Psychiatry* 2000; 157: 514–520.

20. Farde L, Nordstrom L, Wiesel F A *et al.* Positron emission tomographic analysis of central D_1 and D_2 dopamine receptor occupancy in patients treated with classical neuroleptics and clozapine. Relation to extrapyramidal side effects. *Arch Gen Psychiatry* 1992; 49: 538–544.

21. McEvoy J P, Hogarty G E, Steingard S. Optimal dose of neuroleptic in acute schizophrenia. A controlled study of the neuroleptic threshold and higher haloperidol dose. *Arch Gen Psychiatry* 1991; 48: 739–745.

22. Kapur S, Remington G, Jones C *et al.* High levels of dopamine D_2 receptor occupancy with low-dose haloperidol treatment: a PET study. *Am J Psychiatry* 1996; 153: 948–950.

23. Taylor D. Low dose typical antipsychotics – a brief evaluation. *Psychiatr Bull* 2000; 24: 465–468.

24. Taylor D, Paton C, Kerwin R. *The Maudsley Prescribing Guidelines,* 8th edn. London, UK: Taylor and Francis, 2005.

25. Zachariah E, Kumari V, Galea A *et al.* Effects of oral procyclidine administration on cognitive functions in healthy volunteers. *J Clin Psychopharmacol* 2002; 22: 224–226.

26. Sharma T, Galea A, Zachariah E *et al.* Effects of 10 mg and 15 mg oral procyclidine on critical flicker fusion threshold and cardiac functioning in healthy human subjects. *J Psychopharmacol* 2002; 16: 181–185.

27. Addonizio G, Alexopoulos G S. Drug-induced dystonia in young and elderly patients. *Am J Psychiatry* 1988; 145: 869–871.

28. Van Harten P N, Hoek H W, Kahn R S. Acute dystonia induced by drug treatment. *BMJ* 1999; 319: 623–626.

29. Gervin M, Barnes T R E. Assessment of drug-related movement disorders in schizophrenia. *Adv Psychiatr Treat* 2000; 6: 332–343.

30. Caroff S N, Mann S C. Neuroleptic malignant syndrome. *Med Clin North Am* 1993; 77: 185–202.

31. Adnet P, Lestavel P, Krivosic-Horber R. Neuroleptic malignant syndrome. *Br J Anaesth* 2000; 85: 129–135.

32. Levenson J L. Neuroleptic malignant syndrome. *Am J Psychiatry* 1985; 142: 1137–1145.

33. Meltzer H Y, Cola P A, Parsa M. Marked elevations of serum creatine kinase activity associated with antipsychotic drug treatment. *Neuropsychopharmacology* 1996; 15: 395–405.

34. Viejo L F, Morales V, Punal P *et al.* Risk factors in neuroleptic malignant syndrome. A case–control study. *Acta Psychiatr Scand* 2003; 107: 45–49.

35. Suzuki A, Kondo T, Otani K *et al.* Association of the Taql A polymorphism of the dopamine D_2 receptor gene with predisposition to neuroleptic malignant syndrome. *Am J Psychiatry* 2001; 158: 1714–1716.

36. Spivak B, Gonen N, Mester R *et al.* Neuroleptic malignant syndrome associated with abrupt withdrawal of anticholinergic agents. *Int Clin Psychopharmacol* 1996; 11: 207–209.

37. Hasan S, Buckley P. Novel antipsychotics and the new neuroleptic malignant syndrome: a review and critique. *Am J Psychiatry* 1998; 155: 1113–1116.

38. Shiloh R, Valevski A, Bodinger L *et al.* Precautionary measures reduce risk of definite neuroleptic malignant syndrome in newly typical neuroleptic-treated schizophrenia inpatients. *Int Clin Psychopharmacol* 2003; 18: 147–179.

39. Henderson V W, Wooten G F. Neuroleptic malignant syndrome: a pathogenetic role for dopamine receptor blockade? *Neurology* 1981; 31: 132–137.

40. Sachdev P S. The current status of tardive dyskinesia. *Aust NZ J Psychiatry* 2000; 34: 355–369.

41. Burke R E, Fahn S, Jankovic J *et al.* Tardive dystonia late-onset and persistent dystonia caused by antipsychotic drugs. *Neurology* 1982; 32: 1335–1346.

42. Sachdev P. The epidemiology of drug-induced akathisia: part II chronic, tardive, and withdrawal akathisias. *Schizophr Bull* 1995; 21: 451–461.

43. McCreadie R G, Thara R, Kamath S *et al.* Abnormal movements in never-medicated Indian patients with schizophrenia. *Br J Psychiatry* 1996; 168: 221–226.

44. Casey D E. Tardive dyskinesia: pathophysiology and animal models. *J Clin Psychiatry* 2000; 61: 5–9.

45. Kornhuber J, Riederer P, Reynolds G P *et al.* ^{3}H-Spiperdone binding sites in post-mortem brains from schizophrenic patients: relationship to neuroleptic drug treatment, abnormal movements, and positive symptoms. *J Neural Transm* 1989; 75: 1–10.

46. Iakimovski A F, Bobrova I V. Neuromotor dyskinesia occurring during repeated injections of enkephalins into the rat striatum. *Patol Fiziol Eksp Ter* 1991; 6: 20–21.

47. Lohr J B, Kuczenski R, Bracha H S *et al*. Increased indices of free radical activity in the cerebrospinal fluid of patients with tardive dyskinesia. *Biol Psychiatry* 1990; 28: 535–539.

48. Morgenstern H, Glazer W M. Identifying risk factors for tardive dyskinesia among long-term outpatients maintained with neuroleptic medications. *Arch Gen Psychiatry* 1993; 50: 723–733.

49. Muscettola G, Barbato G, Pampallona S *et al*. Extrapyramidal syndromes in neuroleptic-treated patients: prevalence, risk factors, and association with tardive dyskinesia. *J Clin Pyschopharmacol* 1999; 19: 203–207.

50. Chakos M H, Alvir J M J, Woerner M G *et al*. Incidence and correlates of tardive dyskinesia in first episode of schizophrenia. *Arch Gen Psychiatry* 1996; 53: 313–319.

51. Caligiuri M P, Lacro J P, Rockwell E *et al*. Incidence and risk factors for severe tardive dyskinesia in older patients. *Br J Psychiatry* 1997; 171: 148–153.

52. Van O S J, Fahy T, Jones P *et al*. Tardive dyskinesia: who is at risk? *Acta Psychiatr Scand* 1997; 96: 206–216.

53. Lattuada E, Cavallaro R, Serretti A *et al*. Tardive dyskinesia and DRD2, DRD3, DRD4, 5-HT2A variants in schizophrenia: an association study with repeated assessment. *Int J Neuropsychopharmacol* 2004; 7: 489–493.

54. Tiwari A K, Deshpande S N, Rao A R *et al*. Genetic susceptibility to tardive dyskinesia in chronic schizophrenia subjects: I. Association of CYP1A2 gene polymorphism. *Pharmacogenomics* 2005; 5: 60–69.

55. Matsumoto C, Shinkai T, Jori H *et al*. Polymorphisms of dopamine degradation enzyme (COMT and MAO) genes and tardive dyskinesia in patients with schizophrenia. *Psychiatry Res* 2004; 127: 1–7.

56. Yassa R, Lal S, Korpassy A, Ally J. Nicotine exposure and tardive dyskinesia. *Biol Psychiatry* 1987; 22: 67–72.

57. Tollefson G D, Beasley C M Jr, Tamura R N *et al*. Blind, controlled, long-term study of the comparative incidence of treatment-emergent tardive dyskinesia with olanzapine or haloperidol. *Am J Psychiatry* 1997; 154: 1248–1254.

58. Beasley C M, Dellva M A, Tamura R N *et al*. Randomised double-blind comparison of the incidence of tardive dyskinesia in patients with schizophrenia during long-term treatment with olanzapine or haloperidol. *Br J Psychiatry* 1999; 174: 23–30.

59. Correll C U, Leucht S, Kane J M. Lower risk for tardive dyskinesia associated with second-generation antipsychotics: a systematic review of 1 year studies. *Am J Psychiatry* 2004; 161: 414–425.

60. Dolder C R, Jeste D V. Incidence of tardive dyskinesia with typical versus atypical antipsychotics in very high risk patients. *Biol Psychiatry* 2003; 53: 1142–1145.

61. Gafoor R, Brophy J. Three case reports of emergent dyskinesia with clozapine. *Eur Psychiatry* 2003; 18: 260–261.

62. Sharma V. Treatment-emergent tardive dyskinesia with quetiapine in mood disorders. *J Clin Psychiatry* 2003; 23: 415–417.

63. Oosthuizen P P, Emsley R A, Maritz J S *et al.* Incidence of tardive dyskinesia in first-episode psychosis patients treated with low-dose haloperidol. *J Clin Psychiatry* 2003; 64: 1075–1080.

64. Jeste D V, Lacro J P, Palmer B *et al.* Incidence of tardive dyskinesia in early stages of low-dose treatment with typical neuroleptics in older patients. *Am J Psychiatry* 1999; 156: 309–311.

65. Lieberman J A, Saltz B L, Johns C A *et al.* The effects of clozapine on tardive dyskinesia. *Br J Psychiatry* 1991; 158: 503–510.

66. Rosengarten H, Schweitzer J W, Friedhoff A J. Selective dopamine D_2 receptor reduction enhances a D_1 mediated oral dyskinesia in rate. *Life Sci* 1986; 39: 29–35.

67. Emsley R, Turner H J, Schronen J *et al.* A single-blind, randomised trial comparing quetiapine and haloperidol in the treatment of tardive dyskinesia. *J Clin Psychiatry* 2004; 65: 696–701.

68. Nelson M W, Reynolds R R, Kelly D L, Conley R R. Adjunctive quetiapine decreases symptoms of tardive dyskinesia in a patient taking risperidone. *Clin Neuropharmacol* 2003; 26: 297–298.

69. Kinon B J, Jeste D V, Kollack-Walker S *et al.* Olanzapine treatment for tardive dyskinesia in schizophrenia patients: a prospective clinical trial with patients randomized to blinded dose reduction periods. *Progr Neuro-Psychopharmacol Biol Psychiatry* 2004; 28: 985–996.

70. Bai Y M, Yu S C, Lin C C. Risperidone for severe tardive dyskinesia: a 12-week randomized, double-blind, placebo-controlled study. *J Clin Psychiatry* 2003; 64: 1342–1348.

71. Paleau D, Giladi N, Moore O *et al.* Tetrabenazine treatment in movement disorders. *Clin Neuropharmacol* 2004; 27: 230–233.

72. Ondo W G, Hanna P A, Jankovic J. Tetrabenazine treatment for tardive dyskinesia assessment by randomized videotape protocol. *Am J Psychiatry* 1999; 156: 1279–1281.

73. Zhang X Y, Zhou D F, Cao L Y *et al.* The effect of vitamin E treatment on tardive dyskinesia and blood superoxide dismutase: a double-blind placebo-controlled trial. *J Clin Psychopharmacol* 2004; 24: 83–86.

74. Soares K V S, McGrath J J. Vitamin E for neuroleptic-induced tardive dyskinesia. *Cochrane Database of Systematic Reviews* 2001, issue 4. DOI: 10.1002/14651858. CD000209.

75. Walker P, Soares K V S. Benzodiazepines for neuroleptic-induced tardive dyskinesia. *Cochrane Database of Systematic Reviews* 2003, issue 2. DOI: 10.1002/14651858. CD000205.

76. Wonodi I, Adami H, Sherr J *et al.* Naltrexone treatment of tardive dyskinesia in patients with schizophrenia. *J Clin Psychopharmacol* 2004; 24: 441–445.

77. Barnes T R E. The Barnes Akathisia Rating Scale – revisited. *J Psychopharmacol* 2003; 17: 365–370.

78. Simpson G M, Angus J W S. A rating scale for extrapyramidal side effects. *Acta Psychiatr Scand* 1970; 212: 11–19.

79. National Institute for Mental Health: Abnormal Involuntary Movement Scale (AIMS) (U.S. Public Health Service Publication No. MH-9-17). Washington, DC: US Government Printing Office, 1974.

15

Antipsychotics – other adverse effects

Weight gain

Weight gain is an adverse effect common to almost all antipsychotics. The fact that antipsychotics share this effect strongly suggests that any shared pharmacological action is likely to be the root cause of weight gain. Of course, antipsychotics share only one pharmacological action: activity at central dopamine D_2 receptors.

A simplified explanation of this phenomenon is as follows. Dopamine is the key pleasure-inducing transmitter in mammalian reward systems. The reward system is essentially a hard-wired addiction to life-preserving nutrients (water, food) and species-propagating activities (sexual intercourse). Humans deprived of food become dysphoric with hunger. On eating, they become sated and euphoric. Importantly, eating too much causes nausea and dysphoria. All of these effects are mediated via dopamine: too little dopamine causes some type of dysphoria (hunger, thirst, sexual desire); just enough, euphoria; and too much, nausea.

It can be seen that, in relation to food intake, dopamine antagonism is likely to interfere with the reward system in a way that will result in weight gain. A reduction in dopaminergic transmission is likely to result in hunger, reduced capacity to feel satiety and reduced severity of nausea. All of these effects have been noted to occur with antipsychotics. Indeed, many of these drugs are used as antiemetics and some are used as appetite-enhancers in anorexia nervosa.

This simplistic explanation of the effects of antipsychotics on weight provides a broad basis for our understanding of the phenomenon but cannot account for many of the more subtle aspects of the phenomenon. For example, weight-inducing capacity seems not to be in any way associated with dopamine D_2 receptor-binding potential, as might be expected. Several other observations on the pathogenesis of weight gain have been made and may augment theories on the central role of dopamine and reward. Other receptor activities that may provoke weight gain include histamine H_1 antagonism (perhaps via sedation and reduced activity) and 5-hydroxytryptamine $(5HT)_{2C}$ antagonism. Mutation in the gene coding for $5HT_{2C}$ receptors may determine whether or not weight is gained [1, 2] and it is also possible that H_1 receptor genetic mutation plays a similar part [3]. Of particular interest is the observation that mice bred with the $5HT_{2C}$ receptor gene 'knocked out' show severe obesity [4].

Other mechanisms have also been postulated. For example, antipsychotics may induce leptin release and, ultimately, leptin resistance. Leptin is a protein synthesised by adipose tissue which appears to act as an internal messenger which signals the extent of body fat. Its production has the effect of decreasing food intake. Antipsychotics are thought to interfere with this negative feedback by some unknown mechanism [5]. More recent work has suggested that leptin elevation after antipsychotic administration is a consequence rather than a cause of obesity [6]. Another reasonably well-supported theory is that weight gain results from the effects of hyperprolactinaemia on gonadal hormones and insulin [7]. Interestingly, the oestrogen antagonist tamoxifen prevents sulpiride-related obesity [8].

These observations suggest the possibility that the pathogenesis of antipsychotic-induced weight gain is multifactorial. Developing understanding may also allow prediction of weight gain potential with different drugs. To some extent this is possible but it is notable that ziprasidone, a D_2, $5HT_{2C}$, H_1 antagonist, does not cause weight gain.

The relative propensity of different antipsychotics to cause weight gain is the subject of much debate. Two major systematic reviews [9, 10] have provided some insight into the subject. Clozapine and olanzapine seem to have the greatest effect on weight (more than 2 kg (4 lb) over 10 weeks), followed by risperidone, quetiapine, phenothiazines and zotepine, which appear to cause moderate increase in weight (1–1.5 kg (2–3 lb) over 10 weeks). Haloperidol and amisulpride have a still lower risk of weight gain and ziprasidone the lowest risk of all. Some studies not included in the systematic reviews suggest that quetiapine does not result in weight gain in the medium to long term [11, 12]. Aripiprazole was introduced some time after these reviews were published. It appears to cause little or no change in weight [13, 14].

Strategies have been developed to manage antipsychotic-related weight gain and obesity. In most cases, complete withdrawal of antipsychotic medication is not practicable because most people with schizophrenia will relapse. Switching to another antipsychotic is preferred and published data suggest that a switch to quetiapine [15], aripiprazole [16] or, to a lesser extent, risperidone [17] can result in weight loss in subjects who have previously gained weight on other antipsychotics (particularly olanzapine).

However, in perhaps the majority of cases, switching anti-psychotics may not be advisable. This is especially true in patients who have responded well to a particular antipsychotic: switching engenders a risk of relapse which may ultimately be more problematic for the patient than weight gain. Moreover, with clozapine, switching is very likely to cause relapse since clozapine is used only in those unresponsive to other drugs.

There are a number of management options for patients who experience weight gain but who cannot or should not change drug treatment. These options are outlined in Management focus 15.1.

In practice, the management of antipsychotic-related weight gain may involve switching, behavioural intervention and pharmacological intervention, with the last of these options being least used. People with

MANAGEMENT FOCUS 15.1

Managing antipsychotic-induced weight gain [18, 19]

Behavioural methods

Diet change
  Food provision
  Meal plans
  Low glycaemic index [20]
  Weight Watchers [21]
  Calorie control

Increased calorie expenditure
  Exercise at a gym [22]
  Aerobic walking [23]

Pharmacological interventions

Orlistat
  Effective but adverse effects unacceptable to some

Sibutramine
  Effective appetite suppressant but known to cause psychiatric adverse effects

Topiramate
  Effective but sedative/cognitive effects often troublesome

Fluoxetine
  Minimal effect

Metformin
  Minimal effect, but useful in diabetes

schizophrenia often have poor diets [24] and this is often a consequence of poverty (cheaper food is usually processed and high in sugar and fat). Patient education can thus be helpful but only when patients are truly motivated to lose weight. When increased exercise is recommended, it is important to stress the importance of activity (walking instead of catching a bus). Patients with schizophrenia are better able to increase physical activity than to join a gym or to go swimming, for example.

CASE STUDY 15.1

Rose

Rose was a 42-year-old Caucasian with a 15-year history of schizophrenia. She was unresponsive to treatment and continued to believe that she had six children (she had one, in care) and that she was pregnant. She was often elated and giggled to herself while seemingly responding to voices. Rose's appearance was unkempt and she was malodorous.

Rose weighed 146 kg (23 stone) and was 1.83 m (6 ft) tall. Orlistat was started and the patient's access to takeaway food limited. In the first month she lost 7 kg (15 lb).

It was decided to start clozapine. During the first week of treatment Rose was too drowsy to get up and rarely ate. Three months later she weighed 131 kg (20 stone 6 lb), was continuing on orlistat and clozapine and was strongly motivated to lose further weight. Her mental state had improved substantially. Delusions could not be elicited even on direct questioning and mood was normal. Self-care improved and Rose was taking a daily 30-minute walk in the hospital grounds.

Diabetes

Schizophrenia has long been associated with an increased risk of diabetes. Several studies from the 1920s reported impaired glucose tolerance in patients with dementia praecox or schizophrenia and, later, others reported a subdued response to insulin used in insulin coma therapy [25]. Modern studies have noted a higher prevalence of diabetes mellitus in people with schizophrenia compared with the general population [26]. People diagnosed with schizophrenia may be metabolically predisposed to diabetes from or at their first episode: compared with healthy controls those with schizophrenia have higher plasma glucose and insulin resistance [27], more intra-abdominal fat and higher plasma cortisol levels [28]. These metabolic abnormalities are present at onset and so are not a result of the use of antipsychotic drugs.

Antipsychotic drugs are, of course, well known to provoke impaired glucose tolerance and diabetes; this is particularly true of atypical drugs [29]. However, conventional drugs, especially phenothiazines, have an established association with increased risk of diabetes in excess of that seen in schizophrenia itself [30]. Despite popular belief, it is far from clear that atypical drugs give rise to a risk of diabetes over and above that seen in conventionally treated schizophrenia. The main reason for this uncertainty is the flawed nature of the research conducted in this area. Much of our perception of the relative risk of diabetes with different drugs is based on case reports or series and retrospective database studies. Case series reported by Koller and colleagues [31, 32], for example, described large numbers of cases of diabetes, ketoacidosis and, in smaller numbers, death in patients receiving certain atypical antipsychotics. These data are startling because of both the number and severity of adverse effects reported. On the other hand, these reports are difficult to put into context without knowledge of the proportions of patients represented by these figures – the incidence of affected patients per treated patients per year. Nor can they be used to compare drugs: different antipsychotics are prescribed to different numbers of patients over different time periods.

Retrospective database studies have the allure of scientific investigation but are flawed to a similar degree. In such studies prescription records are compared with computer databases containing diagnostic details. Prescriptions for antipsychotics can then be matched against diagnosis of diabetes, prevalence calculated and relative risk with different drugs estimated. Database studies have invariably demonstrated that drugs such as clozapine, olanzapine and (less frequently) quetiapine are more likely to be associated with a diagnosis of diabetes than are conventional antipsychotics [33–35]. It is important to note that these data cannot imply causation since it is possible, if not likely, that screening for diabetes is incomplete and varies between drugs [36]. Different diagnosis rates might then merely reflect different rates of screening.

Other shortfalls in database study methods include use of proxy markers for diabetes (e.g. prescription of oral hypoglycaemics), a failure to account for risk factors for diabetes and a failure to account for variation in antipsychotic treatment over time (e.g. the inability to discount the effect of previous drugs) [37].

Practical measures for screening for and managing antipsychotic-related diabetes are essential (Case study 15.2) because diabetes increases cardiovascular mortality and morbidity, which can be reduced by appropriate treatment. Certainly diabetes screening is worthwhile on the basis that prevalence of diabetes in a population taking antipsychotics is extremely high – approaching 20% [38].

CASE STUDY 15.2

Drug-induced diabetes

JJ is a 29-year-old Jamaican woman with a diagnosis of schizoaffective disorder. She has been treated with chlorpromazine (100 mg t.d.s.) and olanzapine (10 mg o.d.) since admission 11 weeks ago. Her medication notes contain repeated references to instances of nocturnal urinary frequency and two references to the patient's 'raging thirst'. There is no evidence of any prior screening for diabetes mellitus. The pharmacist suggests testing for diabetes. The patient agrees to this but is unable to fast for more than a few hours. A random plasma glucose is reported as 26 mmol/l. Antipsychotic medication is stopped, a strict diet enforced and metformin started at 500 mg t.d.s. Antipsychotic treatment is restarted with amisulpride 800 mg daily. A fasting plasma glucose is later obtained, and the result is 17 mmol/l. JJ is referred to a diabetes specialist.

Given the relatively high incidence of diabetes in schizophrenia itself, annual monitoring of patients is advisable. Fasting plasma glucose is the most useful test but plasma glycosylated haemoglobin is also informative. Even random plasma glucose testing using portable testing kits is clearly more useful than no test at all. For those patients taking clozapine or olanzapine, who are obese or who have a family history of diabetes, testing should be done at 4–6-month intervals.

Where impaired fasting glucose or diabetes is discovered then further testing and/or treatment is indicated. Diabetes may sometimes remit when the offending drug is withdrawn, but not always [39]. The use of oral hypoglycaemics or insulin may then be necessary. When switching antipsychotic drugs because of diabetes, amisulpride, aripiprazole and ziprasidone seem not to alter glucose homeostasis and are generally recommended [40]. Monitoring is however still required with these drugs because of the underlying risk of diabetes in this patient population.

Dyslipidaemias

As previously discussed, bioactive lipids may play a part in the pathogenesis of schizophrenia [41]. Antipsychotic drugs also appear to affect lipid metabolism either via a direct mechanism or as a consequence of increased central adiposity occurring in weight gain [42]. This central adipose tissue enhances release of free fatty acids and accelerates hepatic synthesis of triglycerides. This in turn may inhibit glucose metabolism and lead to type 2 diabetes. Thus antipsychotic-related dyslipidaemia, weight gain and diabetes may occur as a distinct intrarelated syndrome of adverse effects.

Phenothiazine antipsychotics have long been known to raise serum triglycerides and cholesterol [43, 44] – effects not shared by butyrophenones [45]. Amongst atypical antipsychotics, clozapine and olanzapine have been conclusively shown to elevate triglycerides and, to a lesser extent and with less certainty, cholesterol [46, 47]. Quetiapine may have a similar effect [47, 48] but risperidone appears to have a similar (minimal) effect to butyrophenones [46]. Amisulpride, aripiprazole and ziprasidone do not appear to affect serum lipids [49, 50].

In practice, partly because of underlying risk factors for lipid and cholesterol changes, around two-thirds of antipsychotic-treated patients may have some type of dyslipidaemia, regardless of the antipsychotic prescribed [51]. As with diabetes, regular (6–12-monthly) screening for dyslipidaemia is essential if the condition is to be identified and effectively treated [52].

Hyperprolactinaemia

Elevated blood levels of the pituitary hormone prolactin have long been recognised as being associated with the use of antipsychotic drugs. However, in contrast to extrapyramidal and metabolic adverse affects, hyperprolactinaemia has received relatively little attention both academically and clinically. Part of the reason for this is that antipsychotic-related hyperprolactinaemia is often seemingly asymptomatic. That is, patients do not usually have any obvious prolactin-related symptoms or at least do not report them. In fact, hyperprolactinaemia usually has important adverse consequences for patients, some of which may not be apparent for several decades.

Prolactin is a hormone secreted by lactotroph cells in the anterior pituitary. Blood levels of prolactin vary moderately during a 24-hour period but are normally below 500 mU/l (15 mg/l or 0.645 nmol/l). During pregnancy, prolactin levels may reach 6500 mU/l and increase still further during breast-feeding. Prolactin causes breast growth, milk production, decreased libido and reduced fertility. Some of these effects are direct actions of prolactin; others depend on the secondary effect of prolactin on the production of other hormones such as oestrogen.

Control of prolactin production is complex but the major neurotransmitter inhibiting prolactin release is dopamine. Stimulation of D_2 receptors in tuberoinfundibular pathways suppresses prolactin release. Oestrogen, on the other hand, seems to promote prolactin secretion.

Since all available antipsychotics are effectively D_2 receptor antagonists some effect on prolactin levels is to be expected. Most antipsychotics cause prompt and persistent increases in prolactin production and only a very few have little or no effect. Hyperprolactinaemia induced by antipsychotics causes a range of short- and long-term physiological changes which have important consequences. These are described in Adverse-effects focus 15.1.

ADVERSE-EFFECTS FOCUS 15.1

Adverse consequences of drug-induced hyperprolactinaemia [53]
Gynaecomastia (breast enlargement)
Galactorrhoea (breast milk production)
Menstrual changes (e.g. amenorrhoea)
Failure to conceive
Loss of libido
Erectile dysfunction
Acne and hirsutism (in women only – caused by relative excess of testosterone as oestrogen levels decline)
Decreased bone mineral density
Increased risk of breast cancer

The frequency with which prolactin-related adverse effects occur has not been precisely established. Gynaecomastia, for example, is difficult to detect unless profound and there is no reliable evidence of its incidence. Clinical observations suggest a rate of around 1 in 10 patients. Estimates of the prevalence of galactorrhoea are perhaps more reliable and range from 2.2% to around 50% [54]. Much of the variation in estimates is likely to result from patients' reluctance to report such adverse effects. Similarly, the incidence and prevalence of sexual dysfunction are difficult to establish because of problems with patient reporting. On direct questioning, up to half of patients treated with prolactin-increasing antipsychotics report some kind of sexual dysfunction

[55, 56]. Women may be more sensitive to the effects of prolactin than men: prolactin levels are higher, more frequently above normal limits and more often associated with inadequate gonadal function [57].

Two possible long-term effects of raised prolactin levels are the subject of some debate. First, as prolactin reduces oestrogen levels, it is possible that prolonged hyperprolactinaemia reduces bone mineral density (patients are rendered postmenopausal, in effect). Several studies support this assumption [58, 59], although there is little firm evidence that this effect leads to an increased risk of fractures. Second, high prolactin concentrations are known to induce tumours in laboratory animals and it is thought that similar effects may occur in humans [53]. Although published data on this are largely conflicting, two well-conducted studies have found higher rates of breast cancer in people receiving long-term dopamine antagonist drugs [60, 61]. Although confirmation of these findings is required, the possibility of an increased risk of cancer is a powerful impetus for the use of prolactin-sparing antipsychotics.

All conventional antipsychotics cause substantial hyper-prolactinaemia. Amongst atypicals, amisulpride (and sulpiride), risperidone and zotepine are associated with a severity and frequency of hyperprolactinaemia at least as high as that seen with conventional drugs [53, 54]. Thus only clozapine, olanzapine, quetiapine, ziprasidone and aripiprazole are prolactin-neutral [40].

Where hyperprolactinaemia is clearly symptomatic, a switch to one of these drugs is usually effective in normalising prolactin levels and, over a period of several months, reducing symptom levels. A case might be made for switching even those patients who have no obvious symptoms: the risk of longer-term serious adverse effects may be considered reason enough.

For some patients, switching to a prolactin-sparing drug is not a practical option. In the main, these will be patients effectively maintained on depot antipsychotics (at the time of writing all available depots cause hyperprolactinaemia). Where hyperprolactinaemia is problematic in these cases remedial drug treatment is sometimes (albeit rarely) used. Dopamine agonist drugs such as amantadine, bromocriptine [40] and carbergoline [62] can be effective but have the potential to worsen psychosis.

Cardiac adverse effects

Antipsychotics have a range of effects on the cardiovascular system, of which postural hypertension (medicated via adrenergic α_1 blockade) is the most frequent and apparent. Postural hypertension is commonly seen with phenothiazines, clozapine, risperidone, quetiapine and zotepine. Nonetheless, this effect is readily avoided or ameliorated by careful dose titration and is, in any case, usually short-lived. Postural hypertension is, with some antipsychotics, accompanied by transient tachycardia which is of little clinical importance. With clozapine, however, tachycardia may be persistent and associated with other more serious conditions such as myocarditis [40].

Most antipsychotics can be shown to prolong the cardiac QT interval and this may have an important impact on cardiac morbidity and mortality. The QT interval is the time (in milliseconds) from the beginning of the Q wave on the electrocardiogram (ECG) trace to the end of the T wave. As such, it represents the time taken to complete the depolarisation and repolarisation cycle of the ventricles. This cycle involves the movement across cell membranes of sodium, calcium and potassium ions. Antipsychotic drugs, along with many others, seem to prolong the QT interval by binding to certain potassium channels (particularly the delayed rectifier channel, IKr) and delaying completion of the repolarisation phase [63, 64].

It is this delay in completing repolarisation that is thought to be pathogenic. Cardiac tissue consists of several types of cell (myocyte) and drug effects via Ikr may differ from one to another. Some myocytes may generate early after-depolarisations (EADs) during a prolonged repolarisation phase which may in turn generate premature action potentials. These action potentials have the capacity to precipitate multifocal extrasystoles, leading to the ventricular tachyarrhythmia torsade de pointes (TdeP) [64]. This arrhythmia is fatal in a minority of instances and is thought to be the cause of excess cardiac mortality observed with a number of drugs.

The risk presented by individual antipsychotics is very difficult to determine. Almost all can be shown to interact with IKr, a great many prolong the QT interval, some are known to be associated with EADs, some with TdeP, and fewer still with increased mortality. It should not be assumed that any drug interacting with IKr or prolonging the QT interval is inexorably associated with TdeP and increased mortality. Nor can it be assumed that the greater the effect on the QT interval, the greater the risk of arrhythmia: some QT-prolonging drugs (e.g. amiodarone) reduce the risk of arrhythmia.

Risk is therefore most appropriately assessed by reference to epidemiological studies of antipsychotics and sudden cardiac death. Four major studies of this type have been published. These studies are summarised in Adverse-effects focus 15.2. It can be seen that conventional

ADVERSE-EFFECTS FOCUS 15.2

Antipsychotics and cardiac mortality

Reference	Drug evaluated	Outcome measure	Main outcomes
65	Phenothiazines Haloperidol	Sudden cardiac death	Moderate doses of antipsychotics confer 2.39 times increased risk of sudden death compared with no use
66	Phenothiazines Butyrophenones Risperidone Sulpiride Other non-antipsychotics	Sudden unexplained death	Thioridazine increased odds of sudden death by a ratio of 5.3. No increased risk with other drugs
67	Conventional antipsychotics	Sudden cardiac death	Threefold increased rate of sudden death in those receiving antipsychotics compared with no use. Sixfold increased risk with butyrophenones
68	Conventional (mainly haloperidol) and atypical (mainly risperidone) antipsychotics	Admission with ventricular arrhythmia	No increased risk with atypical drugs. Conventional drugs increase risk by 53% compared with no use

antipsychotics, especially thioridazine and haloperidol, are strongly linked to increased cardiac mortality. There appears to be no increased risk with atypical drugs, although the level of investigation is relatively lower.

These findings do not match exactly what is known about the relative effects of antipsychotics on the QT interval. Certainly thioridazine has the most marked QT-prolonging properties of all antipsychotics but haloperidol has only a moderate effect and was for a long time considered to be safe in this respect [69]. Indeed, some studies report that haloperidol has no effect on the QT interval [70]. It is also notable that sertindole, a drug that substantially prolongs the QT interval, appears not to increase mortality and is not known to be associated with TdeP [71]. The same may also be true of droperidol [72], a butyrophenone now withdrawn because of its effects on the QT interval.

These observations make difficult any decisions about recommendations regarding the merits or otherwise of ECG monitoring in people taking antipsychotics. Clearly ECG monitoring is essential with haloperidol and perhaps other conventional drugs. Monitoring is probably not worthwhile with atypical drugs, most of which have little or no effect on the QT interval and appear not to increase the risk of sudden death. ECGs may however be useful in all patients as a means of identifying or accounting for other non-drug risk factors for TdeP and sudden death (e.g. female gender, heart disease, other QT-prolonging drugs) [73, 74].

References

1. Reynolds G P, Zhang Z, Zhang X. Polymorphism of the promoter region of the serotonin 5-HT$_{2C}$ receptor gene and clozapine-induced weight gain. *Am J Psychiatry* 2003; 160: 677–679.

2. Gibson W T, Ebersole B J, Bhattacharyya S *et al.* Mutational analysis of the serotonin receptor 5HT$_{2C}$ in severe early-onset human obesity. *Can J Physiol Pharmacol* 2004; 82: 426–429.

3. Correll C U, Malhotra A K. Pharmacogenetics of antipsychotic-induced weight gain. *Psychopharmacology* 2004; 174: 477–489.

4. Tecott L H, Sun L M, Akana S F *et al.* Eating disorder and epilepsy in mice lacking 5-HT$_{2C}$ serotonin receptors. *Nature* 1995; 374: 542–546.

5. Baptista T, Lacruz A, De Mondoza S *et al.* Body weight gain after administration of antipsychotic drugs: correlation with leptin, insulin and reproductive hormones. *Pharmacopsychiatry* 2000; 33: 81–88.

6. Baptista T, Beaulieu S. Are leptin and cytokines involved in body weight gain during treatment with antipsychotic drugs? *Can J Psychiatry* 2002; 47: 742–749.

7. Baptista T, Lacruz F, Silvera R *et al.* Endocrine and metabolic abnormalities involved in obesity associated with typical antipsychotic drug administration. *Pharmacopsychiatry* 2001; 34: 223–231.

8. Baptista T. Body weight gain induced by antipsychotic drugs: mechanisms and management. *Acta Psychiatr Scand* 1999; 100: 3–16.

9. Allison D B, Mentore J L, Moonseong H *et al.* Antipsychotic-induced weight gain: a comprehensive research synthesis. *Am J Psychiatry* 1999; 156: 1686–1696.

10. Taylor D M, McAskill R. Atypical antipsychotics and weight gain – a systematic review. *Acta Psychiatr Scand* 2000; 101: 416–432.

11. Brecher M, Rak I W, Melvin K, Jones A M. The long-term effect of quetiapine (Seroquel™) monotherapy on weight in patients with schizophrenia. *Int J Psychiatry Clin Pract* 2000; 4: 287–291.

12. Emsley R, Turner HJ, Schronen J *et al.* Effects of quetiapine and haloperidol on body mass index and glycaemic control: a long-term, randomized, controlled trial. *Int J Neuropsychopharmacol* 2005; 8: 175–182.

13. Pigott T A, Carson W H, Saha A R *et al*. Aripiprazole for the prevention of relapse in stabilized patients with chronic schizophrenia: a placebo-controlled 26-week study. *J Clin Psychiatry* 2003; 64: 1048–1056.

14. Potkin S G, Saha A R, Kujawa M J *et al*. Aripiprazole, an antipsychotic with a novel mechanism of action, and risperidone vs placebo in patients with schizophrenia and schizoaffective disorder. *Arch Gen Psychiatry* 2003; 60: 681–690.

15. Gupta S, Masand P S, Virk S *et al*. Weight gain in patients switching from olanzapine to quetiapine. *Schizophr Res* 2004; 70: 57–62.

16. Casey D E, Carson W H, Saha A R *et al*. Switching patients to aripiprazole from other antipsychotic agents: a multicenter randomized study. *Psychopharmacol (Berl)* 2003; 166: 391–399.

17. Ried L D, Renner B T, Bengtson M A *et al*. Weight change after an atypical antipsychotic switch. *Ann Pharmacother* 2003; 37: 1381–1386.

18. Werneke U, Taylor D, Sanders T A B, Wessely S. Behavioural management of antipsychotic induced weight gain: a review. *Acta Psychiatr Scand* 2003; 108: 252–259.

19. Werneke U, Taylor D, Sanders T A B. Options for pharmacological management of obesity in patients treated with atypical antipsychotics. *Int Clin Psychopharmacol* 2002; 17: 145–160.

20. Smith H, White T. Low glycaemic index diet in patients prescribed clozapine: pilot study. *Psychiatr Bull* 2004; 28: 292–294.

21. Ball M P, Coons V B, Buchanan R W. A program for treating olanzapine-related weight gain. *Psychiatr Serv* 2001; 52: 967–969.

22. Ohlsen R I, Treasure J, Pilowsky L S. A dedicated nurse-led service for antipsychotic-induced weight gain. *Psychiatr Bull* 2004; 28: 164–166.

23. Vreeland B, Minsky S, Menza M *et al*. A program for managing weight gain associated with atypical antipsychotics. *Psychiatr Serv* 2003; 54: 1155–1157.

24. McCreadie R G. Diet, smoking and cardiovascular risk in people with schizophrenia. *Br J Psychiatry* 2003; 183: 534–539.

25. Kohen D. Diabetes mellitus and schizophrenia: historical perspective. *Br J Psychiatry* 2004; 184: 564–566.

26. Bushe C, Holt R. Prevalence of diabetes and impaired glucose tolerance in patients with schizophrenia. *Br J Psychiatry* 2004; 184: 567–571.

27. Ryan M C M, Collins P, Thakore J H. Impaired fasting glucose tolerance in first-episode, drug-naïve patients with schizophrenia. *Am J Psychiatry* 2003; 160: 284–289.

28. Thakore J H. Metabolic disturbance in first-episode schizophrenia. *Br J Psychiatry* 2004; 184: 576–579.

29. Mir S, Taylor D. Atypical antipsychotics and hyperglycaemia. *Int Clin Psychopharmacol* 2001; 16: 63–74.

30. Thonnard-Neumann E. Phenothiazines and diabetes in hospitalised women. *Am J Psychiatry* 1968; 124: 138–139.

31. Koller E, Schnedier B, Bennett K, Dubisky G. Clozapine-associated diabetes. *Am J Med* 2001; 111: 716–723.

32. Koller E A, Doraiswamy P M. Olanzapine-associated diabetes mellitus. *Pharmacotherapy* 2002; 22: 841–852.

33. Koro C E, Fedder D O, L'Italien G J *et al*. Assessment of independent effect of olanzapine and risperidone on risk of diabetes among patients with

schizphrenia: population based nested case–control study. *BMJ* 2002; 325: 243–245.

34. Kornegay C J, Vasilakis-Scaramozza C, Jick H. Incident diabetes associated with antipsychotic use in the United Kingdom general practice research database. *J Clin Psychiatry* 2002; 63: 758–762.

35. Sernyak M J, Leslie D L, Alarcon R D *et al.* Association of diabetes mellitus with use of atypical neuroleptics in the treatment of schizophrenia. *Am J Psychiatry* 2002; 159: 561–566.

36. Taylor D, Young C, Esop R *et al.* Testing for diabetes in hospitalised patients prescribed antipsychotics. *Br J Psychiatry* 2004; 185: 152–156.

37. Haddad P M. Antipsychotics and diabetes: review of non-prospective data. *Br J Psychiatry* 2004; 184: 580–586.

38. Taylor D, Young C, Mohamed R *et al.* Undiagnosed impaired fasting glucose and diabetes mellitus amongst inpatients receiving antipsychotic drugs. *J Psychopharmacol* 2005; 19: 182–186.

39. Mir S, Taylor D. Atypical antipsychotics and hyperglycaemia. *Int Clin Psychopharmacol* 2001; 16: 63–74.

40. Taylor D, Paton C, Kerwin R. *The Maudsley Prescribing Guidelines*, 8th edn. London, UK: Taylor & Francis, 2005.

41. Berger G E, Wood S J, Pantelis C *et al.* Implications of lipid biology for the pathogenesis of schizophrenia. *Aust NZ J Psychiatry* 2001; 35: 355–366.

42. Koponen H, Saari K, Savolainen M, Isohanni M. Weight gain and glucose and lipid metabolism disturbances during antipsychotic medication. *Eur Arch Psychiatry Clin Neurosci* 2002; 252: 294–298.

43. Mefferd R B Jr, Labrosse E H, Gawienowski A M, Williams R J. Influence of chlorpromazine on certain biochemical variables of chronic male schizophrenics. *J Nerv Ment Dis* 1958; 127: 167–179.

44. Clark M L, Johnson P C. Amenorrhea and elevated level of serum cholesterol produced by a trifluoromethylated phenothiazine (SKF 5354-A). *J Clin Endocrinol Metab* 1960; 20: 641–646.

45. Sasaki J, Funakoshi M, Arakawa K. Lipids and apolipoproteins in patients with major tranquilizers. *Clin Pharmacol Ther* 1985; 37: 684–687.

46. Smith R C, Lindenmayer J P, Bark N *et al.* Clozapine, risperidone, olanzapine, and conventional antipsychotic drug effects on glucose, lipids, and leptin in schizophrenic patients. *Int J Neuropsychopharmacol* 2005; 8: 183–194.

47. Meyer J M. Effects of atypical antipsychotics on weight and serum lipid levels. *J Clin Psychiatry* 2001; 62: 27–34.

48. Meyer J M. Novel antipsychotics and severe hyperlipidemia. *J Clin Psychopharmacol* 2001; 21: 369–374.

49. Newcomer J W. Metabolic risk during antipsychotic treatment. *Clin Ther* 2004; 26: 1936–1946.

50. Meyer J M, Koro C E. The effects of antipsychotic therapy on serum lipids: a comprehensive review. *Schizophr Res* 2004; 70: 1–17.

51. Paton C, Esop R, Young C, Taylor D. Obesity, dyslipidaemias and smoking in an inpatient population treated with antipsychotic drugs. *Acta Psychiatr Scand* 2004; 110: 299–305.

52. Marder S R, Essock S M, Miller A L *et al.* Physical health monitoring of patients with schizophrenia. *Am J Psychiatry* 2004; 161: 1334–1349.

53. Haddad P M, Wieck A. Antipsychotic-induced hyperprolactinaemia mechanisms, clinical features and management. *Drugs* 2004; 64: 2291–2314.

54. Hamner M B, Arana G W. Hyperprolactinaemia in antipsychotic-treated patients. Guidelines for avoidance and management. *CNS Drugs* 1998; 10: 209–222.

55. Bobes J, Garcia-Portilla M P, Rejas J *et al.* Frequency of sexual dysfunction and other reproductive side-effects in patients with schizophrenia treated with risperidone, olanzapine, quetiapine, or haloperidol: the results of the EIRE study. *J Sex Marital Ther* 2003; 29: 125–147.

56. Knegtering R, Castelein S, Bous H *et al.* A randomized open-label study of the impact of quetiapine versus risperidone on sexual functioning. *J Clin Psychopharmacol* 2004; 24: 56–61.

57. Smith S. Effects of antipsychotics on sexual and endocrine function in women: implications for clinical practice. *J Clin Psychopharmacol* 2003; 23: S27–S32.

58. Meaney A M, Smith S, Howes O D *et al.* Effects of long-term prolactin-raising antipsychotic medication on bone mineral density in patients with schizophrenia. *Br J Psychiatry* 2004; 184: 503–508.

59. Liu-Seifert H, Kinon B J, Ahl J, Lamberson S. Osteopenia associated with increased prolactin and aging in psychiatric patients treated with prolactin-elevating antipsychotics. *Ann NY Acad Sci* 2004; 1032: 297–298.

60. Wang P S, Walker A M, Tsuang M T *et al.* Dopamine antagonists and the development of breast cancer. *Arch Gen Psychiatry* 2002; 59: 1147–1154.

61. Halbreich U, Shen J, Panaro V. Are chronic psychiatric patients at increased risk for developing breast cancer? *Am J Psychiatry* 1996; 153: 559–560.

62. Cavallaro R, Cocchi F, Angelone S M *et al.* Cabergoline treatment of risperidone-induced hyperprolactinemia: a pilot study. *J Clin Psychiatry* 2004; 65: 187–190.

63. Taylor D M. Antipsychotics and QT prolongation. *Acta Psychiatr Scand* 2003; 107: 85–95.

64. Titier K, Girodet P O, Verdoux H *et al.* Atypical antipsychotics from potassium channels to torsade de pointes and sudden death. *Drug Safety* 2005; 28: 35–51.

65. Ray W A, Meredith S, Thapa P B *et al.* Antipsychotics and the risk of sudden cardiac death. *Arch Gen Psychiatry* 2001; 58: 1161–1167.

66. Reilly J G, Ayis S A, Ferrier I N *et al.* Thioridazine and sudden unexplained death in psychiatric in-patients. *Br J Psychiatry* 2002; 180: 515–522.

67. Straus S M J M, Bleumink G S, Dieleman J P *et al.* Antipsychotic and the risk of sudden cardiac death. *Arch Intern Med* 2004; 164: 1293–1297.

68. Liperoti R, Gambassi G, Lapane K L *et al.* Conventional and atypical antipsychotics and the risk of hospitalisation for ventricular arrhythmias or cardiac arrest. *Arch Intern Med* 2005; 165: 696–701.

69. Harrigan E P, Miceli J J, Anziano R *et al.* A randomized evaluation of the effects of six antipsychotic agents on QTc, in the absence and presence of metabolic inhibition. *J Clin Psychopharmacol* 2004; 24: 62–69.

70. Su K P, Shen W W, Chuang C L, Chen K P. A pilot cross-over design study on QTc interval prolongation associated with sulpiride and haloperidol. *Schizophr Res* 2002; 59: 93–94.

71. Wilton L V, Heeley E L, Pickering R M, Shakir S A. Comparative study of

mortality rates and cardiac dysrhythmias in post-marketing surveillance studies of sertindole and two other atypical antipsychotic drugs, risperidone and olanzapine. *J Psychopharmacol* 2001; 15: 120–126.

72. Shale J H, Shale C M, Mastin W D. A review of the safety and efficacy of droperidol for the rapid sedation of severely agitated and violent patients. *J Clin Psychiatry* 2003; 64: 500–505.

73. Frassati D, Tabib A, Lachaux B *et al*. Hidden cardiac lesions and psychotropic drugs as a possible cause of sudden death in psychiatric patients: a report of 14 cases and review of the literature. *Can J Psychiatry* 2004; 49: 100–105.

74. Justo D, Prokhorov V, Heller K, Zeltser D. Torsade de pointes induced by psychotropic drugs and the prevalence of its risk factors. *Acta Psychiatr Scand* 2005; 111: 171–176.

16

Treating schizophrenia with antipsychotics

First-episode schizophrenia

Schizophrenia usually begins insidiously and only comes to the attention of mental health services when psychotic symptoms have developed sufficiently to impair grossly everyday functioning. Many people undergo a period of gradual withdrawal from friends and relatives accompanied by growing feelings of suspiciousness and paranoia. These feelings usually provoke odd behaviour but psychotic symptoms as such may not be experienced or expressed. Eventually it becomes clear that there is severe thought disorder or hallucinatory activity and medical intervention is sought.

Treatment of first-episode psychosis is a matter of some urgency. The duration of untreated psychosis (DUP) is an established predictor of eventual treatment outcome: the longer the DUP, the poorer the response to treatment [1].

Admission to hospital is an invariable consequence of first-episode psychosis. On admission, patients are usually carefully assessed over several days before drug treatment is started. During this time treatment options can be discussed and patients and/or carers can contribute to drug choice. Today, almost all first-episode patients receive an atypical drug as first-line therapy. For some reason, first-episode patients respond to lower doses than that required in chronic schizophrenia. Doses of less than 4 mg/day risperidone [2] and less than 10 mg/day olanzapine [3] are clearly effective, for example.

Drug treatment is usually continued for at least 1 year after symptom remission and there is a return to normal or near-normal functioning (which may take up to a year). After this time consideration may be given to careful, controlled withdrawal from antipsychotic medication. However, stopping antipsychotic medication increases risk of relapse in the 5 years after recovery from an initial episode by almost 500% [4]. In fact, almost all first-episode patients [96%] withdrawing from antipsychotics can be expected to relapse or experience exacerbation of symptoms in the 2 years after stopping antipsychotic treatment [5]. It follows that for most people with a diagnosis of schizophrenia antipsychotic treatment should be continued for several years, usually for life.

Relapse prevention

Antipsychotics reduce the risk of relapse in schizophrenia but do not prevent relapse in all patients. Some of this apparent failure of treatment is undoubtedly a result of poor compliance with prescribed medication (see below). However a substantial proportion of people relapse despite continued compliance with treatment. The reasons for this are not clear but it is notable that, in practice, relapse seems to be relatively much less common in people taking clozapine; indeed, when such people relapse, non-compliance is immediately expected.

It appears that full treatment doses are required to reduce the risk of relapse: dose reduction is usually unsuccessful [6]. Some atypical drugs such as risperidone may be more effective than haloperidol in preventing relapse [7], but again the reasons for this are unclear. Of course, depot or long-acting antipsychotics are widely used to prevent relapse but it remains uncertain as to whether they provide better protection against relapse than oral formulations [8].

Refractory schizophrenia

In first-episode schizophrenia, most people eventually show a substantial response to antipsychotic treatment. However, a small proportion, perhaps 10%, show no response. As the illness progresses, the proportion of those not responding to treatment increases to perhaps as high as 30% of patients [9].

The treatment of choice in those not responding to two or more antipsychotics is clozapine. Clozapine is uniquely effective in this group of patients, showing unparalleled efficacy – more than 50% show a response [10]. Oddly, there seems to be a reluctance to use clozapine despite its clear role. In the only study of its kind [11], clozapine treatment was found to have been delayed by an average of 5 years. In those not responding to clozapine, a variety of augmentation strategies have been developed. Of these, the best supported are the addition of sulpiride, risperidone or lamotrigine [12].

Patient adherence to prescribed regimens

As in other areas of drug treatment, compliance with or adherence to prescribed regimens is rather poor in patients with schizophrenia. Estimates of the proportion of patients not compliant range from around 40% to 50% on average, with single studies reporting non-adherence rates of between 4% and 72% [13]. Non-compliance is made more likely by adverse effects, delusional symptoms, a poor attitude to medication, substance misuse, lack of insight and lack of family support [13, 14].

A wide range of interventions has been evaluated in an attempt to improve adherence rates [15, 16]. No method is particularly effective and some – education, family therapy and (less clearly) assertive community care – seem to have no worthwhile effect at all. Only two methods seem to be effective: behavioural methods (providing concrete instructions and reminders) and motivational or cognitive approaches. In the second of these, patients are encouraged to talk about their attitudes to medication and a therapist attempts to associate patient-defined positive outcomes with medication compliance. This so-called compliance therapy is very effective in improving reported adherence and treatment outcome [17].

It is important to note that informing patients about adverse effects, even serious effects such as tardive dyskinesia, does not seem to reduce adherence to treatment [18, 19], although many prescribers shy away from providing such information [20].

Antipsychotic polypharmacy

The use of two or more antipsychotics for the same patient is common practice in schizophrenia. In the UK, around a third of those receiving antipsychotics for schizophrenia are prescribed more than one antipsychotic [21, 22]. This proportion is fairly stable over time but a reduction in the number of patients receiving typicals and atypicals together may have occurred in recent years [23]. Factors making polypharmacy more likely include younger age, male gender and detention under the Mental Health Act [24].

There is considerable disagreement over the benefits or otherwise of antipsychotic polypharmacy. Some see the practice as intelligent application of science – prescribers choose contributions to affect particular receptors and produce particular patient benefits [25]. There is also evidence that some patients deteriorate when polypharmacy regimens are converted to monotherapy [26]. However, with the exception of clozapine augmentation regimens, polypharmacy of antipsychotics should be avoided where possible. Polypharmacy appears to worsen outcome in the short term [27] and may even increase mortality [28], perhaps because polypharmacy frequently results in high-dose therapy [29]. It is also notable that much polypharmacy is accidental and not associated with clear benefit in relation to psychotic symptoms [30].

Generally, monotherapy is preferred. However, while this might be appropriate for most patients, it is likely that some patients, perhaps a small percentage, do particularly well on certain antipsychotic combinations. The reasons for this are far from clear – a fact which neatly encapsulates our somewhat limited understanding of schizophrenia and its treatment.

References

1. Harris M G, Henry L P, Harrigan S M *et al*. The relationship between duration of untreated psychosis and outcome: an eight-year prospective study. *Schizophr Res* 2005; 79: 85–93.
2. Schooler N, Rabinowitz J, Davidson M *et al*. Risperidone and haloperidol in first-episode psychosis: a long-term randomized trial. *Am J Psychiatry* 2005; 162: 947–953.
3. Sanger T M, Lieberman J A, Tohen M *et al*. Olanzapine versus haloperidol treatment in first-episode psychosis. *Am J Psychiatry* 1999; 156: 79–87.
4. Robinson D, Woerner M G, Alvir J M *et al*. Predictors of relapse following response from a first episode of schizophrenia or schizoaffective disorder. *Arch Gen Psychiatry* 1999; 56: 241–247.
5. Gitlin M, Nuechterlein K, Subotnik K L *et al*. Clinical outcome following neuroleptic discontinuation in patients with remitted recent-onset schizophrenia. *Am J Psychiatry* 2001; 158: 1835–1842.
6. Schooler N R, Keith S J, Severe J B *et al*. Relapse and rehospitalization during maintenance treatment of schizophrenia. The effects of dose reduction and family treatment. *Arch Gen Psychiatry* 1997; 54: 453–463.
7. Csernansky J G, Mahmoud R, Brenner R. A comparison of risperidone and haloperidol for the prevention of relapse in patients with schizophrenia. *N Engl J Med* 2002; 346: 16–22.
8. Adams C E, Fenton M K P, Quraishi S, David A S. Systematic meta-review of depot antipsychotic drugs for people with schizophrenia. *Br J Psychiatry* 2001; 179: 290–299.
9. Meltzer H Y. Treatment resistant schizophrenia – the role of clozapine. *Curr Med Res Opin* 1997; 14: 1–20.
10. Taylor D M, Duncan-McConnell D. Refractory schizophrenia and atypical antipsychotics. *J Psychopharmacol* 2000; 14: 409–418.
11. Taylor D M, Young C, Paton C. Prior antipsychotic prescribing in patients currently receiving clozapine: a case note review. *J Clin Psychiatry* 2003; 64: 30–34.
12. Taylor D, Paton C, Kerwin R. *The Maudsley Prescribing Guidelines*. London, UK: Taylor and Francis, 2005.

13. Lacro J P, Dunn L B, Dolder C R *et al*. Prevalence of and risk factors for medication nonadherence in patients with schizophrenia: a comprehensive review of recent literature. *J Clin Psychiatry* 2002; 63: 892–909.

14. Kampman O, Lehtinen K. Compliance in psychoses. *Acta Psychiatr Scand* 1999; 100: 167–175.

15. Marder S R. Facilitating compliance with antipsychotic medication. *J Clin Psychiatry* 1998; 59: 21–25.

16. Zygmunt A, Olfson M, Boyer C A, Mechanic D. Interventions to improve medication adherence in schizophrenia. *Am J Psychiatry* 2002; 159: 1653–1664.

17. Kemp R, Hayward P, Applewhaite G *et al*. Compliance therapy in psychotic patients: randomised controlled trial. *BMJ* 1996; 312: 345–349.

18. Chaplin R, Kent A. Informing patients about tardive dyskinesia. Controlled trial of patient education. *Br J Psychiatry* 1998; 172: 78–81.

19. Kleinman I, Schachter D, Koritar E. Informed consent and tardive dyskinesia. *Am J Psychiatry* 1989; 146: 902–904.

20. Smith S, Henderson M. What you don't know won't hurt you: information given to patients about the side-effects of antipsychotic drugs. *Psychiatr Bull* 2000; 24: 172–174.

21. Taylor D M. Prescribing of clozapine and olanzapine: dosage, polypharmacy and patient ethnicity. *Psychiatr Bull* 2004; 28: 241–243.

22. Taylor D, Mace S, Mir S, Kerwin R. A prescription survey of the use of atypical antipsychotics for hospital inpatients in the United Kingdom. *Int J Psychiatry Clin Pract* 2000; 4: 41–46.

23. Mace S, Taylor D. A prescription survey of antipsychotic use in England and Wales following the introduction of NICE guidance. *Int J Psychiatry Clin Pract* 2005; 9: 124–129.

24. Lelliott P, Paton C, Harrington M *et al*. The influence of patient variables on polypharmacy and combined high dose of antipsychotic drugs prescribed for in-patients. *Psychiatr Bull* 2002; 26: 411–414.

25. Freudenreich O, Goff D C. Antipsychotic combination therapy in schizophrenia. A review of efficacy and risks of current combinations. *Acta Psychiatr Scand* 2002; 106: 323–330.

26. Suzuki T, Uchida H, Tanaka K F *et al*. Revising polypharmacy to a single antipsychotic regimen for patients with chronic schizophrenia. *Int J Neuropsychopharmacol* 2004; 7: 133–142.

27. Centorrino F, Goren J L, Hennen J *et al*. Multiple versus single antipsychotic agents for hospitalized psychiatric patients: case–control study of risks versus benefits. *Am J Psychiatry* 2004; 161: 700–706.

28. Waddington J L, Youssef H A, Kinsella A. Mortality in schizophrenia. *Br J Psychiatry* 1998; 173: 325–329.

29. Harrington M, Paton C, Okocha C *et al*. The results of a multi-centre audit of the prescribing of antipsychotic drugs for in-patients in the UK. *Psychiatr Bull* 2002; 26: 414–418.

30. Taylor D, Mir S, Mace S, Whiskey E. Co-prescribing of atypical and typical antipsychotics – prescribing sequence and documented outcome. *Psychiatr Bull* 2002; 26: 170–172.

Glossary

Affect: The subjective and immediate experience of emotion attached to ideas or mental representations of objects. Affect has outward manifestations that may be classified as restricted, blunted, flattened, broad, labile, appropriate or inappropriate

Agitation: Severe anxiety associated with motor restlessness

Akathisia: Subjective feeling of motor restlessness manifested by a compelling need to be in constant movement: may show itself as pacing or fidgeting

Alogia: Reduced, slowed or absent speech

Amygdala: Almond-shaped structure in the basal ganglia associated with olfactory sensation

Anxiety: Feeling of apprehension caused by anticipation of danger or hazard

Apathy: Dulled emotional tone associated with detachment or indifference

Ataxia: Lack of coordination, either physical or mental. In neurology, refers to loss of muscular coordination

Auditory hallucination: False perception of sound, usually voices, but also other noises such as music may be 'heard'

Autoreceptor: Presynaptic receptor which, when stimulated, reduces neurotransmitter release

Basal ganglia: Loosely defined grey-matter structures involved in motor function. Consists of corpus striatum, amygdala and putamen

Blunted affect: Disturbance of affect manifested by a severe reduction in the intensity of externalised feeling tone. The failure to show emotional reaction

Catatonia: A condition characterised by physical rigidity and stupor

Cognition: Mental process of knowing and becoming aware; function closely associated with judgement

Command hallucination: False perception of orders that a person may be obliged to obey or unable to resist

Cortex: Outer layer of the brain (grey matter) responsible for motor and sensory function, along with higher cognitive function and intellect

Delusion: False belief, often, but not always, based on incorrect inference about external reality, that is firmly held despite objective and obvious contradictory proof or evidence and despite the fact that other members of the culture do not share the belief

Delusion of grandeur: Exaggerated conception of one's importance, power or identity

Delusion of reference: False belief that the behaviour of others refers to oneself; that events, objects or other people have a particular and unusual significance, usually of a negative nature; derived from idea of reference, in which persons falsely feel that others are talking about them (e.g. belief that people on television or radio are talking to or about the person)

Depression: Mental state characterised by feelings of sadness, loneliness, despair, low self-esteem and self-reproach; accompanying signs include psychomotor retardation or at times agitation, withdrawal from interpersonal contact and vegetative symptoms such as insomnia and anorexia

Dystonia: Extrapyramidal motor disturbance consisting of slow, sustained contractions of the musculature; one movement often predominates, leading to relatively sustained postural deviations; acute dystonic reactions (facial grimacing, torticollis) are occasionally seen with the initiation of antipsychotic drug therapy

Elevated mood: Air of confidence and enjoyment; a mood more cheerful than normal but not necessarily pathological

Flight of ideas: Rapid succession of fragmentary thoughts or speech in which content changes abruptly and speech may be incoherent

Galactorrhoea: Abnormal discharge of milk from the breast; may result from the endocrine influence (e.g. prolactin) of dopamine receptor antagonists, such as phenothiazines

Grandiosity: Exaggerated feelings of one's importance, power, knowledge or identity. Occurs in delusional disorder, manic states

Hallucination: False sensory perception occurring in the absence of any relevant external stimulation. May be auditory, visual, olfactory, gustatory or tactile

Hebephrenia: A condition characterised by shallow or inappropriate affect and silly or childish mannerisms or behaviour

Hippocampus: Cylindrical structure consisting of grey matter forming part of the limbic system and responsible for memory, emotion and the autonomic nervous system

Hypomania: Mood abnormality with the qualitative characteristics of mania but somewhat less intense

Impaired insight: Diminished ability to understand the objective reality of a situation

Insight: Conscious recognition of one's own condition. In psychiatry, it refers to the conscious awareness and understanding of one's own psychodynamics and symptoms of maladaptive behaviour

Loosening of associations: Characteristic schizophrenic thinking or speech disturbance involving a disorder in the logical progression of thoughts, manifested as a failure to communicate verbally adequately; unrelated and unconnected ideas shift from one subject to another

Mania: Mood state characterised by elation, agitation, hyperactivity, hypersexuality and accelerated thinking and speaking (flight of ideas)

Mood: Pervasive and sustained feeling that is experienced internally and that, in the extreme, can markedly influence virtually all aspects of a person's behaviour and perception of the world. Distinguished from affect, the external expression of the internal feeling tone

Neologism: New word or phrase whose derivation cannot be understood; often seen in schizophrenia

Paranoia: Psychiatric syndrome marked by the gradual development of a highly elaborate and complex delusional system, generally involving persecutory or grandiose delusions

Passivity: Feelings of being controlled by others or by outside forces

Pervasive developmental disorder: Group of mental disorders characterised by limitations in the development of language and social skills

Phobia: Persistent, pathological, unrealistic, intense fear of an object or situation; the phobic person may realise that the fear is irrational but, nonetheless, cannot dispel it

Positive signs: In schizophrenia: hallucinations, delusions, thought disorder

Poverty of speech: Restriction in the amount of speech used; replies may be monosyllabic

Pressured speech: Increase in the amount of spontaneous speech; rapid, loud, accelerated speech

Psychosis: Mental disorder in which the thoughts, affective response, ability to recognise reality and ability to communicate and relate to others are sufficiently impaired to interfere grossly with the capacity to deal with reality

Thought disorder: Any disturbance of thinking that affects language, communication or thought content – the hallmark feature of schizophrenia. Manifestations range from simple blocking and mild circumstantiality to profound loosening of associations, incoherence and delusions; characterized by a failure to follow semantic and syntactic rules which is inconsistent with the person's education, intelligence or cultural background

Tremor: Rhythmical alteration in movement, which is usually faster than one beat a second; typically, tremors decrease during periods of relaxation and sleep and increase during periods of anger and increased tension

Ventricle: Fluid-filled structure responsible for secretion of cerebro-spinal fluid

Appendix

Rating scales

Brief Psychiatric Rating Scale

Please enter the score which best describes the patient's condition.

0 = not assessed, 1 = not present, 2 = very mild, 4 = moderate,
5 = moderately severe, 6 = severe, 7 = extremely severe

1. **Somatic concern**   Score
    Degree of concern over present physical health. Rate the   ☐
    degree to which physical health is perceived as a problem by
    the patient, whether complaints have a realistic basis or not.

2. **Anxiety**   Score
    Worry, fear, or over-concern for present or future. Rate solely   ☐
    on the basis of verbal report by patient, not observed anxiety,
    which is rated under Tension.

3. **Depression**   Score
    Includes sadness, unhappiness, anhedonia and preoccupation   ☐
    with depressing topics (can't attend to TV or conversations
    due to depression), hopelessness, loss of self-esteem. Do not
    include vegetative symptoms, e.g. motor retardation, early
    waking or the amotivation that accompanies the deficit
    syndrome.

4. **Suicidality**   Score
    Expressed desire, intent or actions to harm or kill self.   ☐

5. **Guilt**   Score
    Over-concern or remorse for past behaviour. Rate only   ☐
    patient's statements, do not infer feelings from depression,
    anxiety or neurotic defences.

6. **Hostility**   Score

   Animosity, contempt, belligerence, threats, arguments,   ☐
   tantrums, property destruction, fights and any other reports
   of hostile attitudes or actions. Rate solely on the basis of the
   verbal report of feelings and actions of the patient toward
   others. Do not infer hostility from neurotic defences, anxiety
   or somatic complaints. Do not include incidents of appropriate
   anger or obvious self-defence

7. **Elevated mood**   Score

   A pervasive, sustained and exaggerated feeling of well-being   ☐
   cheerfulness, euphoria (implying a pathological mood),
   optimism that is out of proportion to the circumstances. Do
   not infer elation from increased activity or from grandiose
   statements alone.

8. **Grandiosity**   Score

   Exaggerated self-opinion, conviction of special abilities or   ☐
   powers or identity as someone rich or famous. Rate only
   patient's statements about himself, not his demeanour.

9. **Suspiciousness**   Score

   Expressed or apparent belief that others have now, or have   ☐
   had in the past, acted with a malicious or discriminatory intent.
   Include persecution by supernatural or other non-human
   agencies (e.g the devil).

10. **Hallucinations**   Score

    Perceptions without normal external stimulus. Rate only   ☐
    those experiences which are reported to have occurred in the
    last week and which are described as distinctly different from
    the thought and imagery processes of normal people.

11. **Unusual thought content**   Score

    Unusual, odd, strange or bizarre thought content. Rate the   ☐
    degree of unusualness, not the degree of disorganisation of
    speech. Include thought insertion, withdrawal and broadcast.
    Include grandiose, somatic and persecutory delusions, even if
    rated elsewhere.

12. **Bizarre behaviour**   Score

    Reports of behaviours which are odd, unusual or psychotically   ☐
    criminal. Not limited to interview period. Include inappropriate
    sexual behaviour and inappropriate affect.

13. **Self-neglect**   Score

Hygiene, appearance or eating behaviour below usual   ❑
expectations, below socially acceptable standards or
life-threatening.

14. **Disorientation**   Score

Does not comprehend situations or communications such   ❑
as questions asked during the entire interview. Confusion
regarding person, place or time. Do not rate if incorrect
responses are due to delusions.

15. **Conceptual disorganisation**   Score

Degree to which speech is confused, disconnected, vague or   ❑
disorganised. Rate on the basis of integration of the verbal
products of the patient. Do not rate on content of speech.

16. **Blunted affect**   Score

Restricted range in emotional expressiveness of face, voice   ❑
and gestures. Marked indifference or flatness even when
discussing distressing topics.

17. **Emotional withdrawal**   Score

Deficiency in patient's ability to relate emotionally during   ❑
interview situation. Use your own feeling as to the presence of
an 'invisible barrier' between patient and interviewer. Include
withdrawal apparently due to psychotic processes.

18. **Motor retardation**   Score

Reduction in energy level evidenced by slowed movements   ❑
and speech, decreased number of spontaneous body movements.
Rate on basis of observed behaviour of the patient only. Do not
rate on the basis of patient's subjective impression of his own
energy level. Rate regardless of medication effects.

19. **Tension**   Score

Physical and motor manifestations of tension 'nervousness'   ❑
and agitation. Self-reported experiences of tension should be
rated under the item on anxiety. Do not rate if restlessness is
solely akathisia, but do rate if akathisia is exacerbated by
tension.

20. Uncooperativeness   Score

Resistance and lack of willingness to cooperate with interview
The uncooperativeness might result from suspiciousness. Rate
only uncooperativeness in relation to the interview, not
behaviours involving peers and relatives.

21. Excitement   Score

Heightened emotional tone or increased emotional reactivity
to interviewer or topics being discussed, as evidenced by
increased intensity of facial expressions, voice tone, expressive
gestures or increase in speech quantity and speed.

22. Distractibility   Score

Degree to which observed sequences of speech and actions
are interrupted by stimuli unrelated to the interview.
Distractibility is rated when the patient shows a change in the
focus of attention as characterised by a pause in speech or a
marked shift in gaze. Rate even if the distracting stimulus
cannot be identified.

23. Motor hyperactivity   Score

Increase in energy level evidenced in more frequent movement
and/or rapid speech. Do not rate if restlessness is due to
akathisia.

24. Mannerisms and posturing   Score

Unusual and bizarre behaviour, stylised movement or acts, or
any postures which are clearly uncomfortable or inappropriate.
Exclude obvious manifestations of medication side-effects. Do
not include nervous mannerisms that are not odd or unusual.

Total   Score

Positive and Negative Symptom Scale

The Positive and Negative Symptom Scale (PANSS) is a 30-item rating instrument that evaluates positive, negative and other symptoms in people with schizophrenia. It is probably the most commonly used scale in clinical trials.

Seven items are grouped to form a positive subscale. Another seven items constitute the negative subscale and 16 items make up the general psychopathology subscale.

The 30 items in the PANSS are rated on a seven-point scale (1 = absent, 7 = extreme). Ratings are based on information relative to the previous week, devised from both the clinical interview and reports from hospital staff or family members.

In addition to these three scales, a bipolar composite scale expresses the direction and magnitude of difference between positive and negative syndrome. The Composite scale score is determined by subtracting the negative from the positive score and reflects the degree of predominance of one syndrome or another.

The potential ranges of scores are 7–49 for the Positive and Negative scales and 16–112 for the General Psychopharmacology scale. In addition to these measures the composite scale yields a bipolar index that ranges from −42 to +42.

Those who score 'moderate' or higher on at least three of the seven positive items are considered to have predominantly positive symptoms. Similarly, those who score 'moderate' or higher on at least three of the seven negative items thus have negative-type schizophrenia. Those that score at least three moderate ratings are regarded as 'mixed-type'.

A 20% reduction in the total PANSS score is usually defined as a response.

The Positive and Negative Syndrome Scale

For each item below enter the code that best describes the patient's psychopathology.

Positive scale

P1.   Delusions: Beliefs which are unfounded, unrealistic   **Score**
and idiosyncratic.   ❏

Basis for rating: thought content expressed in the interview
and its influence on social relations and behaviour.

1 =   Absent – Definition does not apply.

2 = Minimal – Questionable pathology; may be at the upper extreme of normal limits.

3 = Mild – Presence of one or two delusions which are vague, uncrystallised and not tenaciously held. Delusions do not interfere with thinking, social relations or behaviour.

4 = Moderate – Presence of either a kaleidoscope array of poorly formed, unstable delusions or of a few well-formed delusions that occasionally interfere with thinking, social relations or behaviour.

5 = Moderate severe – Presence of numerous well-formed delusions that are tenaciously held and occasionally interfere with thinking, social relations and behaviour.

6 = Severe – Presence of a stable set of delusions which are cystallised, possibly systematised, tenaciously held, and clearly interfere with thinking, social relations and behaviour.

7 = Extreme – Presence of a stable set of delusions which are either highly systematised or very numerous and which dominate major facets of the patient's life. This frequently results in inappropriate and irresponsible action, which may even jeopardise the safety of the patient or others.

P2. **Conceptual disorganisation:** Disorganised process of thinking characterised by the disruption of goal-directed sequencing (e.g, circumstantiality, tangentiality, loose associations, *non sequiturs*, gross illogicality or thought block).

Score ❏

Basis for rating: cognitive–verbal processes observed during the course of the interview.

1 = Absent – Definition does not apply.

2 = Minimal – Questionable pathology; may be at the upper extreme of normal limits.

3 = Mild – Thinking is circumstantial, tangential or paralogical. There is some difficulty in directing thoughts toward a goal, and some loosening of associations may be evidenced under pressure.

4 = Moderate – Able to focus thoughts when communications are brief and structured, but becomes loose or irrelevant when dealing with more complex communications or when under minimal pressure.

5 = Moderate severe – Generally has difficulty in organising thoughts, as evidenced by frequent irrelevancies, disconnectedness or loosening of associations when under pressure.

6 =   Severe – Thinking is seriously derailed and internally inconsistent, resulting in gross irrelevancies and disruption of thought processes, which occur almost constantly.

7 =   Extreme – Thoughts are disrupted to the point where the patient is incoherent. There is marked loosening of associations, which results in total failure of communication (e.g. 'word salad') or mutism.

P3.   **Hallucinatory behaviour:** Verbal report or behaviour indicating perceptions which are not generated by external stimuli. These may occur in the auditory, visual, olfactory or somatic realms.

    Score ☐

Basis for rating: verbal report and physical manifestations during the course of the interview as well as reports of behaviour by primary care workers or family.

1 =   Absent – Definition does not apply.

2 =   Minimal – Questionable pathology; may be at the upper extreme of normal limits.

3 =   Mild – One or two clearly formed but infrequent hallucinations, or else a number of vague abnormal perceptions which do not result in distortions of thinking or behaviour.

4 =   Moderate – Hallucinations occur frequently but not continuously, and the patient's thinking and behaviour are affected only to a minor extent.

5 =   Moderate severe – Hallucinations are frequent, may involve more than one sensory modality and tend to distort thinking and/or disrupt behaviour. Patient may have delusional interpretation of these experiences and respond to them emotionally and, on occasion, verbally as well.

6 =   Severe – Hallucinations are present almost continuously, causing major disruption of thinking and behaviour. Patient treats these as real perceptions, and functioning is impeded by the frequent emotional and verbal responses to them.

7 =   Extreme – Patient is almost totally preoccupied with hallucinations, which virtually dominate thinking and behaviour. Hallucinations are provided with a rigid delusional interpretation and provoke verbal and behavioural responses, including obedience to command hallucinations.

P4.   Excitement: Hyperactivity as reflected in accelerated motor behaviour, heightened responsivity to stimuli, hypervigilance or excessive mood lability.

Basis for rating: behavioural manifestations during the course of the interview as well as reports of behaviour by primary care workers or family.

1 =   Absent – Definition does not apply.

2 =   Minimal – Questionable pathology; may be at the upper extreme of normal limits.

3 =   Mild – Tends to be slightly agitated, hypervigilant or mildly overaroused throughout the interview, but without distinct episodes of excitement or marked mood lability. Speech may be slightly pressured.

4 =   Moderate – Agitation or overarousal is clearly evident throughout the interview, affecting speech and general mobility, or episodic outbursts occur sporadically.

5 =   Moderate severe – Significant hyperactivity or frequent outbursts of motor activity are observed, making it difficult for the patient to sit still for longer than several minutes at any given time.

6 =   Severe – Marked excitement dominates the interview, delimits attention, and to some extent affects personal functions such as eating or sleeping.

7 =   Extreme – Marked excitement seriously interferes with eating and sleeping and makes interpersonal interactions virtually impossible. Acceleration of speech and motor activity may result in incoherence and exhaustion.

P5.   Grandiosity: Exaggerated self-opinion and unrealistic convictions of superiority, including delusions of extraordinary abilities, wealth, knowledge, fame, power and moral righteousness.

Basis for rating: thought content expressed in the interview and its influence on behaviour.

1 =   Absent – Definition does not apply.

2 =   Minimal – Questionable pathology; may be at the upper extreme of normal limits.

3 =   Mild – Some expansiveness or boastfulness is evident, but without clear-cut grandiose delusions.

4 = Moderate – Feels distinctly and unrealistically superior to others. Some poorly formed delusions about special status or abilities may be present but not acted upon.

5 = Moderate severe – Clear-cut delusions concerning remarkable abilities, status or power are expressed and influence attitude but not behaviour.

6 = Severe – Clear-cut delusions of remarkable superiority involving more than one parameter (wealth, knowledge, fame, etc.) are expressed, notably influence interactions, and may be acted upon.

7 = Extreme – Thinking, interactions and behaviour are dominated by multiple delusions of amazing ability, wealth, knowledge, fame, power and/or moral stature, which take on a bizarre quality.

P6. Suspiciousness/Persecution: Unrealistic or exaggerated ideas of persecution, as reflected in guardedness, a distrustful attitude, suspicious hypervigilance or frank delusions that others mean harm.

Score
❑

Basis for rating: thought content expressed in the interview and its influence on behaviour.

1 = Absent – Definition does not apply.

2 = Minimal – Questionable pathology; may be at the upper extreme of normal limits.

3 = Mild – Presents a guarded or even openly distrustful attitude, but thoughts, interactions and behaviour are minimally affected.

4 = Moderate – Distrustfulness is clearly evident and intrudes on the interview and/or behaviour, but there is no evidence of persecutory delusions, and it does not seem to affect the patient's attitude or interpersonal relations.

5 = Moderate severe – Patient shows marked distrustfulnesss, leading to major disruption of interpersonal relations, or else there are clear-cut persecutory delusions that have limited impact on interpersonal relations and behaviour.

6 = Severe – Clear-cut pervasive delusions of persecution which may be systematised and significantly interfere in interpersonal relations.

7 = Extreme – A network of systematised persecutory delusions dominates the patient's thinking, social relations and behaviour.

P7. Hostility: Verbal and non-verbal expressions of anger and resentment, including sarcasm, passive–aggressive behaviour, verbal abuse and assaultiveness.

Score

Basis for rating: interpersonal behaviour observed during the interview and reports by the primary care workers or family.

1 = Absent – Definition does not apply.
2 = Minimal – Questionable pathology; may be at the upper end of normal limits.
3 = Mild – Indirect or restrained communication of anger, such as sarcasm, disrespect, hostile expressions and occasional irritability.
4 = Moderate – Presents an overly hostile attitude, showing frequent irritability and direct expression of anger or resentment.
5 = Moderate severe – Patient is highly irritable and occasionally verbally abusive or threatening.
6 = Severe – Uncooperativeness and verbal abuse or threats notably influence and seriously impact upon social relations. Patient may be violent and destructive but is not physically assaultive toward others.
7 = Extreme – Marked anger results in extreme uncooperativeness, precluding other interactions, or in episode(s) of physical assault towards others.

Negative scale

N1. Blunted affect: Diminished emotional responsiveness as characterised by a reduction in facial expression, modulation of feelings and communicative gestures.

Score

Basis for rating: observation of physical manifestations of effective and emotional tone during the course of the interview.

1 = Absent – Definition does not apply.
2 = Minimal – Questionable pathology; may be at the upper extreme of normal limits.
3 = Mild – Changes in facial expression and communicative gestures seem to be stilted, forced, artificial or lacking in modulation.
4 = Moderate – Reduced range of facial expression and few expressive gestures result in a dull appearance.

5 = Moderate severe – Affect is generally 'flat', with only occasional changes in facial expression and a paucity of communicative gestures.

6 = Severe – Marked flatness and a deficiency of emotions exhibited most of the time. There may be unmodulated extreme affective discharges, such as excitement, rage or inappropriate uncontrolled laughter.

7 = Extreme – Changes in facial expression and evidence of communicative gestures are virtually absent. Patient seems constantly to show a barren or 'wooden' expression.

N3. Emotional withdrawal: Lack of interest in, involvement with, and affective commitment to life's events.

Score ❏

Basis for rating: reports of functioning from primary care workers or family and observation of interpersonal behaviour during the course of the interview.

1 = Absent – Definition does not apply.

2 = Minimal – Questionable pathology; may be at the upper end of normal limits.

3 = Mild – Usually lack initiative and occasionally may show deficient interest in surrounding events.

4 = Moderate – Patient is generally distanced emotionally from the milieu and its challenges but, with encouragement, can be engaged.

5 = Moderate severe – Patient is clearly detached emotionally from persons and events in the milieu, resisting all efforts at engagement. Patient appears distant, docile and purposeless but can be involved in communication at least briefly and tends to personal needs, sometimes with assistance.

6 = Severe – Marked deficiency of interest and emotional commitment results in limited conversation with others and frequent neglect of personal functions, for which the patient requires supervision.

7 = Extreme. Patient is almost totally withdrawn, uncommunicative and neglectful of personal needs as a result of profound lack of interest and emotional commitment.

N3. Poor rapport: Lack of interpersonal empathy, openness in conversation and sense of closeness, interest or involvement with the interviewer. This is evidenced by interpersonal distancing and reduced verbal and non-verbal communication.

Score ☐

Basis for rating: interpersonal behaviour during the course of the interview.

1 = Absent – Definition does not apply.

2 = Minimal – Questionable pathology; may be at the upper extreme of normal limits.

3 = Mild – Conversation is characterised by a stilted, strained or artificial tone. It may lack emotional depth or tend to remain on an interpersonal, intellectual plane.

4 = Moderate – Patient is typically aloof, with interpersonal distance quite evident. Patient may answer questions mechanically, act bored or express disinterest.

5 = Moderate severe – Disinvolvement is obvious and clearly impedes the productivity of the interview. Patient may tend to avoid eye or face contact.

6 = Severe – Patient is highly indifferent, with marked interpersonal distance. Answers are perfunctory, and there is little non-verbal evidence of involvement. Eye and face contact are frequently avoided.

7 = Extreme – Patient is totally uninvolved with the interviewer. Patient appears to be completely indifferent and consistently avoids verbal and non-verbal interactions during the interview.

N4. Passive/Apathetic social withdrawal: Diminished interest and initiative in social interactions due to passivity, apathy, anergy or avolition. This leads to reduced interpersonal involvements and neglect of activities of daily living.

Score ☐

Basis for rating: reports on social behaviour from primary care workers or family.

1 = Absent – Definition does not apply.

2 = Minimal – Questionable pathology; may be at the upper extreme of normal limits.

3 = Mild – Shows occasional interest in social activities but poor initiative. Usually engages with others only when approached first by them.

4 =   Moderate – Passively goes along with most social activities but in a disinterested or mechanical way. Tends to recede into the background.

5 =   Moderate severe – Passively participates in only a minority of activities and shows virtually no interest or initiative. Generally spends little time with others.

6 =   Severe – Tends to be apathetic and isolated, participating very rarely in social activities and occasionally neglecting personal needs. Has very few spontaneous social contacts.

7 =   Extreme – Profoundly apathetic, socially isolated and personally neglectful.

N5. Difficulty in abstract thinking: Impairment in the use   **Score**
of the abstract–symbolic mode of thinking, as evidenced   ☐
by difficulty in classification, forming generalisations and
proceeding beyond concrete or egocentric thinking in
problem-solving tasks.

Basis for rating: responses to questions on similarities and proverb interpretation, and use of concrete versus abstract mode during the course of the interview.

1 =   Absent – Definition does not apply.

2 =   Minimal – Questionable pathology; may be at the upper extreme of normal limits.

3 =   Mild – Tends to give literal or personalised interpretations to the more difficult proverbs and may have some problems with concepts that are fairly abstract or remotely related.

4 =   Moderate – Often utilises a concrete mode. Has difficulty with most proverbs and some categories. Tends to be distracted by functional aspects and salient features.

5 =   Moderate severe – Deals primarily in a concrete mode, exhibiting difficulty with most proverbs and many categories.

6 =   Severe – Unable to grasp the abstract meaning of any proverbs or figurative expressions and can formulate classifications for only the most simple of similarities. Thinking is either vacuous or locked into functional aspects, salient features and idiosyncratic interpretations.

7 =   Extreme – Can use only concrete modes of thinking. Shows no comprehension of proverbs, common metaphors or similes, and simple categories. Even salient and functional attributes do not serve as a basis for classification. This rating may apply to those who cannot interact even minimally with the examiner due to marked cognitive impairment.

N6. Lack of spontaneity and flow of conversation:
Reduction in the normal flow of communication associated with apathy, avolition, defensiveness or cognitive deficit. This is manifested by diminished fluidity and productivity of the verbal–interactional process.

Score
❏

Basis for rating: cognitive–verbal processes observed during the course of interview.

1 = Absent – Definition does not apply.
2 = Minimal – Questionable pathology; may be at the upper extreme of normal limits.
3 = Mild – Conversation shows little initiative. Patient's answers tend to be brief and unembellished, requiring direct and leading questions by the interviewer.
4 = Moderate – Conversation lacks free flow and appears uneven or halting. Leading questions are frequently needed to elicit adequate responses and proceed with conversation.
5 = Moderate severe – Patient shows a marked lack of spontaneity and openness, replying to the interviewer's questions with only one or two brief sentences.
6 = Severe – Patient's responses are limited mainly to a few words or short phrases intended to avoid or curtail communication (e.g. 'I don't know', 'I'm not at liberty to say'). Conversation is seriously impaired as a result, and the interview is highly unproductive.
7 = Extreme – Verbal output is restricted to, at most, an occasional utterance, making conversation not possible.

N7. Stereotyped thinking: Decreased fluidity, spontaneity and flexibility of thinking, as evidenced in rigid, repetitious or barren thought content.

Score
❏

Basis for rating: cognitive–verbal processes observed during the interview.

1 = Absent – Definition does not apply.
2 = Minimal – Questionable pathology; may be at the upper extreme of normal limits.
3 = Mild – Some rigidity shown in attitudes or beliefs. Patient may refuse to consider alternative positions or have difficulty in shifting from one idea to another.

4 = Moderate – Conversation revolves around a recurrent theme, resulting in difficulty in shifting to a new topic.

5 = Moderate severe – Thinking is rigid and repetitious to the point that, despite the interviewer's efforts, conversation is limited to only two or three dominating topics.

6 = Severe – Uncontrolled repetition of demands, statements, ideas or questions, which severely impairs conversation.

7 = Extreme – Thinking, behaviour and conversation are dominated by constant repetition of fixed ideas or limited phrases, leading to gross rigidity, inappropriateness and restrictiveness of patient's communication.

General Psychopathology Scale

G1. Somatic concern: Physical complaints or beliefs about   Score
bodily illness or malfunctions. This may range from a   ❏
vague sense of ill-being to clear-cut delusions of
catastrophic physical disease.

Basis for rating: thought content expressed in the
interview.

1 =   Absent – Definition does not apply.
2 =   Minimal – Questionable pathology; may be at the upper extreme
of normal limits.
3 =   Mild – Distinctly concerned about health or somatic issues, as
evidenced by occasional questions and desire for reassurance.
4 =   Moderate – Complains about poor health or bodily malfunction,
but there is no delusional conviction, and overconcern can be
allayed by reassurance.
5 =   Moderate severe – Patient expresses numerous or frequent
complaints about physical illness or bodily malfunction, or else
patient reveals one or two clear-cut delusions involving these
themes but is not preoccupied by them.
6 =   Severe – Patient is preoccupied by one or a few clear-cut
delusions about physical disease or organic malfunction, but
affect is not fully immersed in these themes, and thoughts can
be diverted by the interviewer with some effort.
7 =   Extreme – Numerous and frequently reported somatic delusions,
or only a few somatic delusions of a catastrophic nature, which
totally dominate the patient's affect and thinking.

G2. Anxiety: Subjective experience of nervousness, worry,   Score
apprehension or restlessness, ranging from excessive   ❏
concern about the present or future to feelings of panic.

Basis for rating: verbal report during the course of
interview and corresponding physical manifestations.

1 =   Absent – Definition does not apply.
2 =   Minimal – Questionable pathology; may be at the upper
extreme of normal limits.
3 =   Mild – Expresses some worry, over-concern or subjective
restlessness, but no somatic and behavioural consequences
are reported or evidenced.

4 = Moderate – Patient reports distinct symptoms of nervousness, which are reflected in mild physical manifestations such as fine hand tremor and excessive perspiration.

5 = Moderate severe – Patient reports serious problems of anxiety which have significant physical and behavioural consequences, such as marked tension, poor concentration, palpitations or impaired sleep.

6 = Severe – Subjective state of almost constant fear associated with phobias, marked restlessness or numerous somatic manifestations.

7 = Extreme – Patient's life is seriously disrupted by anxiety, which is present almost constantly and, at times, reaches panic proportion or is manifested in actual panic attacks.

G3. Guilt feelings: Sense of remorse or self-blame for real or imagined misdeeds in the past.

Score ☐

Basis for rating: verbal report of guilt feelings during the course of interview and the influence on attitudes and thoughts.

1 = Absent – Definition does not apply.

2 = Minimal – Questionable pathology; may be at the upper extreme of normal limits.

3 = Mild – Questioning elicits a vague sense of guilt or self-blame for a minor incident, but the patient clearly is not overly concerned.

4 = Moderate – Patient expresses distinct concern over his responsibility for a real incident in his life but is not preoccupied with it, and attitude and behaviour are essentially unaffected.

5 = Moderate severe – Patient expresses a strong sense of guilt associated with self-deprecation or the belief that he deserves punishment. The guilt feelings may have a delusional basis, may be volunteered spontaneously, may be a source of preoccupation and/or depressed mood, and cannot be allayed readily by the interviewer.

6 = Severe – Strong ideas of guilt take on a delusional quality and lead to an attitude of hopelessness or worthlessness. The patient believes he should receive harsh sanctions for the misdeeds and may even regard his current life situation as such punishment.

7 = Extreme – Patient's life dominated by unshakable delusions of guilt, for which he feels deserving of drastic punishment, such as life imprisonment, torture or death. There may be associated suicidal thoughts or attribution of others' problems to one's own past misdeeds.

G4. **Tension:** Overt physical manifestations of fear, anxiety **Score** and agitation, such as stiffness, tremor, profuse sweating ☐ and restlessness.

Basis for rating: verbal reports attesting to anxiety and, thereupon, the severity of physical manifestations of tension observed during the interview.

1 = Absent – Definition does not apply.

2 = Minimal – Questionable pathology; may be at the upper extreme of normal limits.

3 = Mild – Posture and movements indicate slight apprehensiveness, such as minor rigidity, occasional restlessness, shifting of position or fine rapid hand tremor.

4 = Moderate – A clearly nervous appearance emerges from various manifestations, such as fidgety behaviour, obvious hand tremor, excessive perspiration or nervous mannerisms.

5 = Moderate severe – Pronounced tension is evidenced by numerous manifestations, such as nervous shaking, profuse sweating and restlessness, but conduct in the interview is not significantly affected.

6 = Severe – Pronounced tension to the point that interpersonal interactions are disrupted. The patient, for example, may be constantly fidgeting, unable to sit still for long or show hyperventilation.

7 = Extreme – Marked tension is manifested by signs of panic or gross motor acceleration, such as rapid restless pacing and inability to remain seated for longer than a minute, which makes sustained conversation not possible.

G5. **Mannerisms and posturing:** Unnatural movements or **Score** posture as characterized by an awkward, stilted, ☐ disorganized or bizarre appearance.

Basis for rating: observation of physical manifestations during the course of interview as well as reports from primary care workers or family.

1 =   Absent – Definition does not apply.

2 =   Minimal – Questionable pathology; may be at the upper
      extreme of normal limits.

3 =   Mild – Slight awkwardness in movements or minor rigidity
      of posture.

4 =   Moderate – Movements are notably awkward or disjointed,
      or an unnatural posture is maintained for brief periods.

5 =   Moderate severe – Occasional bizarre rituals or contorted
      posture are observed, or an abnormal position is sustained
      for extended positions.

6 =   Severe – Frequent repetition of bizarre rituals, mannerisms
      or stereotyped movements, or a contorted posture is sustained
      for extended periods.

7 =   Extreme – Functioning is seriously impaired by virtually
      constant involvement in ritualistic, manneristic or stereotyped
      movements or by an unnatural fixed posture which is
      sustained most of the time.

G6. Depression: Feelings of sadness, discouragement,   **Score**
helplessness and pessimism.   ☐

Basis for rating: verbal report of depressed mood during
the course of interview and its observed influence on
attitude and behaviour.

1 =   Absent – Definition does not apply.

2 =   Minimal – Questionable pathology; may be at the upper
      extreme of normal limits.

3 =   Mild – Expresses some sadness or discouragement only on
      questioning, but there is no evidence of depression in general
      attitude or demeanour.

4 =   Moderate – Distinct feelings of sadness or hopelessness, which
      may be spontaneously divulged, but depressed mood has no
      major impact on behaviour or social functioning, and the patient
      usually can be cheered up.

5 =   Moderate severe – Distinctly depressed mood is associated with
      obvious sadness, pessimism, loss of social interest, psychomotor
      retardation and some interference in appetite and sleep. The
      patient cannot be easily cheered up.

6 =   Severe – Markedly depressed mood is associated with sustained
      feelings of misery, occasional crying, hopelessness and
      worthlessness. In addition, there is a major interference in
      appetite and/or sleep as well as in normal motor and social
      functions, with possible signs of self-neglect.

7 = Extreme – Depressive feelings seriously interfere in most major functions. The manifestations include frequent crying, pronounced somatic symptoms, impaired concentration, psychomotor retardation, social disinterest, self-neglect, possible depressive or nihilistic delusions and/or possible suicidal thoughts or actions.

G7. **Motor retardation:** Reduction on motor activity as reflected in slowing or lessening of movements and speech, diminished responsiveness to stimuli and reduced body tone.   Score ❑

Basis for rating: manifestations during the course of the interview as well as reports by primary care workers or family.

1 = Absent – Definition does not apply.
2 = Minimal – Questionable pathology; may be at the upper extreme of normal limits.
3 = Mild – Slight but noticeable diminution in rate of movements and speech. Patient may be somewhat underproductive in conversation and gestures.
4 = Moderate – Patient is clearly slow in movements, and speech may be characterized by poor productivity, including long response latency, extended pauses or slow pace.
5 = Moderate severe – A marked reduction in motor activity renders communication highly unproductive or delimits functioning in social and occupational situations. Patient can usually be found sitting or lying down.
6 = Severe – Movements are extremely slow, resulting in a minimum of activity and speech. Essentially the day is spent sitting idly or lying down.
7 = Extreme – Patient is almost completely immobile and virtually unresponsive to external stimuli.

G8. **Uncooperativeness:** Active refusal to comply with the will of significant others, including the interviewer, hospital staff or family, which may be associated with distrust, defensiveness, stubbornness, negativism, rejection of authority, hostility or belligerence.   Score ❑

Basis for rating: interpersonal behaviour observed during the course of interview as well as reports by primary care workers or family.

1 = Absent – Definition does not apply.

2 = Minimal – Questionable pathology; may be at the upper extreme of normal limits.

3 = Mild – Complies with an attitude of resentment, impatience or sarcasm. May inoffensively object to sensitive probing during the interview.

4 = Moderate – Occasional outright refusal to comply with normal social demands, such as making own bed, attending scheduled programmes, etc. The patient may project a hostile, defensive or negative attitude but usually can be worked with.

5 = Moderate severe – Patient frequently is incompliant with the demands of his milieu and may be characterised by others as an 'outcast' or having 'a serious attitude problem'. Uncooperativeness is reflected in obvious defensiveness or irritability with the interviewer and possible unwillingness to address many questions.

6 = Severe – Patient is highly uncooperative, negativistic and possibly also belligerent. Refuses to comply with most social demands and may be unwilling to initiate or conclude the full interview.

7 = Extreme – Active resistance seriously impacts on virtually all major areas of functioning. Patient may refuse to join in any social activities, tend to personal hygiene, converse with family or staff and participate even briefly in an interview.

G9. Unusual thought content: Thinking characterised by strange, fantastic or bizarre ideas, ranging from those which are remote or atypical to those which are distorted, illogical and patently absurd.

Score
☐

Basis for rating: thought content expressed during the course of interview.

1 = Absent – Definition does not apply.

2 = Minimal – Questionable pathology; may be at the upper extreme of normal limits.

3 = Mild – Thought content is somewhat peculiar or idiosyncratic, or familiar ideas are framed in an odd context.

4 = Moderate – Ideas are frequently distorted and occasionally seem quite bizarre.

5 = Moderate severe – Patient expresses many strange and fantastic thoughts (e.g. being the adopted son of a king, being an escapee from death row) or some which are patently absurd (e.g. having hundreds of children, receiving radio messages from outer space through a tooth filling).

6 = Severe – Patient expresses many illogical or absurd ideas or some which have a distinctly bizarre quality (e.g. having three heads, being a visitor from another planet).

7 = Extreme – Thinking is replete with absurd, bizarre and grotesque ideas.

G10. Disorientation: Lack of awareness of one's relationship to the milieu, including persons, place and time, which may be due to confusion or withdrawal.

Score ☐

Basis for rating: responses to interview question on orientation.

1 = Absent – Definition does not apply.

2 = Minimal – Questionable pathology; may be at the upper extreme of normal limits.

3 = Mild – General orientation is adequate but there is some difficulty with specifics. For example, patient knows his locations but not the street address; knows hospital staff names but not their functions; knows the month but confuses the day of week with an adjacent day; or errs in the date by more than two days. There may be narrowing of interest evidenced by familiarity with the immediate but not extended milieu, such as ability to identify staff but not the Mayor, Governor or President.

4 = Moderate – Only partial success in recognising persons, places and time. For example, patient knows he is in hospital but not its name; knows the name of his city but not the borough or district; knows the name of his primary therapist but not many other direct care workers; knows the year and season but is not sure of the month.

5 = Moderate severe – Considerable failure in recognising persons, place and time. Patient has only a vague notion of where he is and seems unfamiliar with most people in his milieu. He may identify the year correctly or nearly so but not know the current month, day of the week, or even the season.

6 =   Severe – Marked failure in recognising persons, place and time. For example, patient has no knowledge of his whereabouts; confuses the date by more than 1 year; can name only one or two individuals in his current life.

7 =   Extreme – Patient appears completely disoriented with regard to persons, place and time. There is gross confusion or total ignorance about his location, the current year, and even the most familiar people, such as parents, spouse, friends and primary therapist.

G11. Poor attention: Failure in focused alertness manifested by poor concentration, distractibility from internal and external stimuli, and difficulty in harnessing, sustaining or shifting focus to new stimuli.

Score

☐

Basis for rating: manifestations during the course of interview.

1 =   Absent – Definition does not apply.

2 =   Minimal – Questionable pathology; may be at the upper extreme of normal limits.

3 =   Mild – Limited concentration evidenced by occasional vulnerability to distraction or faltering attention toward the end of the interview.

4 =   Moderate – Conversation is affected by the tendency to be easily distracted, difficulty in long sustaining concentration on a given topic, or problems in shifting attention to new topics.

5 =   Moderate severe – Conversation is seriously hampered by poor concentration, distractibility and difficulty in shifting focus appropriately.

6 =   Severe – Patient's attention can be harnessed for only brief moments or with great effort due to marked distraction by external or internal stimuli.

7 =   Extreme – Attention is so disrupted that even brief conversation is not possible.

G12. Lack of judgement and insight: Impaired awareness or understanding of one's own psychiatric condition and life situation. This is evidenced by failure to recognize past or present psychiatric illness or symptoms, denial of need for psychiatric hospitalisation or treatment, decisions characterised by poor anticipation of consequences and unrealistic short-term and long-range planning.

Score

☐

Basis for rating: thought content expressed during the interview.

1 = Absent – Definition does not apply.

2 = Minimal – Questionable pathology; may be at the upper extreme of normal limits.

3 = Mild – Recognises having a psychiatric disorder but clearly underestimates its seriousness, the implications for treatment or the importance of taking measures to avoid relapse. Future planning may be poorly conceived.

4 = Moderate – Patient shows only a vague or shallow recognition of illness. There may be fluctuation in acknowledgement of being ill or little awareness of major symptoms which are present, such as delusions, disorganised thinking, suspiciousness and social withdrawal. The patient may rationalise the need for treatment in terms of its relieving lesser symptoms, such as anxiety, tension and sleep difficulty.

5 = Moderate severe – Acknowledges past but not present psychiatric disorder. If challenged, the patient may concede the presence of some unrelated or insignificant symptoms, which tend to be explained away by gross misinterpretation or delusional thinking. The need for psychiatric treatment similarly goes unrecognised.

6 = Severe – Patient denies ever having a psychiatric disorder. He disavows the presence of any psychiatric symptoms in the past or present and, though compliant, denies the need for treatment and hospitalisation.

7 = Extreme – Emphatic denial of past and present psychiatric illness. Current hospitalisation and treatment are given a delusional interpretation (e.g. as punishment for misdeeds, as persecution by tormentors, etc.), and the patient may thus refuse to cooperate with therapists, medication or other aspects of treatment.

G13. **Disturbance of volition:** Disturbance in the wilful initiation, sustenance and control of one's thoughts, behaviour, movements and speech.

Score ☐

Basis for rating: thought content and behaviour manifested in the course of interview.

1 = Absent – Definition does not apply.

2 = Minimal – Questionable pathology; may be at the upper extreme of normal limits.

3 =   Mild – There is evidence of some indecisiveness in conversation and thinking, which may impede verbal and cognitive processes to a minor extent.

4 =   Moderate – Patient is often ambivalent and shows clear difficulty in reaching decisions. Conversation may be marred by alternation thinking, and in consequence verbal and cognitive functioning are clearly impaired.

5 =   Moderate severe – Disturbance of volition interferes with thinking as well as behaviour. Patient shows pronounced indecision that impedes the initiation and continuation of social and motor activities, and which also may be evidenced in halting speech.

6 =   Severe – Disturbance of volition interferes in the execution of simple, automatic motor functions, such as dressing and grooming, and markedly affects speech.

7 =   Extreme – Almost complete failure of volition is manifested by gross inhibition of movement and speech, resulting in immobility and/or mutism.

G14. Poor impulse control: Disordered regulation and control of action on inner urges, resulting in sudden, unmodulated, arbitrary or misdirected discharge of tension and emotions without concern about consequences.

Score
☐

Basis for rating: behaviour during the course of interview and reported by primary care workers or family.

1 =   Absent – Definition does not apply.

2 =   Minimal – Questionable pathology; may be at the upper extreme of normal limits.

3 =   Mild – Patient tends to be easily angered and frustrated when facing stress or denied gratification but rarely acts on impulse.

4 =   Moderate – Patient gets angered and verbally abusive with minimal provocation. May be occasionally threatening, destructive or have one or two episodes involving physical confrontation or a minor brawl.

5 =   Moderate severe – Patient exhibits repeated impulsive episodes involving verbal abuse, destruction of property or physical threats. There may be one or two episodes involving serious assault, for which the patient requires isolation, physical restraint, or prn sedation.

6 = Severe – Patient is frequently impulsively aggressive, threatening, demanding and destructive without any apparent consideration of consequences. Shows assaultive behaviour and may also be sexually offensive and possibly respond behaviourally to hallucinatory commands.

7 = Extreme – Patient exhibits homicidal attacks, sexual assaults, repeated brutality or self-destructive behaviour. Requires constant direct supervision or external constraints because of inability to control dangerous impulses.

G15. Preoccupation: Absorption with internally generated thoughts and feelings and with autistic experiences to the detriment of reality orientation and adaptive behaviour.

Score ☐

Basis for rating: interpersonal behaviour observed during the course of interview.

1 = Absent – Definition does not apply.

2 = Minimal – Questionable pathology; may be at the upper extreme of normal limits.

3 = Mild – Excessive involvement with personal needs or problems, such that conversation veers back to egocentric themes and there is diminished concern exhibited toward others.

4 = Moderate – Patient occasionally appears self-absorbed, as if daydreaming or involved with internal experiences, which interferes with communication to a minor extent.

5 = Moderate severe – Patient often appears to be engaged in autistic experiences, as evidenced by behaviours that significantly intrude on social and communicational functions, such as the presence of a vacant stare, muttering or talking to oneself, or involvement with stereotyped motor patterns.

6 = Severe – Marked preoccupation with autistic experiences, which seriously delimits concentration, ability to converse and orientation to the milieu. The patient frequently may be observed smiling, laughing, muttering, talking or shouting to himself.

7 = Extreme – Gross absorption with autistic experiences, which profoundly affects all realms of behaviour. The patient constantly may be responding verbally and behaviourally to hallucinations and show little awareness of other people or the external milieu.

G16. Active social avoidance: Diminished and social involvement associated with unwarranted fear, hostility or distrust.

Score ❏

Basis for rating: reports of social functioning by primary care workers or family.

1 = Absent – Definition does not apply.

2 = Minimal – Questionable pathology; may be at the upper extreme of normal limits.

3 = Mild – Patient seems at ease in the presence of others and prefers to spend time alone, although he participates in social functions when required.

4 = Moderate – Patient begrudgingly attends all or most social activities but may need to be persuaded or may terminate prematurely on account of anxiety, suspiciousness or hostility.

5 = Moderate severe – Patient fearfully or angrily keeps away from many social interactions despite others' efforts to engage him. Tends to spend unstructured time alone.

6 = Severe – Patient participates in very few social activities because of fear, hostility or distrust. When approached, the patient shows a strong tendency to break off interactions, and generally appears to isolate himself from others.

7 = Extreme – Patient cannot be engaged in social activities because of pronounced fears, hostility or persecutory delusions. To the extent possible, he avoids all interactions and remains isolated from others.

Clinical Global Impression

The Clinical Global Impression is a scale that assesses treatment response in all categories of patients.

The scale consists of two items:

Item 1: Severity of illness – rated on a seven-point scale (1 = normal, 7 = among the most severely ill patients). Assessed from previous week's experience.

Item 2: Global improvement – rated on a seven-point scale (very much improved, 7 = very much worse). Assessed from when current treatment was started.

Each item is evaluated separately and the overall score is not calculated.

Clinical Global Impression

Severity of illness

Considering your total clinical experience with this particular population, what is the severity of illness of this patient now?

	Score (post-treatment)
0 = Not assessed	
1 = Very much improved	
2 = Much improved	
3 = Minimally improved	
4 = No change	
5 = Minimally worse	
6 = Much worse	
7 = Very much worse	

Global improvement

Compared to the patient's condition on admission, how much has the patient changed?

0 = Not assessed	Score		
1 = Normal, not ill at all	Pre-treatment	Post-treatment 1	Post-treatment 2
2 = Borderline mentally ill			
3 = Mildly ill			
4 = Moderately ill			
5 = Markedly ill			
6 = Severely ill			
7 = Among the most severely ill patients			

Barnes Akathisia Scale

This is a rating scale for drug-induced akathisia. It incorporates diagnostic criteria for pseudoakathisia and mild, moderate and severe akathisia. It comprises items for rating the observable, restless movements that characterise the condition, the subjective awareness of restlessness and any distress associated with akathisia.

The scale consists of four items, each rated according to severity. The patient should be observed while they are seated and then standing while engaged in neutral conversation (for a minimum of 2 minutes in each position). Symptoms observed in other situations, for example, while engaged in activity on the ward, may be noted. Subsequently, the subjective phenomena should be elicited by direct questioning.

The Barnes Akathisia Scale can be done at any time to assess akathisia. It may be particularly useful where medication has been changed (because of akathisia) to an atypical drug.

A rating of 2 or more is considered diagnostic for akathisia.

Barnes Akathisia

Patients should be observed while seated, and then standing while engaged in neutral conversation (for a minimum of 2 minutes in each position). Symptoms observed in other situations, for example, while engaged in activity on the ward, may also be rated. Subsequently, the subjective phenomena should be elicited by direct questioning.

Objective   Score

☐

0 =   Normal, occasional fidgety movements of the limbs.
1 =   Presence of characteristic restless movements: shuffling or
      tramping movements of the legs and feet or swinging of one leg,
      while sitting, and/or rocking from foot to foot or 'walking on
      the spot' when standing, but movements present for less than
      half the time observed.

2 = Observed phenomena, as described in (1) above, which are present for at least half the observation period.
3 = Patient is constantly engaged in characteristic restless movements, and/or has the inability to remain seated or standing without walking or pacing, during the time observed.

Subjective   Score

Awareness of restlessness

0 = Absence of inner restlessness.
1 = Non-specific sense of inner restlessness.
2 = Patient is aware of an inability to keep the legs still, or a desire to move the legs, and/or complains of inner restlessness aggravated specifically by being required to stand still.
3 = Awareness of an intense compulsion to move most of the time and/or reports a strong desire to walk or pace most of the time.

Distress related to restlessness

0 = No distress.
1 = Mild.
2 = Moderate.
3 = Severe.

Global clinical assessment of akathisia   Score

0 = Absent – no evidence of awareness of restlessness. Observation of characteristic movements of akathisia in the absence of a subjective report of inner restlessness or compulsive desire to move the legs should be classified as pseudoakathisia.
1 = Questionable – non-specific inner tension and fidgety movements.
2 = Mild akathisia – awareness of restlessness in the legs and/or inner restlessness worse when required to stand still. Fidgety movements present, but characteristic restless movements of akathisia not necessarily observed. Condition causes little or no distress.
3 = Moderate akathisia – awareness of restlessness as described for mild akathisia above, combined with characteristic restless movements such as rocking from foot to foot when standing. Patient finds the condition distressing.

4 = Marked akathisia – subjective experience of restlessness includes a compulsive desire to walk or pace. However the patient is able to remain seated for at least 5 minutes. The condition is obviously distressing.

5 = Severe akathisia – the patient reports a strong compulsion to pace up and down most of the time. Unable to sit or lie down for more than a few minutes. Constant restlessness which is associated with intense distress and insomnia.

Total

Reproduced with the permission of the Royal College of Psychiatrists.

Simpson–Angus Scale (SAS)

It is a 10-item scale used to measure drug-induced extrapyramidal side-effects (EPSEs). It is also known as the Extrapyramidal Side-Effects Rating Scale. Seven of the 10 scale items measure rigidity (e.g. shoulder shaking, arm dropping, and elbow and wrist rigidity). There are also items for tremor and pooling of saliva in the mouth. The scale does not address subjective rigidity or slowness and several of the rigidity items (e.g. 'leg pendulousness' and 'head dropping') are difficult to evaluate. However, this scale is commonly used in clinical trials for parkinsonian side-effects.

This instrument consists of 10 items rated on a five-point scale (0 = complete absence of the condition, 4 = presence of the condition in extreme form).

The Simpson–Angus Scale can be done at any time to assess EPSEs. It may be particularly useful where medication has been changed (because of side-effects) to an atypical drug.

Simpson–Angus Scale

Enter appropriate code in boxes below

1. **Gait**   Score

   The patient is examined as he walks into the examining
   room: his gait, the swing of his arms, his general posture,
   all form the basis for an overall score for this item. This
   is rated as follows:

   0 – Normal.
   1 – Mild diminution in swing while patient is walking.
   2 – Marked diminution in swing suggesting shoulder rigidity.
   3 – Stiff gait with little or no arm swing noticeable.
   4 – Stooped shuffling with propulsion and repropulsion.

2. **Arm dropping**   Score

   The patient and the examiner both raise their arms to
   shoulder height and let them fall to their sides. In a
   normal subject, a stout slap is heard as the arms hit the
   sides. In the patient with extreme Parkinson's syndrome,
   the arms fall very slowly:

0 – Normal, free fall with loud slap and rebound.

1 – Fall slowed slightly with less audible contact and little rebound.

2 – Fall slowed, no rebound.

3 – Marked slowing, no slap at all.

4 – Arms fall as though against resistance, as though through glue.

3. Shoulder shaking   Score

The subject's arms are bent at a right angle at the elbow ☐ and are taken one at a time by the examiner who grasps one hand and also clasps the other around the patient's elbow. The subject's upper arm is pushed to and fro and the humerus is externally rotated. The degree of resistance from normal to extreme rigidity is scored as follows:

0 – Normal.

1 – Slight stiffness and resistance.

2 – Moderate stiffness and resistance.

3 – Marked rigidity and difficulty in passive movement.

4 – Extreme stiffness and rigidity with almost a frozen shoulder.

4. Elbow rigidity   Score

The elbow joints are separately bent at right angles and ☐ passively extended and flexed, with the subject's biceps observed and simultaneously palpated. The resistance to this procedure is rated. (The presence of cogwheel rigidity is noted separately.) Scoring is 0–4 as in the shoulder-shaking test.

0 – Normal.

1 – Slight stiffness and resistance.

2 – Moderate stiffness and resistance.

3 – Marked rigidity with difficulty in passive movement.

4 – Extreme stiffness and rigidity with almost a frozen elbow.

5. Wrist rigidity   Score

The wrist is held in one hand and the fingers held by the ☐ examiner's other hand, with the wrist moved to extension flexion and both ulnar and radial deviation. The resistance to this procedure is rated as in items 3 and 4.

0 – Normal.
1 – Slight stiffness and resistance.
2 – Moderate stiffness and resistance.
3 – Marked rigidity with difficulty in passive movement.
4 – Extreme stiffness and rigidity with almost a frozen wrist.

6. **Leg pendulousness**   Score ☐

   0 – The legs swing freely.
   1 – Slight diminution in the swing of the legs.
   2 – Moderate resistance to swing.
   3 – Marked resistance and damping of swing.
   4 – Complete absence of swing.

7. **Head dropping**   Score ☐

   0 – The head falls completely with a good thump as it hits
       the table.
   1 – Slight slowing in fall, mainly noted by lack of slap as head
       meets the table.
   2 – Moderate slowing in the fall quite noticeable to the eye.
   3 – Head falls stiffly and slowly.
   4 – Head does not reach examining table.

8. **Glabellar tap**   Score ☐

   0 – 0–5 blinks.
   1 – 6–10 blinks.
   2 – 11–15 blinks.
   3 – 16–20 blinks.
   4 – 21 and more blinks.

9. **Tremor**   Score ☐

   0 – Normal.
   1 – Mild finger tremor, obvious to sight and touch.
   2 – Tremor of hand or arms occurring spasmodically.
   3 – Persistent tremor of one or more limbs.
   4 – Whole-body tremor.

10. Salivation

Score

0 – Normal.

1 – Excess salivation to the extent that pooling takes place if the mouth is open and tongue raised.

2 – When excess salivation is present and might occasionally result in difficulty in speaking.

3 – Speaking with difficulty because of excess salivation.

4 – Frank drooling.

Abnormal Involuntary Movement Scale

(A) **Examination procedure:** Either before or after completing the examination procedure, observe the patient unobtrusively, at rest (e.g. in waiting room). The chair to be used in this examination should be a hard, firm one without arms.

1. Ask the patient to remove shoes and socks.
2. Ask the patient if there is anything in his or her mouth (e.g. gum, candy); if there is, to remove it.
3. Ask the patient about the current condition of his or her teeth. Ask the patient if he or she wears dentures. Do teeth or dentures bother the patient now?
4. Ask the patient whether he or she notices any movements in mouth, face, hands or feet. If yes, ask to describe and to what extent they currently bother patient or interfere with his or her activities.
5. Have the patient sit in a chair with hands on knees, legs slightly apart and feet flat on floor. (Look at entire body for movements while in this position.)
6. Ask the patient to sit with hands hanging unsupported. If male, between legs, if female and wearing a dress, hanging over knees. (Observe hands and other body areas.)
7. Ask the patient to open mouth. (Observe tongue at rest in mouth.) Do this twice.
8. Ask the patient to protrude tongue. (Observe abnormalities of tongue movement.) Do this twice.
9. Ask the patient to tap thumb, with each finger, as rapidly as possible for 10–15 seconds; separately with right hand, then with left hand. (Observe facial and leg movements.)
10. Flex and extend patient's left and right arms (one at a time). (Note any rigidity.)
11. Ask the patient to stand up. (Observe in profile. Observe all body areas again, hips included.)
12. Ask the patient to extend both arms outstretched in front with palms down. (Observe trunk, legs and mouth.)
13. Have the patient walk a few paces, turn and walk back to chair. (Observe hands and gait.) Do this twice.

(B) Rating sheet

Patient name		Rater name	
Patient #	**Data group:** Abnormal Involuntary Movement Scale	Evaluation date	

Instructions: Complete the above examination procedure before making ratings. For movement ratings, circle the highest severity observed.	Code: 0: None 1: Minimal, may be extreme of normal 2: Mild 3: Moderate 4: Severe

Facial and oral movements	1. **Muscles of facial expression** e.g. movements of forehead, eyebrows, periorbital area, cheeks. Include frowning, blinking, smiling and grimacing.	0 1 2 3 4
	2. **Lips and perioral area** e.g. puckering, pouting, smacking.	0 1 2 3 4
	3. **Jaw** e.g. biting, clenching, chewing, mouth-opening, lateral movement.	0 1 2 3 4
	4. **Tongue** Rate only increase in movements both in and out of mouth, *not* the inability to sustain movement.	0 1 2 3 4
Extremity movements	5. **Upper** (arms, wrists, hands, fingers) Include choreic movements (i.e. rapid, objectively purposeless, irregular, spontaneous), athetoid movements (i.e. slow, irregular, complex, serpentine). Do *not* include tremor (i.e. repetitive, regular, rhythmic).	0 1 2 3 4
	6. **Lower** (legs, knees, ankles, toes) e.g. lateral knee movement, foot tapping, heel dropping, foot squirming, inversion and eversion of the foot.	0 1 2 3 4

(B) Rating sheet *Continued*

Trunk movements	7. Neck, shoulders, hips e.g. rocking, twisting, squirming, pelvic gyrations.	0 1 2 3 4
Global judgements	8. Severity of abnormal movements	0 1 2 3 4
	9. Incapacitation due to abnormal movements	0 1 2 3 4
	10. Patient's awareness of abnormal movements Rate only patient's report.	0 1 2 3 4
Dental status	11. Current problems with teeth and/or dentures	0: No 1: Yes
	12. Does the patient usually wear dentures?	0: No 1: Yes

Index